D1496422

Praise for *Head to Head*

"Anyone who has read any of Lenny Shulman's previous books and his features in *Bloodhorse* knows what an excellent writer he is, but here he demonstrates his uncanny skills as an interviewer. Shulman, with genuine interest in his subjects and an infectious sense of humor, has a knack for putting people at ease and bringing out the kind of candid comments that make this a must-read book for anyone who wants to get inside the minds of racing's leading personalities."—Steve Haskin, Hall of Fame turf writer and author

"This compilation of interviews is a mixture of insightful information and entertainment. It represents Lenny Shulman at his witty best. He interviewed me on two occasions. Afterwards, I realized that I had revealed things I never knew about myself. *That's* a great interviewer."—Tom Durkin, Hall of Fame track announcer

"As a turf writer, Lenny Shulman coaxed Penny Chenery to tell lesser-known stories and historical accounts about Secretariat. She always looked forward to her interviews with him, and enjoyed and respected his literary talents and insights into the sport."—Leonard Lusky, *Secretariat.com*

HEAD TO HEAD

HEAD TO HEAD

Conversations with a Generation of Horse Racing Legends

Lenny Shulman

UNIVERSITY PRESS OF KENTUCKY

Copyright © 2021 by The University Press of Kentucky

Scholarly publisher for the Commonwealth,
serving Bellarmine University, Berea College, Centre
College of Kentucky, Eastern Kentucky University,
The Filson Historical Society, Georgetown College,
Kentucky Historical Society, Kentucky State University,
Morehead State University, Murray State University,
Northern Kentucky University, Transylvania University,
University of Kentucky, University of Louisville,
and Western Kentucky University.
All rights reserved.

Editorial and Sales Offices: The University Press of Kentucky
663 South Limestone Street, Lexington, Kentucky 40508-4008
www.kentuckypress.com

Library of Congress Cataloging-in-Publication Data

Names: Shulman, Lenny, author.
Title: Head to head : conversations with a generation of horse racing legends /
     Lenny Shulman.
Description: Lexington, Kentucky : The University Press of Kentucky, [2021]
Identifiers: LCCN 2021006480 | ISBN 9780813181271 (hardcover) |
     ISBN 9780813181288 (pdf) | ISBN 9780813181295 (epub)
Subjects: LCSH: Jockeys—United States—Biography. | Horse racing—United
     States—Biography. | Thoroughbred horse—United States.
Classification: LCC SF336.A2 S475 2021 | DDC 798.40092/273 [B]—dc23

This book is printed on acid-free paper meeting
the requirements of the American National Standard
for Permanence in Paper for Printed Library Materials.

Manufactured in the United States of America

  Member of the Association
of University Presses

Much of this material has appeared within articles in *Bloodhorse* magazine. The author offers his thanks to the *Bloodhorse* for its permission to reprint it. Minor edits for clarity have been made to the interview transcripts.

Contents

Part IV. Kentucky Hardboots

Part V. Veterinarians

Part VI. Kentucky Derby–Winning Owners

Introduction

It is a depiction of being close to the action when one is said to have a front-row seat.

I have been more fortunate still.

For more than twenty years and counting, I've had a field pass to the world of Thoroughbred racing. I stood next to trainer Richard Mandella for ten minutes while he nervously waited for the photo-finish sign to come down to see if his Johar had won the 2003 Breeders' Cup Turf (he did, in a dead heat). Earlier that year I rode in the famous yellow school bus to Belmont Park with the owners of Funny Cide to see him try to win the Triple Crown (he didn't). I watched next to Bobby Frankel on the Keeneland rail as Sightseek flew by us to win the Raven Run Stakes and establish herself as a superior horse. ("Yeah, she might be all right," Frankel said in joking understatement.)

I've visited with Penny Chenery in her home and had lunch with Sam Shepard. I've run my hands over American Pharoah and Justify and Zenyatta. I've fed mints to A. P. Indy and walked a field with Seattle Slew. Even before I became employed full-time in the industry, I saw up close Affirmed and Unbridled, Mr. Prospector and Danzig. I stood at his paddock fence while twenty-six-year-old Forego sprinted around his field, showing he still had it.

I listened while Charles Nuckols Jr. and Arthur Hancock III recited generations of pedigrees. I spent the hour immediately preceding the race talking strategy and philosophy with Paul Reddam before his I'll Have Another won the 2012 Kentucky Derby. I spent the morning with the Zayat family in a trailer at Belmont Park on the day in 2015 their American Pharoah became the first horse in thirty-seven years to win the Triple Crown.

I have been in the stall watching a foal being born on a freezing February night. I have stayed up all evening with a night watchman in an ice-cold trailer on a lush Kentucky farm making sure horses made it through the dark hours OK. I have asked questions in dozens of beautifully appointed farm offices and in bare, cramped, freezing ones in barns at major racetracks.

I tell you this not to brag or try to show how important I am. I don't do the former, and I'm not the latter. It's simply been my job, for an entire generation, to document the Thoroughbred world from all angles. And, as part of an oath I took when I joined the *Bloodhorse* magazine full-time in 2000, to further and help the industry through my efforts.

I have participated in this great sport but tangentially. I have never bred or raised or owned or trained or ridden a racehorse. I've inspired a couple of racehorse names, although the horses attached to them could barely outrun me. But I've been told enough times that I write OK and tell a good-enough story that I've come to believe I've contributed in a small way, that I've upheld that oath and have played a small part in pushing this heavy industry a little bit forward.

All these experiences have snowballed into enough knowledge whereby some of it has seeped into my head and given me a foundation. I have been able, through the years, to build relationships, small trust by small trust, and gain access to the men and women who are and have been hands-on in this world.

And that has provided me with the gift of documenting a slice of history, a snapshot in time at the beginning of the twenty-first century. As with all history, it is important to pay attention to the experienced, to learn the lessons they convey before they pass from the scene. And it is crucial to spot the coming trends and document the onrushing generation and understand why they are here, so that we may perpetuate this affair we have with this great game, this one-time Sport of Kings that, through evolution, has become attainable for nonroyals as well.

I've been allowed to ask the questions that I've deemed important to a wide variety of horse lovers and industry participants, and to craft their answers into articles that tell their stories. An interviewer must prove himself knowledgeable and worthy in his subjects' eyes to elicit a measure of respect and ease. Gaining trust is a must. Sharing a laugh becomes useful. The subjects must be relaxed and confident that their responses will be conveyed with the meaning and in the spirit in which they are spoken. Only then will they put forth their true thoughts. In these pages live those raw questions and answers, forming a history told without filter or distillation into another form.

It is a particular stroke of good fortune that I have been able to hand off to readers a piece of the passion that was instilled in me by my father's having taken me to Belmont Park a few times in my formative years. And by my having snuck away, a few years later, for dozens of evenings to attend the harness races at the fondly remembered and tragically defunct gem that was Roosevelt Raceway in my hometown of Westbury, New York.

A second piece of luck came with the gift of having seen the film *Inherit the Wind* when I was a child, which magically sent me along the trail of wanting to be a writer, inspired by Gene Kelly's portrayal of the greatest newspaperman of them all, H. L. Mencken.

It has been a happy marriage, this writing about horses. I hope it serves as inspiration.

Lenny Shulman
Nonesuch, Kentucky

Part I

Legends of the Industry

"LARGER THAN LIFE." THE TERM IS RESERVED FOR THOSE FEW PEOPLE WHOSE NAMES AND IMPACT ARE IMMEDIATELY REC‑OGNIZABLE NOT MERELY TO FRIENDS AND ACQUAINTANCES but to strangers. Their fame is unquestioned, their faces are familiar to all, and their influence lingers on long past their years.

Invariably, they are risk-takers and pioneers, because raising a standard requires rising above the status quo, and just a small percentage of people among us display that willingness, and fewer still boast great accomplishment above their bravado.

In an enterprise such as horse racing that has been with us for hundreds of years, it is more difficult still to find wheels to reinvent. To take part in a world that carries such tradition and make it greater still, that gift comes to just a few. They must be hardworking, resourceful, creative, and fearless. Inside them burns an inner confidence, manifested in actions bold and subtle, and in words spoken loudly and softly.

They are not always the most beloved. Their advance through life leaves others behind. Often there are, through competition, hard feelings and jealousy. One's success is another's failure. Making friends for them can be a by-product, but it is not a goal. They are driven by other voices.

Many participate. Some attain the status of stars and champions. A very few become game-changers. In each generation, they fill the history books with their achievements. Within this section reside the game-changers whose stories I've been fortunate enough to tell.

1

Helen "Penny" Chenery

PENNY (TWEEDY) CHENERY WAS the most recognizable face in the sport of horse racing for the last forty-five years of her life. Her ostensible ticket to fame was owning the greatest racehorse since at least Man o' War, with that clock still ticking today. Secretariat dominated opponents during 1972 and 1973, shattering time records in each of his Triple Crown victories. But Penny's true genius lay in her perseverance, in her willingness to tear down fences and ceilings, to defy every norm of her day.

Consider that she was one of the first female graduates of university business school. When her siblings wanted to sell off their father's horse interests after he had taken sick, she alone fought to keep his name and stable extant. She battled for his legacy and was rewarded with consecutive Kentucky Derby and Belmont Stakes winners in Riva Ridge and Secretariat, and of course gained glory when the latter won the Triple Crown. There is no more iconic image in racing than Penny Chenery standing at her box seat at Belmont Park, her hands clenched and then waving above her head, acknowledging the roar of the patrons after Secretariat's thirty-one-length triumph in the Belmont Stakes.

She was as kind and sweet as your favorite grandmother, and equally tough and driven when it came to business. She had left her young family behind in Colorado while she guided the careers of her racehorses—bred by her father—back East. She fiercely protected the reputation of her stars through all her life and also gave back to the sport in every conceivable manner.

She became the first woman to head a variety of industry organizations. And until the end she remained the sport's greatest ambassador. Forty years after Secretariat's Triple Crown, fans would still queue up from one side of the giant plant to the other when she graced Belmont Park on Belmont Stakes day to sign photos and memorabilia. She had a kind word for them all and wanted nothing more than to make more fans for racing.

We spoke on many occasions, with formal interviews a handful of times, including on the fortieth anniversary of Secretariat's magical three-year-old season. During those last sessions, and having passed ninety, she was finally ready to

Penny Chenery (Keeneland Association by John Wyatt)

confess the mistakes she had made while desperately trying to squeeze every race she could out of her superstar horse before his retirement to stud. Forty years after the fact, I got the scoop.

Not many people have a Hollywood film made about them. Penny deserved a far better one than she received.

2005

Interviewed in her Lexington home

Lenny Shulman: *What was your childhood like?*
Penny Chenery: I was born in New York and was a daddy's girl. I adored my dad [Christopher Chenery], and whatever he did, I wanted to do. He taught me all about horsemanship. I always rode with him. We spent our summers in Connecticut and cut trails and rode through the hills. My job was to clean tack and groom horses.

Girls didn't wear trousers in those days. I took my first riding lesson in gym bloomers, and I got such blisters. And he said, "Well, Helen, how did you like it?" And I said, "Daddy, I love it." And then he bought me some trousers.

He heard about the horse sales in Saratoga and went and came home with three Thoroughbreds. That's when I started learning pedigrees, from the names on the halters.

LS: *Did you think you'd end up working with the horses?*
PC: Dad didn't need help; he needed an audience. So I was allowed to ask questions and learn, but I couldn't make suggestions. I graduated from college during World War II and worked for an architect who was building landing craft for the invasion of Normandy. Then I went overseas as a nurse and came back home and went to business school.

He wanted me to marry. He wanted a son-in-law to help with his business, not a daughter. Once I married and moved to Colorado, I had a different life. I learned to fly-fish and shoot ducks and ski, which I loved. I always figured my mother would outlive Dad and probably run the stable, but she died and he got Alzheimer's, and I, somewhat reluctantly, because I'd been around horses, agreed I ought to take care of the stable.

I sat in Denver and read the *Morning Telegraph* and the *Bloodhorse* and the *Thoroughbred Record,* just to learn the lingo. I knew nothing about racing. I'd come back East, and people would say, "Who is this yahoo?"

LS: *Did anyone help you?*
PC: I had three years of self-education, and I had [Claiborne Farm's] Bull Hancock, who was my dad's friend. When I was thrown into the fire, Bull was wonderful to me.

LS: *And at some point you left your family in Colorado and moved across the country?*
PC: I couldn't wait; I needed a challenge. We'd had some pretty good horses—Hill Prince, First Landing, Cicada, Sir Gaylord. I'd fly East for the big races. Dad had incorporated the farm in 1958 and put me on the board, so I knew the workings of that end of it.

LS: *You wanted to continue his legacy?*
PC: I shared his dream and then adopted his dream. I knew more than anything he wanted to win the Kentucky Derby. He'd come so close—Hill Prince was second; First Landing was third. Dad was still alive when we went with Riva

Ridge in 1972, and I thought if we could do this and fulfill his dream, that would be great.

LS: *What were your emotions like at Riva's Derby?*
PC: I don't know why, but I was very optimistic. He'd won his prep races in Florida, but he was very unprepossessing. He was what John Nerud called a "one-holer." He looked as though his front legs came out of the same hole. He was lop-eared and had been a sickly weanling, but he had speed. He was afraid of other horses and ran because of fear.

I got so excited during the race, screaming, "Riva's winning," and I was pounding on Clay Hancock, who was in the box in front of me. He was the ugly duckling who came along and saved the farm. It was just a great relief to win.

With Alzheimer's, it is a long, slow process. Dad hadn't spoken for seven months, and the nurse was feeding him dinner and had the television on, and she told him, "Mr. Chenery, Mr. Chenery, your horse has won the Kentucky Derby." And tears came down his face. So we knew that he knew. I thought, "OK, I've done it. This is it. Now I can retire." Which I didn't.

LS: *You had already made changes to the stable.*
PC: Before Riva came along, I had asked Bull to suggest a trainer for the stable, and the names he gave me were Henry Forrest, Roger Laurin, and Woody Stephens. The first person who answered the phone was Roger Laurin. He came downtown to Dad's office to meet me and Elizabeth Ham, who was Dad's secretary and my strength, because she kept the books, paid the bills, and made the stable run.

Roger walks in all dressed up, and we were like, "This is a trainer?" But he had trained for Captain Guggenheim, and we decided to give it a try, and he was a lifesaver. He culled our horses by half, and we started to make money. Hydrologist, a good two-year-old, became a stakes winner, and we started getting good horses again.

LS: *But there was pressure from your family to sell the operation?*
PC: Yes, my brother and sister felt I was the only one having any fun with this, and that Dad didn't know what was going on. And they wanted to sell the horses and invest the money in the stock market. And I said, "These are Dad's horses, and as long as he's alive, we can't do that." Fortunately, my act was successful. At that point I was doing it more for myself than for Dad.

LS: *And then Roger left?*

PC: Yes, Eddie Neloy, who had been training the Phipps horses, died. Bull suggested to Ogden Phipps he should have Roger run Phipps Stable. And Roger told me his father, Lucien, was about to retire, but perhaps he could help us out. He was a very shrewd judge of young horses.

LS: *In your wildest dreams, did you think you could win another Derby?*

PC: No. When Riva won, I thought that was it. We accomplished what Dad wanted. He was a homebred and was a tribute to all of Dad's skill and effort.

But Lucien knew. He came down to the farm in Virginia to watch the yearlings train and picked out one horse who he said might be something. He wanted to take him to Florida, which we weren't doing because it was expensive and we had a training track at home. But Lucien insisted on taking that Bold Ruler colt with him. And all spring he kept on downplaying him, complaining about how he didn't show anything and couldn't outrun a fat man. Looking back, I should have realized the fact he talked about him so often . . .

Lucien wanted to run him for the first time July 1, but my husband had taken a job, and we were in the process of moving, and I couldn't get there for the race, so Lucien said he'd wait a few more days, which also should have told me something. So on July 4 he ran and didn't win, and Lucien stood up and kicked a chair across the box and said, "Damn, that horse should never get beat." And that's when I knew what he really thought of Secretariat.

LS: *How much of that time was pure fun for you, and how much was pressure from having to run the operation?*

PC: It was a wonderful time, but I did have to deal with some things. My brother and sister were somewhat resentful because everyone would be talking about "Mrs. Tweedy's horse" [Penny was married to John Tweedy], and of course he wasn't my horse. He raced in the name of the family's Meadow Stable. And my husband did not share my enthusiasm. He wanted it to be over so I would go back home and be a wife and mother. But I had the bit in my teeth. I was not going back.

In terms of running the stable, there had been many women who were owners. Being overseas with the Red Cross, and then going to Columbia Business School, I was used to being one of the few women in a man's world, and I just didn't pay any attention to it. If people did not accept me, I was not aware of it. I was doing my job. Dad taught me I could do anything anyone else could.

LS: *And you became the sport's greatest ambassador.*
PC: I wasn't intimidated by crowds. When you have a really good horse, fans love you and holler at you and want an autograph. All they want is an acknowledgment of their admiring your horse. I'm basically a friendly person, and if you want to tell me I'm wonderful, I'm delighted to hear it. So all the love for the horse spilled over to Lucien and me.

I felt it was my job to be the spokesman for the horse and, in a sense, for the industry. That has really been my mission—to let people in on the fun of racing. It's such a simple thing, to share. I think it's important not to be a small tribe. We need the fans and the potential owners to see what fun it is.

LS: *Secretariat opened a lot of doors for you.*
PC: I was invited to be in The Jockey Club and made it to the chairman's table, and all the heavy players wanted to talk to me because I had Secretariat. It's amazing, the power of that horse. I think it's the thirty-one lengths, but also it's the thirteen years he spent at Claiborne, where people could see him. And he was such a ham. He never just stood there when people were around. He'd come charging off the hill and slam on the brakes and almost run into you, or he'd throw a stick in the air. Always performed, and I think that's when people learned to love him as much as for his racetrack performance.

LS: *In your mind, was he the greatest horse of the century?*
PC: That's a very hard question because I never saw Man o' War, who had a better record. It would have been fascinating to see them race because they both had that determination. My feelings are not hurt when people call Secretariat the best horse of the second half of the twentieth century. We'll share the century with Man o' War.

LS: *You've been raising money for a statue of Secretariat at the Kentucky Horse Park?*
PC: Yes, I've worked really hard and found it difficult to do. I've sold memorabilia and worked at fundraising. It costs nearly a half-million dollars. But I feel he was the outstanding horse of his time, and I want people to get the feeling of the dignity and elegance and excitement of the horse. You glorify your past to ensure your future. People see something that radiates strength and vitality, and maybe they'll go out to the racetrack. I can't let his legacy die with me, and it won't, because he'll be in pedigrees forever.

LS: *What would you like your legacy to be?*
PC: Someone who loved racing and loved horses. Secretariat's Mom—that's how I want to be remembered.

2013

On the 40th anniversary of Secretariat's Triple Crown, Chenery, then past ninety, looked back at her superstar's 1973 campaign and was of the mind to unburden herself of feelings she'd kept private all those decades. Interviewed from her home in Colorado.

Lenny Shulman: *Secretariat had been named champion two-year-old, he'd finished first in eight straight races, but did you carry any doubts he'd progress as he'd need to from two to three?*
Penny Chenery: Sure. Because he was precocious and big, and you'd hear all about the Bold Rulers not wanting to go that far. He was a flashy two-year-old, but can he carry it through to three? My philosophy was just to wait and see. If he can do it, let him show me. And the fact we'd won the Derby and Belmont with Riva Ridge the previous year added to my doubts. We got lucky once. Now, really, can we expect it again?

I talked to [trainer] Lucien [Laurin] a lot over that winter. Elizabeth Ham and I met with Lucien on Long Island, and we laid out a plan for the three-year-old season, assuming all went well. Lucien explained his choices, and I learned to trust him. It gave him the freedom to make the plans and know I wasn't going to go to the press and say something else. So the plan was in place. But it changed.

LS: *The big news over that winter was the syndication of the horse, which would end up affecting a lot of decisions, knowing that he would be retired after his three-year-old season.*
PC: Yes. Daddy had died, and there were the inheritance taxes. The syndication took the financial pressure off me, and it wasn't going to be money coming out of my pocket if it wasn't successful. But I didn't like the syndication deal. I thought Secretariat should go for $200,000 a share. But my lawyer was influenced by the Claiborne lawyer. Buckpasser had gone for $180,000, and Mr. Phipps didn't want Secretariat to go for that much more than Buckpasser. I had to accept the $190,000 to save the Phippses' pride. I was so green when it came to that whole deal. I knew about riding and breeding but not this territory.

Lucien didn't want to run the horse until the syndication was complete. Partly because he got a share, and he didn't want to see it lose value if the horse didn't go on successfully. There were a lot of angles. I never have told anybody this. But Mr. Phipps is gone, Lucien is gone, and the lawyers are gone. Nothing is as straightforward as you expect it to be.

LS: *Were you able to attend his races early in 1973?*

PC: I lived in New York at that time. My husband had taken a job there, which was very handy because I wanted to be at every race. I remember Secretariat being big, gleaming, and gorgeous before the first race that year. He had a lot of self-confidence and was enjoying himself. I didn't get to every workout, but it was pretty much my life.

LS: *His first race was the Bay Shore on March 17. What do you remember about it?*

PC: To be truthful, the races are kind of a blur. But I recall he split horses, which certainly gave us hope and confidence. I do remember the look on his face: "I could go around, but I'll just go through." He did it with such confidence that I felt we were set up for a big, strong spring. I had lots of confidence anyway. I didn't say so, because I didn't want to look like a chump. Having been through it the year before made things much easier for me. I knew what the moments were like and where the pitfalls were, and who to turn to for help.

LS: *In the Gotham April 7, he went straight to the lead.*

PC: He had never run that way before. I was OK with it. I had lots of faith. I was just waiting to see what would happen when a horse came to him. He was training well, and Lucien had learned you had to put a lot of work into this horse. The harder he trained, the better he went. He'd work five-eighths in the days before every race, and if he missed that, it never worked out as well. He won the Bay Shore and the Gotham by daylight, which made the Wood quite a shock.

LS: *He ran third in the Wood Memorial April 21, his last prep before the Kentucky Derby.*

PC: I was confused by his performance. And there were a lot of second-guessers. The syndicate members were instructed not to talk to me, but that doesn't mean I didn't get looks. That was when the tension was greatest. Obviously, I was disappointed, but we'd had everything go so well, and sometimes it's healthy to face some adversity. Get a loss under our belt and be more realistic. I didn't know at the time why he'd run so poorly, beaten four lengths. It was years before I knew. Nobody told me he had an abscess in his mouth. Lucien maintained he didn't know. He wasn't a hands-on trainer; he wasn't in the stall at five in the morning feeling ankles. Plus, he was out of town at a funeral that week.

Seth Hancock, who'd done the syndication and would stand the horse at Claiborne, called and said something like, "It was an unfortunate outcome." It was my right to manage the horse through the end of that year, and I told him so. Someone asked how many more times I would allow him to be defeated, and I said, "Hopefully, none, but that is my right." Once you let people start helping you manage the horse, there would be no peace. It was regrettable that he lost, but I was going to keep managing his career. I can be strong. I was guarding my territory. There were people who wanted to retire him at two, when he was Horse of the Year and had done enough. My thought was I didn't know where the bottom of this horse was, so let's not be chicken.

LS: *What did that defeat do to your confidence moving forward to the Derby?*
PC: I was willing to think it was an aberration. But you wouldn't have wanted to be in the car when Lucien and I were driving out of Aqueduct after the Wood. I gave him such hell. He trained the winner, Angle Light, and I told him he had an investment in Secretariat too, and why would he let him get beat by Angle Light? We both had tempers. I show mine less often, but when I'm mad, I'm mad.

Lucien and I became very good friends. With a horse that prominent, nobody else knows what kind of pressure you're under. He was my confidante. But he sure didn't tell me about the abscess. Lucien had a lot of professional pride, and he may have felt it reflected poorly on him.

LS: *The week of the Derby you held a rather infamous meeting with Lucien and [jockey] Ron [Turcotte].*
PC: I wanted to remind Ronny and Lucien that they were—with this horse—working for me. I wanted to make sure we were all on the same page. And I wanted Ronny's full attention. I had talked to Lucien about taking Ronny off the horse. I didn't seriously consider doing that; what I wanted to do was scare Ronny.

LS: *How calm or nervous were you in general before a big race?*
PC: I wasn't nervous. I was realistic, and pretty confident because I really thought I had the best horse.

LS: *He began slowly in the Derby, and dropped well off the pace. Did that concern you?*
PC: Ron told me years later that he broke slowly because it took him that long to get his big rear end in gear. I wasn't concerned, because generally that's how he ran. And then he made that long, strong, grinding move. After he won, I was swallowed up by well-wishers. It was a hot day, and I wanted to do it right, but

I wished we could get back to the barn and congratulate the horse and join the party. But we were in the press box being interviewed for forty minutes.

There was a sense of pressure being lifted off my shoulders. I thought we might get tripped up by something, but all things being equal, I had the best horse. I was happy, relieved, but I wasn't screaming, "Oh my God, we did it!" Just, "We did it." I was not surprised or overwhelmed by winning the Derby. Having won it the year before was a huge difference. It made it a lot easier. It was, "OK, we won the first one and now we have to win the second one."

LS: *What do you remember about the Preakness?*
PC: The horse was fine coming out of the Derby. But Preakness day was a horror show. They banged up my car and stole my husband's wallet. Then we couldn't get into the track. They didn't have our credentials. We were supposed to go in a special entrance to avoid the mosh pit, and that got fouled up somehow. But I knew they needed us.

The thing that amused me was Lucien brought some nuns with him. I don't know where he found them, but in the photos of us watching the race, there are these three nuns. It was bizarre. I never even knew Lucien went to church.

LS: *Secretariat had no trouble getting his rear end into gear that day.*
PC: No. I thought Ronny had lost his mind. I thought, "We don't run this way. What are you doing?" But he made that spectacular move to the lead on the first turn. For dramatic effect, it was wonderful. There was concern he moved too soon and somebody would catch him, but no. So now we had the second.

LS: *Nobody had won the Triple Crown in twenty-five years, and now here was this superstar horse. Was it a frenzy?*
PC: It was Hell Week leading up to the Belmont. Just brutal. I like people and enjoy being interviewed, but that was just too much. I did three magazine covers [Secretariat appeared on the covers of *Time, Newsweek,* and *Sports Illustrated* in the same week] and that was exhausting. It takes an hour per interview, and it's a great deal of repetition, and everybody thinks their story is the most important. That part was work.

There was a problem with my brother and sister, because they owned as much of the horse as I did, but he was in Boston, she was in Tucson, and the media called him my horse because I was the one who was there. They were upset by that, and I don't blame them. We had issues going back to when we were five years old.

LS: *Now we come to the Belmont, probably the most famous race of the century. Any doubts going in?*

PC: I had a nagging thought that maybe it was Sham's turn. His speed might make a difference, and there was the doubt about Bold Rulers getting a mile and a half. But I had faith in my horse. He got into that steady rhythm. By the time the horse got to the Belmont, he understood the game. He was on his home track. He enjoyed the early part of the Belmont, going stride for stride with Sham. He really got in the zone after he pulled away. I was in awe. I'd never seen anything like it. I wish I'd seen Count Fleet. Horses that are comfortable on the lead and within themselves, it's a beautiful, wonderful thing to see.

LS: *When the camera finds you after the race, there's pure joy on your face.*

PC: There's a bit of a backstory. [New York governor] Hugh Carey was there, and earlier in the afternoon the crowd had booed him. And so when my moment came, I thought, "They won't boo me." And I did the double-handed wave, which was inspired by Hugh. I didn't want them to boo me.

I wish my father could have been there. I don't think he would have done the double-handed wave, but he would have been mighty thrilled. A lifetime goal achieved. I was gratified by the people who came to the trustees' room to congratulate me, people like Paul Mellon and Jock Whitney. Important men. I knew my dad would have been pleased with their recognition of his horse, and I was highly gratified by that.

LS: *You ran Secretariat again three weeks later at Arlington Park. What was behind that decision?*

PC: Money and overoptimism. We were bragging that the horse could do anything. The original plan had been to wait for Saratoga, and we made a poor decision. We knew we only had until the end of the year, and we thought, "Let's see how much we could do." But it was a put-up race. They didn't even have a trophy. It was more like an exhibition than a race. But the crowd was great, and it was nice to show him off to a new place, and he won by nine lengths.

LS: *And then you did run at Saratoga a month later in the Whitney.*

PC: We sensed he wasn't well when we got to Saratoga. He had a low-grade fever. But we really thought this horse could do anything. I wasn't thinking straight. "Greedy" is the word that comes to mind. I was trying to get prestige, money, records, everything I could. And this was a prestigious race. And so we tested his limits.

I watched the Whitney in disbelief [Secretariat ran second, beaten a length by Onion]. How could this be? I didn't make good decisions during this time. Secretariat needed medical attention after that race.

LS: *He got nearly six weeks off until his next start in the Marlboro Cup in mid-September.*
PC: The Marlboro Cup proposal at first was for a match race between him and Riva Ridge, and then they both got beat at Saratoga, so we had to regroup and open the race up. Lucien said he could get Secretariat ready in time to race against a top field of older horses. And it was for a lot of money, $250,000, and that was appealing. They had just created the race that year.

Both horses came into the race doing very well. Riva set a record in the Brooklyn and won a million dollars before Secretariat did, a fact lost in history. But in my heart, I knew Secretariat could outrun Riva. I just wanted them to run 1–2. There were good horses in there, and Cougar made a strong move at the end and almost caught Riva. Kennedy Road was very good as well, and Key to the Mint. But Secretariat won by three and a half lengths.

LS: *After the Marlboro Cup there was another change in your plans?*
PC: The plan was to run on the grass three weeks later in the Man o' War [October 8]. Riva was supposed to run in the Woodward (September 29). But then it rained, and Riva hated to run in the mud. So we threw Secretariat into the Woodward without his usual preparations. We were kind of floundering around, and unfortunately we took liberties that didn't work. That one didn't work [Prove Out defeated Secretariat by four and a half lengths].

LS: *But then Secretariat came back and won the Man o' War just nine days later, his first time on turf.*
PC: I loved the Man o' War. He was actually better on the grass. That was a glorious race. We were running out of time, and it was kind of a Hail Mary. But it was absolutely a thrill to see him do so well on the grass [he won by five lengths].

I was always aware there was a time limit with him. There was no point in retiring him early because he was already syndicated. So we went up to Woodbine for the Canadian International [October 28]. We went there as a favor to E. P. Taylor, who had been a friend and adviser to me. Plus, both Lucien and Ronny were Canadian, and I thought it was suitable that they have the chance to race him there. [Turcotte, having been suspended in New York, couldn't ride Secretariat in the Canadian International, as Eddie Maple guided him to a six-and-a-half-length victory on the turf.] The fans were so wonderful and appreciative. It was a grandstanding move that worked.

It was otherworldly. I remember the steam coming out of his mouth and nose in the fog.

LS: *What were your emotions after that, knowing the ride with Secretariat was over?*
PC: I was so sad. I'm a big girl, and I knew what the contract said, and the end was the end. But still . . . I went on the plane with him to Kentucky, and that was really hard. Of course, I wanted another year with him. But we owed this huge tax bill and didn't have the money.

After that I kept breeding, always thinking that it happened once, it could happen again. But I've had a lot of years to realize . . . "No."

2

James E. "Ted" Bassett III

JAMES E. "TED" BASSETT knew next to nothing about the horse industry when he was hired by Keeneland in 1968. He was long on life experience, however. His defining development came as a US Marine lieutenant serving in the Pacific theater during World War II, and then as head of the Kentucky State Police, in charge of helping to integrate a state that wasn't keen on the concept.

Bassett brought Keeneland into the modern era, overseeing a new sales pavilion, a race-caller (previously the races there had been run in silence), and dozens of other advancements large and small. While maintaining Keeneland's tradition, Bassett shaped it as a cutting-edge company at the vanguard of trying new technologies. He also served as president of the Breeders' Cup during its formative years.

He is, at this writing, ninety-eight and still going strong, a force in so many ways, including fundraising. His efforts saved the Calumet Farm trophy collection and helped build the Marine Corps Museum in Virginia, the Kentucky Blood Center in Lexington, and statues around the country honoring the World War II equine hero Sgt. Reckless. Various local charities and organizations benefit from his (often anonymous) largesse.

It is one of life's pleasures to visit with Mr. Bassett at his office in a cottage on the Keeneland grounds, and one of which I've taken regular advantage.

2006

Interviewed at Keeneland Race Course, Lexington

Lenny Shulman: *Did you have any background with horses?*
Ted Bassett: None to speak of, except my father was the farm manager of Greentree Stud for the Whitneys. I worked summers at the farm, basically as a laborer cutting grass. Graduated from a mower to a tractor, but never quite suited anyone with the patterns I made.

James E. "Ted" Bassett III at Keeneland (Keeneland Association)

LS: *What type of man was your father?*
TB: He was a disciplinarian. He had standards he expected my brother and me to adhere to. Punctuality was a big thing. Neatness, courtesy, and politeness. Grades were very important once I got to the Kent School and then to Yale.

LS: *Serving in the Marine Corps during World War II was a defining time in your life. How did that affect you?*
TB: Kent was a strict, spartan place with a structured life. That was the formation of whoever I am. It wasn't an easy time in the Marine Corps—nobody has an easy time on Parris Island—but having that experience at Kent made me more

21

adaptable to that life. I couldn't have been better trained than what the Marine Corps provided—the intensive basic training for sixteen weeks at Parris Island and then six months of officer training school. There was tremendous pressure.

Three dozen of us second lieutenants were put through intensive landing practices. We were sent to the Pacific to fill in for casualties right before Christmas 1944; shipped over to Guadalcanal. The Marine Corps didn't have the manpower to build battalions; we had raider battalions that excelled in amphibious operations. Macho-type people. Having the opportunity to serve with those people and with that leadership was very meaningful to me.

I don't believe I would have been effective in heading the state police if I hadn't had that extensive training and also the building of self-confidence that almost anything is attainable if you try hard enough and work hard enough. The experience fortified you with an inner confidence.

LS: *You worked at a variety of things after the war.*
TB: I took a summer off and sailed around New England. I had no idea what I wanted to do, no definitive course. When you look at my career, there is no real path. It's been a series of 90-degree turns. I went to work for the Great Northern Paper Company, which was owned by the Whitney family, selling newsprint. I spent nine months up north of Bangor, Maine, in the backwoods. I worked up and down the East Coast for eight years, and it was a great experience.

LS: *But eventually you moved back to Kentucky.*
TB: When you marry a Kentucky girl, the pull to return home is greater than the gravitational pull of the universe. So I started to farm with my father-in-law, raising tobacco and sheep and cattle. Pete Widener, who was the commissioner of the state police, began recruiting me. He'd take me to the pistol range and to the aircraft field and the polygraph lab, and the hook began to take.

But there were political problems. My wife's family were prominent Republicans who had opposed the Democratic governor, Happy Chandler. I was an independent, but I registered as a Democrat, which caused some eyebrow-raising in the family.

But it worked out. They were creating a new Department of Public Safety, which is where I got my start. My first day on the job we had an integration blowup in Sturgis, trying to integrate the schools there. The trauma of those small children—seven, eight, nine years old—I never forgot that. That was my first day.

I figured I'd stay for six months. I did eleven years. It was a fascinating period of my life—school integration, open housing, vicious coal strikes, floods. I felt very strongly about the need for improved training standards, selection standards, and discipline. I'm proud of my time there.

LS: *Keeneland must have been easy after all that.*
TB: *(laughs).* No, it wasn't. The first six months here was quite an experience. Here was somebody from the outside, an industry nonentity, brought onto a staff of experts. They were polite, but I knew they had a lot of questions about me.

I had just left an environment where if I raised an eyebrow, you'd hear a click of heels. If I raised two eyebrows here, I was lucky to evoke a yawn. People wanted to know what the heck was happening at Keeneland that they had to bring in a state police guy, and the truth is if things were going along swimmingly, there wouldn't have been a need for me. Which was also true later at the Breeders' Cup.

LS: *What was your view of Keeneland when you came to work here?*
TB: It wasn't just a racetrack. It was an institution that was respected and revered throughout the community. Its board members were prominent citizens and leaders. It put more emphasis on the tradition and sporting aspects of racing as opposed to strictly the gambling side. Equally important was contributing a portion of its profits to the community. So I came in feeling extremely fortunate to have the opportunity.

LS: *What would we find surprising today looking back at Keeneland in 1968?*
TB: The lack of a public-address announcer—a race-caller—brought the most public reaction. The Daily Double may have been in place, but no other exotic wagering. Sunday racing was just about to start. We were perceived as conservative, if not stodgy, but the truth is we are not ultraconservative. Yes, we emphasize tradition, but today we are on the absolute cutting edge with the Polytrack racing surface and the Trakkus timing system, and our safety initiatives.

It's a lot less conservative today than when I started. I have changed, too. I would have probably been labeled as one of the stodgiest of the staff, concentrating on the mission of Keeneland and the provisions of its charter.

LS: *What changed you?*
TB: My experience with the Breeders' Cup, for one thing. That was an eye-opening experience and a divergent path. There was an aggressive marketing and promotion plan there, with new ideas, new technology, and dealing with creating an international championship. The mission there was to promote and market racing to attract new fans, so they were open to new ideas. We crossed swords many times in the beginning because the marketing guys were streetwise New Yorkers

who knew the advertising and TV businesses but felt that anyone outside three miles of the Hudson River had IQs of about two. That grated on me, even though it might have been true. But I learned from those guys, and some are still friends.

LS: *What were your most memorable moments from Breeders' Cups?*
TB: A lot of us probably have the same races in mind, at least the ones we didn't have a personal involvement in. Personal Ensign, undefeated, coming from near dead last in the cold and dark and mud to barely get up. Alysheba racing in the dark, the only lights being the photo-finish ones.

Then there was Hurricane Andrew tearing the roofs off several barns at Gulfstream Park. The fires at Santa Anita; the day before the races you couldn't see across the track from the apron. The threatened strike by the pari-mutuel clerks at Woodbine.

Personally, the race that stands out was Adoration winning the 2003 Distaff. She was a horse that my wife, Lucy, bred. And Northern Spur winning the Turf at Belmont, owned by my old friend Charlie Cella.

LS: *Has there been a Golden Age for Keeneland?*
TB: I think it's been a progressive Golden Age. We've been able to grow with the times, make changes to the facilities that are subtle, seamless. Being able to expand without losing the ambiance. Initiate new programs without changing the traditional feel or philosophy of Keeneland.

LS: *Is the Keeneland model transferrable to other racetracks?*
TB: I would be extraordinarily hesitant to advise other tracks, because what we have here is God-given, and the founders were smart enough to work on the premise of "just enough, not too much." We're blessed with having six weeks of the most beautiful seasons Kentucky or anyplace can have, three in April and three in October. We've always resisted expanding that, and we don't have to pay dividends to shareholders.

LS: *What are some of the things here of which you're most proud?*
TB: I don't take credit for being a genius. This goes back way before me. We have changed without seeming to change. Look at the library here, the entertainment center, the toteboard. They're relatively new but have the feel and understanding of what Keeneland is about. We use architects and contractors who understand how we want things to appear.

I'd be comfortable to be remembered as someone who believed in tradition and tried to, within the framework of the founders' vision, move forward.

LS: *You've also been instrumental in raising money for projects in the community, and beyond.*

TB: Starting back in school, I was taught you have to participate. Take whatever talent you have and lend it to the community when the bureaucracy falls short. There was a need for a new Blood Center in town, so I chaired the capital fund. It's never easy, fundraising. It's perseverance. The Calumet trophies, that would have been a tragedy if they had been sold off piecemeal. The YMCA, I chaired the campaign to build that. You knock on doors and keep going, and it becomes a game.

I'm passionate about the Marine Corps Museum in Quantico, Virginia. We're dedicating it this year. We started out trying to raise $50 million, and we raised $60 million. It's a game, particularly when they say, "You can't do it."

I'm going to try and ease off a little bit. But I'm also not going to sit here and look at the four walls. You can't retire from life.

3

Bobby Frankel

BOBBY FRANKEL WAS NEVER well understood from the outside. His reputation was that of a man-eater who devoured in a barrage of vitriol those of whom he was not fond. For many of us, the opposite was true. He was an urchin from the streets of Brooklyn who, for sure, didn't suffer fools. But below the surface he was a charming, funny, bright man who rose from a guy climbing fences to get into the racetrack for free, to one of the greatest trainers of all time. He also was the rare racetracker who loved to talk about things outside horse racing, being a connoisseur of ethnic food and a follower of current events.

He succeeded Charlie Whittingham (whom I've written about but never had the opportunity to interview) as the top trainer in California, starting with cheap claiming horses and eventually rising to work with a barn full of star runners. His skill caught the eye of Khalid Abdullah, a Saudi prince whose Juddmonte Farms has been a superior breeding and racing operation worldwide for many decades. Frankel's reputation was sealed by his success with helping make great Juddmonte families, mostly on the turf but also in winning the Belmont Stakes with Empire Maker.

Asked about the irony of a Jewish kid from Brooklyn partnering with a Saudi Arabian prince, Frankel brushed the question aside. "He's under enough pressure," Frankel said of Khalid Abdullah.

Juddmonte held Frankel in such esteem that, following his death in 2009, it named its best prospect after him, and the four-legged Frankel became one of the greatest racehorses of all time, winning all fourteen of his races, and has continued to shine as a stallion.

Frankel would have flashed his Cheshire cat smile at that one.

2005

Interviewed in a Thai restaurant in West Los Angeles, California

Lenny Shulman: *Your family had no ties to horse racing. How did you get started in it?*

Bobby Frankel (Keeneland Association by Bill Straus)

Bobby Frankel: When I was ten or eleven, my folks watched the trotters on TV one night a week. They took me to Roosevelt Raceway, and I'm there holding the program and starting to handicap at fifteen, and they give me a few bucks and I'm betting. The gambling part of it clicked.

How I got on the racetrack is the best part. My father took me to Belmont Park, and I got into the Thoroughbreds more than the harness. It was challenging, and the *Form* looked like Chinese to me. The harness horses all ran a mile, but now with the Thoroughbreds you see seven-eighths; a mile and a quarter; turf. You have to figure it all out, and I'm starting to get hooked on it. I'd go down to the candy store in Far Rockaway every night at 8:00 p.m. when the *Form* got dropped off. I'd handicap all night and go to the races the next day.

I met a guy who ponied horses, and I went out with him real early the next morning, and he introduced me to a trainer named Joe Williams, who had two horses. He put me on his badge list as a hotwalker, which meant I got a free pass and a parking sticker—that's three dollars I'm saving going to the races, a big score.

I went to Florida and walked hots for Buddy Bellew. I was making two hundred dollars a month and gambling. I made friends around the track. Back in New York, I was introduced to a guy who owned horses at Finger Lakes who said he'd let me train a horse. The first horse I bought was off Allen Jerkens, named Pink Rose. I went from a hotwalker to a trainer in three months. At Saratoga I bought 'Taint Funny, also a Jerkens horse, at a sale for $3,500. The guy from Finger Lakes sent me Double Dash, who was my first winner. Then 'Taint Funny won the first time I ran her, and then I won three in a row with Pink Rose.

LS: *Did you know what you were doing?*
BF: I was guessing. Didn't really have a clue. I got friendly with [trainer] Buddy Jacobson and went to Maryland with a bunch of his horses. He went to Florida, leaving me to take care of them. He'd call every day and tell me to look at his horses, and he'd tell me what to do with them. So through that communication I picked up and learned a lot.

After Kenny Noe turned me down for stalls at Hialeah, I went to California with [owner] Bill Frankel's [no relation] horses. California looked pretty good to me. I moved out there the following year. I'd asked for thirty-five stalls, and they gave them to me, and I had about eighteen horses. So I began claiming horses and had a great meet at Hollywood Park right away.

I won sixty races from 180 starts. Everything I ran . . . I was winning three a day like nothing, y'know? It was unbelievable.

LS: *You became bicoastal.*
BF: I went back to Saratoga because all my help was from New York. But the next year I stayed out West. Personally, I didn't have any trouble adjusting because all I did was work. Get up, go to the barn, and stay all day until six at night. I fed every horse myself. When I went home, I went to sleep. It was a good experience. Hey, when you're winning, it's a good experience. I wasn't paying attention to what the next guy was doing. I was trying to prove to the world that I could do it.

LS: *But you must have been influenced . . . ?*
BF: Charlie Whittingham was a great influence on other trainers. His style, to get these horses going, just training them into races instead of running in a bunch of races. He is why trainers in California don't believe you need prep races. I train mine up to races quite a bit, probably more than anybody. I've found that when you get your horses real good, especially on grass, it doesn't require as much hard training as the dirt horses. I get them in real good condition, as sound as they can be, and they're happy, and I'd rather not waste them on a prep race. I'd rather go for the bucks.

LS: *Other trainers have said that you changed the way people train horses out here.*
BF: Eat some of this food. I'm gonna kill myself here. When I first came out here the trainers would work a horse as fast as it could go. I guess I was giving them more easy breezes, and when I started winning, some people began changing.

LS: *What differentiates trainers?*
BF: It's the feel you have—when you should do things and when you shouldn't. You have to watch the way each individual horse trains. Some fillies put a lot into their gallops and don't need the breezes that a laid-back filly would have.

When you get soundness problems, you have to change your training with that particular horse. Anyone can train a sound horse who can run, but you rarely find those kind of horses. So you have to give and take with the training, knowing when to go and when to slow down.

LS: *But you need an owner who allows you to slow things down.*
BF: You wouldn't believe it—I don't have one owner who pushes me. They don't even suggest when I should run. My job is just training, and calling them up and saying, "Your horse is in Thursday."

LS: *Most aren't so lucky.*
BF: I realize that. When I started training for Mr. Frankel, he was that way and gave me the confidence to do what I wanted when I wanted. And that's the way I've been.

LS: *People—those not from New York—comment about your attitude, colorful language, and your ability to intimidate. Is that just a case of you not suffering fools well?*
BF: That's pretty much what it is. I can't stand listening to bullshit, especially if people don't know what they're talking about. I just try and stay away from it, because it will just upset me, and then I'll open my mouth. Bob Baffert's got his thing—he wants to be on the stage. I don't want that. I'm happy with my life. I just want to do my thing and enjoy my life my way, y'know? I don't need the rest of it. There's no right or wrong. It's whatever you want in your life.

LS: *Describe your relationship with Juddmonte, with whom you're most closely associated.*
BF: It's real easy to train for them. I'm very relaxed because there's no pressure. I just try to do the best I can. There's nobody looking over my shoulder critiquing me or telling me where to run. It's like they're my horses, so it's a real easy job. I ask if it's OK to send a horse here or there, but pretty much I can do what I think is right.

LS: *Do you think about the irony of a Saudi prince [Khalid Abdullah] joining forces with a Jewish guy from Brooklyn?*
BF: He's under enough pressure, so I don't want to say anything about that.

LS: *You've had great success with horses from other parts of the world. What is the secret to training European imports?*
BF: Oftentimes the difference is patience. Instead of trying to rush them and risk not getting them to the races, I can give them four or six months off. When you're spending certain people's money, you have to go on with it. How can you tell an owner that you have to stop on a horse he just spent $300,000 on? I have the luxury of doing that.

You don't try to change them too much. Let them do their thing, y'know? Get along with them. Most guys get these horses and think they have no speed, and they try to put speed into them. Worst thing you can do. You ruin them that way. Guys like Billy Mott and Chris Clement are really good with them.

LS: *Is it the same deal with horses from South America?*
BF: The way they train down there is more Americanized. There's a lot of dirt racing, and you can train them a lot harder than you can the Europeans. They're sounder than the European horses. I've got a few now, and they're easy to train. Lido Palace will be a very serious horse. Happyanunoit is a New Zealand–bred, and she's going to be good. [Frankel would train Lido Palace to more than $2 million in North American earnings and Happyanunoit to more than $1.4 million in earnings. Each won three grade 1 races under him.] The negative thing about the South American horses is that they're six months younger, which is why they need a little time to catch up. And with the fillies, their cycling is the opposite of North American fillies, so they need almost a year to adapt. But they're nice to train.

LS: *How different is it training turf horses versus dirt horses?*
BF: With my style of not pressing hard on them, it seems like I can get them ready easier to run on turf. If they don't show they have speed, I don't force them. I can get them ready to run long first time out on turf. And if they don't run that great on turf, I'll switch them to dirt.

I'd rather they have an easy go of it first time out, and you have a better shot of that on the grass. Coming out of there in :22 and :45, you can ruin a lot of horses. If you want to stretch them out after that, they run off with you. You can ruin a good turf horse running them on the dirt like that first time out, y'know?

LS: *You have been pretty outspoken when talking about jockeys.*
BF: I have a lot of grass horses, and I look for riders that can get horses to relax. My horses basically come from behind, and I look for riders who are cool and can do that. Do I put too much pressure on them? I get a lot of fucked-up rides. So maybe I do put too much pressure on them. Maybe they're scared when they ride for me. Despite my reputation, I don't give them much instruction. I pretty much leave it up to them, and a lot of times I wish I *had* said things to them. But things change so much during a race you hate to have them blow a race by giving them bad instructions.

Everyone gets bad rides, I guess. But at the current meet I should have won another six or seven races; two or three big stakes. There are some riders who make less mistakes than others.

LS: *Watching you the other day, you had a big smile when Marine came back to the winner's circle. Is it still as big a kick as ever when you win one?*
BF: Oh yeah, definitely. You know, you're going to get beat most of the time. There are trainers out there who worry about their percentages and want to be so careful where they run their horses. And they'll go for an allowance race instead of a stakes race.

Me? I'm not a percentage trainer. I don't go for singles. I'm a home-run hitter. That's the way I think. I'm trying to go for home runs all the time.

4

Tony Leonard

A FORMER NIGHTCLUB SINGER who picked up a camera one day to earn extra cash, **Tony Leonard** forever changed the way horses are presented on the page. Once stallion owners saw how well their charges looked through Leonard's lens, they clamored for his services, and he soon gave up crooning to shoot stud horses throughout Kentucky. He became known as the king of the conformation shot.

Leonard knew how he wanted his horses to be posed, even though it might take hours for a handler to get the horse to stand correctly. Hence, he wasn't necessarily very popular with workers, but he certainly was with the farm owners who were seeking to attract mares to their stallions.

Leonard was an engaging and highly likable guy, a character who fit beautifully into the beat of the racetrack, which were once populated by a seemingly unending parade of colorful personalities. He shot the great horses of racing's Golden Era of the 1970s and was a favorite of Queen Elizabeth II in her travels to North America.

Leonard's rich collection of work was thankfully saved from the trash bin by the efforts of John Adger, Bobby Shiflet, and David Sorrell, and his work has been displayed in exhibitions in Kentucky and New York.

2004

Interviewed in Lexington

Lenny Shulman: *What is your background?*
Tony Leonard: I was born Leonard Anthony Bergantino in Cincinnati and went to the college of music there. In the Army I was stationed in Calcutta. I saw Gandhi being carried through the streets. Armed Forces Radio gave me a show while I was stationed there. Of three thousand on my ship, three of us were kept behind in port and didn't have to go to the war. Most of those guys got killed in Burma. My whole life is luck.

LS: *And you continued your music career after the Army.*

TL: I had a nightclub act doing Broadway songs, Gershwin, and pop. Played on Bourbon Street in New Orleans. My wife, Adele, was a dancer—legitimate—and I sang. We worked out of Chicago. In the mid-1960s I got booked into La Flame in Lexington. Over time we developed a nice following. The girls who worked on the big farms would come in on Saturday nights.

LS: *How did the photography start?*

TL: One week after I bought a camera, a stripper named Boots King asked me to take her picture in Cincinnati. She came in with her boyfriend and told me what I did was better than the top man in Chicago. She turned to her boyfriend and told him to give me a hundred bucks. I was making seventy-five dollars a week singing. I said, "Whoa, I think I may have hit on something."

A fellow named Max, who liked to drink, came into the club in Lexington and eventually taught me how to pose horses. Skeets Meyers had all the business then, but in his photos the horses looked like they were always getting ready to sit down. He didn't have them balanced. A woman named Louise who worked at Spendthrift Farm told me she'd introduce me to [Spendthrift owner] Leslie Combs, and I could see if he'd let me take pictures of the horses.

I did nine sessions with Majestic Prince and never charged Combs for it. I guaranteed my work: if they couldn't use the picture, I didn't charge them. That was a bad move. Everybody found fault in everything (*laughs*). The first picture I took at Spendthrift, I balanced the horse. And Leslie Combs said, "Tony, you want to work for us?" I ended up doing Darby Dan, Spendthrift, and on and on.

Some liked a low-headed horse; some like their stallions to be high-headed like Man o' War. So I had to learn what each one wanted.

LS: *Your career really took off after your incident with the great racehorse and stallion Ribot.*

TL: That put me on the map. He was at Darby Dan, and Olin Gentry was the farm manager. Gentry was heading out to New York, and I asked if I could go into Ribot's paddock and take pictures. Gentry wasn't paying attention to anything I was saying, so he waved me off with, "Yeah, do whatever."

So I went to Ribot's groom, Floyd, and asked him how bad the horse was, because he had a reputation as a rogue. Floyd said, "He's alright. Don't worry, I'll go in with you." We go in, and Floyd is against the fence peeling a banana, and Ribot is calm, like an old broodmare. I start walking around shooting, and I got three or four bad pictures, because I had the wrong kind of camera.

And all of a sudden it clicks inside his head that I'm in his paddock. With full force that &%#$* comes right at me. I knew he was from Italy, so I started cursing him out in Italian, and that shook him up just enough to save my life. He slid into me and put his nose right on my lens. We're three feet apart, and he threw his head back and looked at me as if to say, "I'm gonna kill you." The veins start popping out of his eyes. I would love to have had that picture.

He charged at me three times. The last time, I had gotten to the gate, which was just big enough to get through. Just as I open it, I hear "Boom, boom, boom" coming right at me. He slid into that gate. I turned to Floyd. I said, "Why did you tell me this horse is alright?" He said, "He is to me." I said, "I could have been killed." He said, "I know."

I couldn't sell those shots. I gave them to *Daily Racing Form,* and they ran them over an entire page. I got a lot of publicity from that.

LS: *You also got famous shots of Secretariat and Ruffian.*
TL: At the Belmont in 1973 I got a finish-line shot of Secretariat that was out of focus. But I had taken four pictures of him in the paddock, three of which were atrocious. The fourth one was good. My wife airbrushed out the entire background because it looked like Eddie Sweat, the groom, had no head. So it was just the horse walking by himself—no shank, no anything. I gave it to Penny Chenery, and she auctioned it off for charity years later for two thousand dollars. Belmont used it for the program cover for the Marlboro Cup one year. The programs were all snapped up before the second race.

But Secretariat's Belmont was my favorite race. I enjoy the racetrack more than conformation photos because of the excitement. There's nothing like standing at the finish line listening to those hoofs coming at you, knowing they're giving it their all. Oh man. But I didn't get the shot that day. Thirty-one lengths he won by. I remember the woman who owned Our Native, who finished third, asked me if I had gotten a shot of her horse. I told her, "Not only did I get a picture of him, I changed rolls of film first."

Some people talked [trainer] Frank Whiteley into letting me do a conformation shot of Ruffian. Whiteley was a real bastard—he'd do whatever he could to screw up the press. So I go over there, and he looks at his watch and says, "You've got three minutes." I begged him not to do that to me, to at least give me fifteen minutes. He wouldn't. Then he takes her out, and out of spite he sets her up in front of a muck pile. I got the picture. Whiteley called later and said that's the best picture ever taken of her, and he hangs up. So I quoted him in an ad I took out. He hit the roof. Grabbed me and threatened me.

LS: *Your experience with Queen Elizabeth went better than that.*
TL: Yes. Will Farish called me and said Queen Elizabeth was coming to Lane's End Farm and he needed a photographer. I jumped at the chance. I had to get fixed up with the Secret Service. They were great. Even pulled the limo up a few feet to center a shot. I gave them all pictures, and they gave me a money belt with "Secret Service" on it.

I was the only one allowed to shoot her. I followed her around to all the farms. The one shot that stands out is from Calumet, with her standing on one side of the frame and Alydar standing under a tree at the other side.

On her second trip to Lexington, the queen gets out of the limo and looks at me and says, "Mr. Leonard, is that you?" And I said, "Yes, Your Highness. Welcome to Kentucky." And she brought me over and introduced me to all her people from Buckingham Palace—eleven limos full of people. I told her I loved her, which was very American of me, and she said, "Oh, Mr. Leonard, no, really?"

LS: *You became synonymous with conformation photos of stallions.*
TL: I was the first one to pay attention to the details of taking a conformation picture. Combs told me that if you can't make the horse look better than what he is, then don't take the picture. I changed the conformation pose, and everyone around the world copied my style. Then I had to do something a little different. If I opened up the front legs just a little, you could see the knee on the other side. By spreading a little bit, the balance is perfect.

LS: *You are famous, or infamous, for taking a lot of time to get a shot you like.*
TL: It takes three minutes to three and a half hours. Mrs. Woolworth, from the five-and-dime stores, had a son named Norman who wanted me to take a shot of his mother's horse up in Chicago. I stayed three and a half hours. She was standing great, but she never stopped swishing her tail. The groom finally said he had an idea, and he stood behind the mare, and as the tail came back, he touched the top of it and it stopped swishing. I said, "Where were you three hours ago?"

I learn a lot of tricks from the grooms. They despise me when it comes to holding the horses for a long period, but they like me because they know I won't have to come back when we get it right. It's not easy. They think I take too long, but I don't. I go when you get the horse right. Sometimes you have to put them away and try again the next day. Horses can be moody. I was in Canada shooting Vice Regent and couldn't get him right. I told the groom something was wrong with him. He died the next day.

Good pictures are all about having a good eye. With great horses, I beg to do two sessions because invariably I do it better the second time.

Another trick was my wife used to whinny to get the stallions' ears upright, but she got hoarse, and I decided to replace her with a tape recorder. I got a recording of a mare whinnying, and the studs hear that and go bonkers. Their ears go straight up.

When Genuine Risk had her first foal, I got an exclusive. I heard some profanity over that one. I only had twenty minutes because the foal had come out of surgery. But I got a wonderful shot of the mare looking back at the foal. It's all luck.

LS: *Do people want to tweak the conformation shot?*
TL: Now the big farms are competing with each other so much they want you to try different shots. Someone started with the twisting of the head, and it bothers me because it's not natural; it does not give the full complement to how the horse really looks. They want something that stands out, but I wouldn't go to that. In my opinion, I've been doing it right all along.

I was in Italy once being interviewed, and they asked me about my competitors, and I said I only had one, but he died. They asked me who it was, and I said, "Michelangelo." The guy was laughing so hard he had to stop the interview.

LS: *You had another singing engagement recently, at Yankee Stadium.*
TL: Oh man, yeah. Years ago, I ran into George Steinbrenner at the Campbell House in Lexington and played him a tape of me singing, and he invited me to New York to sing the national anthem. I wasn't a singer anymore, so I wasn't nervous. The organist hit the wrong pitch, and I started and stopped. Then I started again, and it went fine. The thought goes through your mind that Babe Ruth and Lou Gehrig stood where you're standing. Oh man. It's been a great life.

5

Cot Campbell

COT CAMPBELL CHANGED THE game of horse racing ownership more than any other person in history. After watching his father go bust on a horse-farming operation, Campbell, saddled with a taste for whiskey that once caused him to set ablaze his own rooming house, tried a variety of occupations.

But he found his way after studying the syndication model of other businesses and applied the partnership concept to horse racing. At first shunned by traditionalists who saw him as a barbarian at the gates, Campbell arrived in full bloom after his Dogwood Stable's Summer Squall won the 1990 Preakness Stakes. Soon, Campbell's partnerships were populated by titans of industry as well as regular folk looking to get their feet wet in the thrill of owning a racehorse.

Campbell, who was based in Aiken, South Carolina, was a fixture annually at Saratoga. Along with his partner in hospitality, Anne, he made the racing experience an unfailingly fun time, an ongoing party that they hosted for decades with southern gentility and a gleam in their eyes.

Today, partnerships make up the ownership of nearly every racehorse in training, and Campbell's vision has been vindicated as the backbone of racing. He lived to see himself lauded as the George Washington of this great change that made racing accessible to thousands of owners, and to be inducted into its Hall of Fame.

2011

Interviewed in Lexington

Lenny Shulman: *Not too many people know you were quite a rider at one point.*
Cot Campbell: My father was interested in horses. He was a Coca-Cola bottler in Des Moines, Iowa, and was a great fella who was up and down in business. When he was flush with cash, he had some saddle horses. I rode them and did pretty well; I was a championship rider in Missouri, Nebraska, and Iowa. Then he decided to sell his Coca-Cola plant in 1940 and go into racehorses, which he knew nothing about. He wasn't gonna make it anyway, but World War II came along and helped sink him. But he had built a racetrack on his farm in Tennessee,

Cot and Anne Campbell (Keeneland Association by John Wyatt)

and I was exposed to racehorses. Went to the Derby in 1942 and fell in love with it.

LS: *You lived a bit of a gypsy lifestyle for a while.*
CC: I worked at everything, from being a mortician to a newspaper reporter, among other things. Alcohol played a large role, and when I started a fire that burned off a floor of the boardinghouse where I was living, that was the wake-up call. I moved to Atlanta, got sober, and cofounded a successful advertising agency.

LS: *How did you start in horse ownership?*
CC: I raced a few claiming horses with friends in a partnership agreement. My father had become an oil wildcatter and used to syndicate drilling leases, and he mentioned it to me. So I did a limited partnership with a few pals. In 1971 we bought a filly with crooked ankles for five thousand dollars. She won the Alcibiades Stakes at Keeneland. That was Mrs. Cornwallis. And the *Wall Street Journal* took notice and ran a front-page piece on this novel concept of horse ownership.

The next thing you know, people were calling and asking about it. We gained momentum, and it blossomed out to people around the country. Soon, I had forty investors and eighteen horses. I had to decide between the ad business and the horses, and the only person who thought it was a good idea to choose the horses was my wife, Anne. She was all for it. We had great enthusiasm, which is half the battle.

LS: *And it didn't hurt that your Dogwood Stable enjoyed some early success.*

CC: Yes, winning the Bernard Baruch with Dominion did a lot for us. He criss-crossed the country; he didn't win every race, but he was right there on Saturday afternoons, and he put us in the limelight. If there was a horse who was closest to my heart, it would have to be him. Then, certainly Summer Squall was a break-through. We thought we were going to win the [Kentucky] Derby [in 1990] for about thirty seconds, but winning the Preakness with him was a great thing. It was like throwing a stone in a pool. The ripples keep coming out, and nobody can ever take that away from you. It's like stamping your report card with a big A+ on it.

LS: *But you weren't readily accepted among the racing elite?*

CC: It was not a popular thing within the industry. We represented a break from tradition as far as the Kentucky horsemen were concerned. When we won the Alcibiades, Keeneland scraped up a few people for the postrace celebration, and Duval Headley said to me, "I'm not familiar with your nom de course." I didn't know what a "nom de course" was, but perhaps he was inquiring in a subtle way, "What's the deal here?" It was not originally embraced . . . until we started winning.

It's interesting to me today that some of the Kentucky breeders who scoffed at partnerships and looked down their noses are now putting together partner-ships. It was an idea whose time had come then. It was just logical as a way to own a racehorse and participate at a high level while limiting your exposure.

LS: *You spawned many copycats.*

CC: In the early days people would call, wanting to see our legal agreement. They were trying to go to school on it. I would get frantic about it then, but I don't give a damn now. I'm happy to tell how we do it. I'm relaxed about it, and should be.

Centennial Farms came around about ten years after us, and it was involved in a brokerage firm in Boston, so it made sense for them. Brokerage houses embraced partnerships for a period of time. That concept flourished, then sub-sided, and a wave of relatively informal partnerships came in.

I have a very pleasant relationship with Terry Finley of West Point Thoroughbreds, and I admire what he's done. He wants to be bigger than I ever wanted to be. I wanted it to provide me with a great way of life, which it has. I just wanted to be involved in racing and have a good time.

LS: *With the Dogwood newsletter you send out with pictures of all the parties, and costumes, it seems you really have tried to stress the social aspect of horse racing.*
CC: It's supposed to be fun. People who have gotten involved with us know full well the likelihood of profit is small. We were very straightforward about that. But we've not let it get too heavy, and we've not taken ourselves too seriously. We've always had a little zaniness about us.

And I've got great resiliency. My God, I really do. So does Anne. No matter what, I can walk out of the racetrack with a smile on my face. It may hit me two or three nights later at four o'clock in the morning, but I'm not gonna let anybody see it.

Anne and I are both gifted at keeping things moving along and stimulated. We take our best shot at making a day at the races a happy occasion. We're not nervous wrecks about whether everybody is doing well. Our people, for the most part, feel comfortable at the races.

I've always screened prospective clients. I remember a guy came to the farm to see some horses, but he wanted to show me his business plan. And I tried to show him the horses, but he wanted to talk about his business plan, with which, according to his calculations, we could make $23,418. I told him that both of us are going to be happier if we don't do business together.

In a nutshell, I tell people this is something that might make money, but chances are it won't, so don't count on it. And if it doesn't, you're going to have a good tax write-off, and it's going to put a good deal of zest, excitement, and glamour in your life.

LS: *And you have introduced many people to the game, plenty of whom have gone on to own horses themselves.*
CC: We've brought about one thousand people into the sport as clients. Paul Oreffice, the former chairman of Dow Chemical, has been in on every one of our horses. You'd think a strong man like that would be a pain in the neck, but as head of a big company he knows about delegating, and he believes in me and has grinned the entire time. He's been wonderful.

We've had Will Farish, Warner Jones, Jim Tafel, George Strawbridge, Bob Lewis, Tommy Valando. Real blue-chip guys. Those who have gone on and wanted to move their own checkers, I absolutely understand that. No hard feelings when somebody moves on.

LS: *What is it you love most about the horse game?*
CC: The characters, certainly. The people who are in this have sporting blood; they're gamblers in one way or another. They're a little bit off the mark. And, yes, we have people who get into this business who have a slight bent toward larceny. But most are smart, and they know it's smarter to be honest than to be larcenous. I've known a few of each kind. But they're wonderful characters. The great thing here is that everyone is equalized. You see grooms speaking up to a millionaire in the shedrow. That's great.

The horse business has kept me young. I'm not as young as I want to be, but I'm better off for having been in the horse business. I love to get up in the morning and go to the barn. That gives you a fresh outlook, and I love that part of it. Saratoga and Keeneland are some of the great things in our lives.

LS: *Do you and Anne have hobbies?*
CC: We read a lot and love to go to the theater. I've taken up golf. We make sure our lives are not immersed in only horses. We've traveled quite a bit. Several years ago, I took up the ukulele. The banjo player in the Dixieland band at Saratoga, Reggie's Red Hot Feet Warmers, gave me lessons. I made the horrible mistake on three occasions of playing it in front of other human beings. And I will never do that again.

6

Tom Durkin

TOM DURKIN BROUGHT HORSE racing out of the black-and-white world and into full color. Prior to his arrival, racetrack announcers were file clerks, giving out horses' names and the lengths that separated them from one another. Durkin, however, painted flowing pictures with his verbal descriptions of a race. Without sacrificing accuracy, he placed each race into the context of telling a story.

There is no count of how many fans he helped create for horse racing. But I guarantee it is more than one might imagine. And I know, because I was hooked back into the sport in the early 1990s while listening to the brilliant California race-caller Trevor Denman, who made requisite viewing of and listening to his nightly television recap show. I would never have immersed myself in horse racing if not for Denman's brilliance, and I am confident thousands of others feel the same after having heard him and Durkin.

Durkin was undoubtedly a core reason why racing attracted lucrative contracts from TV networks for its biggest days early in the twenty-first century.

Durkin's popularity has only grown after his retirement from the microphone. He is the unofficial godfather of all things horse racing around his home in Saratoga Springs, New York. His tours of the National Museum of Racing and Hall of Fame are the toughest ticket in town, and he contributes his genius to charitable causes in all facets of the racing world, including calling bingo games as part of Saratoga's Backstretch Worker Appreciation program. He cannot walk five paces in public without being stopped by a fan wanting to share a favorite race call.

2006

Interviewed from New York

Lenny Shulman: *What were your career ambitions early in your life?*
Tom Durkin: There was a time when I wanted to be pope. I grew up Catholic and had a great respect for clergy, and I thought being pope was a pretty good idea. But then I realized the celibate lifestyle and vows of poverty and obedience would not suit my personality, and soon after I came upon the idea of wanting to be a race-caller.

LS: *You have brought an element of theater to your job.*
TD: The track is an exciting place to be. Growing up in Chicago, we had a very charismatic race-caller in Phil Georgeff, my childhood hero. I have no predilection toward horses; I'm not a hands-on horseperson at all. In fact, I'm allergic to them. But I love the game and the horses. My personality is more bent toward performance. Some people are managers, some are builders, negotiators. I'm a performer. At the track there are only two performers—the announcer and the bugler. And I can't play the trumpet. I did acting in college, majored in theater as a vehicle to perform as a race-caller. There is no race-calling major yet that I know of.

LS: *What was the first Breeders' Cup like in 1984 at Hollywood Park?*
TD: It was absurd, really. It was an orgy of money. There had never been anything like it moneywise. When Chief's Crown crossed the wire in the Juvenile, which was the first Breeders' Cup race, I said, "A champion is crowned. And it's Chief's Crown." And that's when I realized that this is the finals, and if you win, you're the definitive champ. You couldn't really say it up till that moment.

After the Breeders' Cup races were over, I really needed a drink. Here I was, three years removed from being the announcer at Cahokia Downs. So I walk into the party room, and I ask the security guard if he'll watch my binoculars while I get a drink. And he says, "Sure, but when my guy goes, I've got to leave." I ask him who his guy is, and he points over his shoulder, and it's [former President] Gerald Ford. And then I look in the room and there's Elizabeth Taylor, Frank Sinatra, Cary Grant, Zsa Zsa Gabor, Merv Griffin, and Fred Astaire. I didn't talk to any of them.

LS: *Do announcers ever get together and tell war stories?*
TD: An announcers' reunion? We don't see each other much. If we did, we'd bitch about work and how we don't get paid enough. Of the guys I know, Larry Lederman is the funniest. One thing I will say about nearly every announcer I know, including myself: We all have a legitimate, diagnosable, mental health problem. And I'm right near the top of that list.

LS: *Do you listen to other guys call races?*
TD: When I prepared for Breeders' Cup by going over tapes, I'd turn down the volume because I'd find myself listening too much to the announcers. I don't want to put in my subconscious certain things about the horses, for fear they would come out again during the Breeders' Cup call. No disrespect, but I don't want somebody else's ideas in my mind. But I listen to others on simulcasts, sure.

LS: *Are there calls you've made that are "one and done," that you never use again?*
TD: Yes. Here, I'll show you my book full of words. See, there are certain things I cross off. I crossed out the word "sublime," which is the word I ascribed to Barbaro in the Derby. That's retired. There are a few of those in here.

LS: *Let's play word association with some Breeders' Cup moments. Arazi.*
TD: Greatest two-year-old ever. Spectacular move on the far turn at Churchill. I'd never seen any of his races, even on tape.

LS: *Tiznow winning in New York after 9/11 ("Tiznow wins it for America.").*
TD: A shade jingoistic, but appropriate. Exciting. Gallant. I stand by that call. These are stories, and the story that day was the pall that 9/11 cast over the place. There were SWAT guys standing two feet above me with machine guns. Here was an American horse against foreign horses, and there was great patriotic fervor. What you try to do is describe stories, and there are issues, and that was an issue.

LS: *Arcangues winning the 1993 Classic at 132–1.*
TD: He's one reason why I have more gray hair, and less hair in general. The hard part in calling races is horses that look alike, and he looked exactly like Ezzoud. And to boot they have the exact same colors [silks]. They switched places on me at some point in the race—Ezzoud was closer to the front, and then he took back, and Arcangues was in the back and all of a sudden rushed up into the spot Ezzoud had been in.

Arcangues had a little white diamond on his forehead, and they're coming down the stretch, and I'm saying to myself, "There's that diamond, but it can't be Arcangues." I was fortunate in my research that I had a picture in my head of that diamond, and I just called his name and crossed my fingers. Because if I say, "Arcangues wins the Breeders' Cup Classic, he's 99–1," and it's Ezzoud, that's the end of my career right there.

2014

Upon his retirement from race-calling, interviewed in Saratoga Springs, New York

Lenny Shulman: *Why retire now?*
Tom Durkin: I could have played out this string another four, five, six years. But I didn't ever want to come in here one day and not be able to do my best, so I think it's best to get off the stage before that happens.

LS: *Any plans?*

TD: I hope to keep my hand in racing in some way. I go to Italy every year for an extended visit. I did a voice-over for an ad today. Never got any calluses doing voice-over work.

LS: *I saw a banner up on Nelson Avenue with a picture of you that read, "Thanks for the memories, Tom." How are you handling these accolades?*

TD: Not well. It's overwhelming. I had no idea the reaction from people would be like this. Some people start crying. The media attention is crazy. I'm doing two interviews a day. Sentiments are very deep. People love horse racing, and they're uncomfortable with change. I'm emotionally overwhelmed. I didn't realize. I mean, people have been very nice to me right along. They've sent mail, they stop me on the street and have something really nice to say. I've never been very good taking compliments. That's just my nature. This has been a bit tough to handle.

LS: *You helped take race-calls from simply intoning names and lengths to telling a story.*

TD: I view it as an entertainment. It's really plot and narrative. The narrative is the lengths and margins and times. The plot is in the footnotes, and I tried to pay more attention to those, and expanding on those. I got a thesaurus. "Blocked" could become "stymied." People will accept you being clever. With humor, you have to tread lightly because people are betting, and you'd better choose your spots. But I've tried to make it exciting and lively.

LS: *I've watched you here. You can't take three steps before somebody comes up to you with a memory.*

TD: People remember stuff. They'll say, "I remember when you said this . . . And I'll say, "Yeah, yeah," but I don't remember whatsoever. It means more if they cash a ticket on it. One time I said, "So and so leaves so and so in his wake." And a guy comes up to me and tells me it was the funniest thing he ever heard. And I said, "What's so funny about that?" And he repeated the call: "The Undertaker leaves him in his wake." And I had no idea when I said it. Your subconscious works like that.

LS: *Things you won't miss?*

TD: The stress. That's the biggie. I won't miss my crayons and putting down the colors of the horses before every race. I'm looking forward to reading more, traveling more, golfing, cooking. I want to live a meaningful and relevant life. That's my goal. I didn't find a cure for cancer, and I could have done better. But it's turned out to be pretty good.

7

Bob Baffert

IN BASEBALL, THE TOUGHEST ball for an outfielder to play is the line drive hit directly at him, because the speed and height are difficult to quickly determine.

Trainer **Bob Baffert** is like a fiercely struck line drive for those of us chronicling the first couple of decades of this century. We know he is at the top of the game, but we don't fully understand where his ball will land in the broader historical context.

We do know he's moved past Wayne Lukas as the all-time winningest trainer of Triple Crown races, and that his two Triple Crown triumphs put him alongside the legendary "Sunny" Jim Fitzsimmons as the only two trainers to accomplish that. He won't end up with the most wins or stakes wins over his career because his barn is based much more on quality than it is quantity, but Baffert will have pages devoted to him in the history books as the greatest trainer of his time.

More than that, he has taken over from Lukas as the face of horse racing to the public at large, a responsibility he has embraced since the late 1990s, when he began winning Kentucky Derbys. He is the first top trainer to have grown up in the television age, and the first to embrace the cameras pointed in his direction. Although his sense of humor has not always been appreciated by those he's vanquished, his antics, such as placing the Preakness trainer's trophy cup upside-down on his head, have won the sport a new generation of fans, ones who grew up rooting for a different breed of sports hero such as Muhammad Ali and Joe Namath.

Like each of the others named here, there is no doubt Baffert is a Legend of the Industry.

2007

Interviewed at Santa Anita Park after a lull in his career

Lenny Shulman: *It's interesting that you've said, "Don't call this a comeback, because I've never left."*

Bob Baffert: I've been working every day; haven't had a vacation. I've had a lot of good horses, but without the big clients you don't have the numbers to work with, and this is a numbers game. One guy can come with a horse and get lucky and

"Boom," you're off. But to keep it going and stay at the top for years with runner after runner . . .

LS: *Major clients of yours like Prince Ahmed Salman, Bob Lewis, and John Mabee passed away in a short amount of time. That must have hurt.*
BB: It made a huge difference. The numbers have suffered, and the process has changed. A lot of the big guys now have agents or racing managers. Those guys have a tough job, and they need results. What's hurt me is I like to pick out my own horses at sales, because I'm the one who has to live with them. It's like a marriage. So these agents figure if they commit to me, they're not going to be able to pick out the horses.

LS: *You must have heard the whispers the past couple of years that it was over for you.*
BB: A jockey agent saw me at Del Mar and said, "Look, it's dead man walking." It wasn't working for me there with the synthetic track. It's the first time in my career I got scared. I thought, "If this is the future of racing in California, I'm in trouble." I was in a total funk. I decided to take horses to Saratoga, which is the best thing that could have happened. Those horses started winning—More Happy, Maimonides; Indian Blessing broke the track record. It lit a fire under me.

LS: *You're the closest thing to a rock star this sport has seen. Why is that?*
BB: Horse racing is like boxing: tough and dangerous. So I've tried to stay on the lighter side and have fun. I want to make it enjoyable. Horsemen go to big races with horses and they're stressed out, worried about this and that. I'd rather take it like, "I'm so lucky to be here, let's make the most out of it." And when I have a good horse, I want to share it with everybody. I remember when Bill Mott brought Cigar to Del Mar, and I ran up there with my brother to watch him train. To me, as a fan, watching him go by was awesome.

I decided if I ever had a good horse, I was going to share him like that, because there are people like me who truly love horses, and they appreciate stuff like that. So if somebody comes by and asks to take a look at a horse, I'm like, "Yeah, come on in." And they'll remember that for the rest of their life.

LS: *What's your relationship with other trainers?*
BB: We work long hours, and everyone's tired. I don't go out to dinner with any of them. At Saratoga I hung out with [Bobby] Frankel, a no-BS kind of guy. Nothing phony. He's competitive. There was a time when I liked [Wayne] Lukas, and then for a time I didn't. I was jealous of him he was beating me. But I worked harder and got up there, and I was able to like him again.

LS: *What did you learn from your quarter horse days that still serves you well?*

BB: I learned everything from my father. I was like a sponge, constantly asking him stuff. I learned good horsemanship; I learned how to break my own horses; I learned how to get them ready. It was a lot of trial and error. Mostly error. You had to learn how to fix problems. In those days there was no medication. You used Absorbine and alcohol, and you rubbed legs for hours until the filling was gone. You learn legs; you learn how much they can handle. To this day I still go back and sort of Google my mind to when I had this problem before, and you remember some off-the-wall remedy that worked on some quarter horse.

LS: *What was your first Kentucky Derby like?*

BB: When Cavonnier won the Santa Anita Derby [in 1996], that was a thrilling moment for me. Because it really meant you have a shot to run in the Kentucky Derby. You won the playoff, and you're going to the Super Bowl with a legit shot.

I remember arriving at Churchill Downs with Cavonnier, and there was one guy—a photographer—there to greet me. And he always reminds me he was the only guy there. The excitement of that year; when you have a good horse, it brings so many people together.

When he got beat a nose, oh, that was horrible. The night before, I was hoping to hit the board. If he'd lost by three lengths and run second, I'd have been so happy. But being in front all the way to the wire and having it snatched away, that was cruel. I figured I at least got the worst loss of my life out of the way. Nothing could top that beat. And then two years later, Real Quiet gets beat a nose for the Triple Crown. But he'd already given us the Kentucky Derby and the Preakness, and he ran great. But that Derby . . .

People asked me how I could take those losses so well. How many guys even get that chance, to get so close? If you saw the tracks I trained on in Arizona, believe me, I haven't forgotten where I came from. Training at those bush tracks, I never imagined . . .

LS: *And you won the Derby the next year for Bob Lewis, and then the year after that for your great friend Mike Pegram.*

BB: I learned a lot from Bob Lewis. I believe in karma, or fate, or whatever you want to call it. Winning with Silver Charm—I could have bought that horse for anybody, but it was Bob Lewis who got him. I had nothing running well for Bob at that time, and Silver Charm saved me with him. And then to come back with Real Quiet for Mike, who had come to the winner's circle for Silver Charm, and I had dedicated that win to him for getting me started, and he had tears in his eyes.

LS: *What have you learned from your time in the spotlight?*
BB: Don't talk when you're upset. You say something in the moment, and it may have sounded good to you, but then when you read it somewhere, it's like, "Oh, hell, what was I thinking?" And you can't take it back. If you keep talking about it, you just dig yourself in deeper. People think you're an asshole, and it gets you in trouble.

I try to be the fun guy I've always been. I did that deal where I dressed up like Austin Powers. I don't go out looking for that stuff; people think I'm a ham. They [TV producers] come to you and ask. I did that stuff to promote the sport because I love it and want it to go on forever. I want my younger kids to be at a Derby where they can appreciate it. That's the way I can give back. I give to charities. These horses have been so good to me. My family loves the sport.

That Breeders' Cup [in 2007 Baffert won the Breeders' Cup Juvenile Fillies with Indian Blessing and the Sprint with Midnight Lute] brought everything back, gave me the confidence that I'm not finished, I'm not washed up. Given the right tools, I can still get it done. I still have it. I want to be a trainer that, with the right horse in my hands, I'm dangerous. I can get it done no matter how I'm doing at the time.

2018

Baffert had been inducted into the Hall of Fame in 2009, had won the Triple Crown in 2015 with American Pharoah, and was just beginning to train Justify up to the 2018 Triple Crown. Interviewed at Santa Anita Park

Lenny Shulman: *You just turned sixty-five. How does that feel?*
Bob Baffert: Once you turn sixty, you don't want anybody to know how old you are. [Jockey] Mike Smith has been fifty the last four years. I don't feel sixty-five, but it's hard for me to say. People will be describing somebody as pretty old, and you ask how old they are, and they say, "Sixty-five."

LS: *Do you ever think about doing something else?*
BB: It's too late. I missed my window. When I was younger, I always wanted to learn how to play the guitar and be in a rock band. But the talent wasn't there. So this is it. There's no turning back now.

LS: *You're in the Hall of Fame, you've won the Triple Crown. Do you have to fight the sense of "been there, done that" to stay fresh?*

BB: Not really. I always thought what it would be like to win the Triple Crown. Once we won it, I remember on the walk to the winner's circle thinking, "Now I know what it feels like," but the bad thing was my parents weren't there to share it with me. I wish it would have happened earlier. It was just my own personal accomplishment, but when they were alive, my accomplishments were their accomplishments, too, that their boy did it.

So I didn't feel like, "OK, I got that out of the way" when I won it. That whole experience was incredible with American Pharoah. At the Derby, we knew we had the horse, and the way he won the Preakness was one of his best races. It's always been said that the number-one quality of a great horse is speed. And the second-best quality of a great horse is more speed. And that's what American Pharoah had.

I always thought about why I came up short in all those other Triple Crown attempts. Now I know why. I didn't have that extra-extraordinary horse with that kind of talent. He just kept going and getting stronger with every race.

I think my drive—once you've been spoiled to have all these great horses— you want to keep it going. You want the party to keep going, and the only way that's going to happen is to keep working hard. Trainers are only as good as their last good horse. And you better come with one in the next few years or else they're going to forget about you. So Pharoah, Arrogate, West Coast, McKinzie, Justify— we don't know what kind of horse he is. But you need those clients, those big guys that buy those horses.

LS: *But it must be easier now that people are calling you instead of you needing to go out and hustle up owners?*
BB: I've endured a lot of things. [Wife] Jill is my biggest cheerleader. Whenever I get down, she'll ask me if I'm the best. And I'll go, "Yeah." And she says, "Then you have nothing to worry about." And so that's what keeps clients. I think I'm the best. I may not *be* the best, but in my mind, I think I'm the best.

LS: *Are you getting better at your job?*
BB: I think I'm a better trainer than I was ten years ago. I'm a little bit more patient instead of trying to force something to happen. When you do that, it's not going to happen. I have a clientele now that knows when I have a good horse, I'm going to do right by it and take my time. Also, I used to have to go out and buy my own horses. Now, the big outfits are sending horses, which makes it so much easier. If you don't have the big players, you're going to have a tough time. Sure, you can get lucky once in a while. You might luck into a freak.

LS: *What was that moment like of winning the Triple Crown?*
BB: It was a beautiful moment. That day went so smooth, and it was magical. I remember [Baffert's friend and Los Alamito executive] Brad McKinzie in 1988 invited my brother and me to a World Series game at Dodger Stadium, the game where Kirk Gibson hit the walk-off home run and everybody was screaming and carrying on. One of the greatest sports moments in history. And the Belmont was the same way. So loud, and for a long time. He was coming down the stretch, and it was the first time I didn't say a word. I was watching it happen and waiting for the story to go bad. "OK, here comes Frosted. This is where it ends."

And then Frosted started gassing it, and Pharoah was moving away, and I was, "Wow." I was in awe. I didn't say a word, never cheered for my horse coming down the stretch. I was like, "Is this really happening? I'm going to win the Triple Crown, and I don't know how to act." I was shocked, like everyone else.

LS: *Talk about the ups and downs you go through training horses.*
BB: When you have a good horse and you win a big race, there's no feeling like it. But you really have to have the right type of personality for horse racing, because it can beat you up. You need clientele who know the brutal part of the sport but also know the end game can be unbelievable, and they live for that.

After Gary West won the Travers last year we went to dinner, and Jill asked him how it felt when West Coast turned for home on the lead. He said, "I was waiting for all of them to pass him." Then he said, "It was the best day of my life." And he got very emotional. Here's a billionaire, obviously very successful, and he cried. That's what these horses mean. That's the kind of passion they bring out.

LS: *What do you hope [son] Bode takes away from your success?*
BB: I don't encourage him to become a horse trainer because there are too many disappointments and a lot of failure. You need the right personality for it. There are times when you get really down and have to fight through it. There are times I've wanted to quit, when I didn't want to be a trainer because I couldn't take the disappointment.

It happened back when I was with my dad in the quarter horses. He owned the fastest qualifier, and she came back and ran fifth. I couldn't take it. I thought, "This is bullshit." And I quit. I came back a year later because somebody offered me a job taking care of some mares and maybe having one racehorse. It bothered me that I'd never won a stakes race, so I gave it another try to just get that one stakes win.

LS: *When you go to Kentucky now, your graduates are standing at stud at virtually every farm in the Bluegrass.*
BB: I love that history of it. I'll spend hours on YouTube watching Dr. Fager, Man o' War, Slew. They were all great in their time. I know you can't really compare horses from all these various times. But Bode and I were watching Man o' War win a race by like one hundred lengths. He was looking up all the Derby winners and trying to compare Pharoah. I got in some hot water last year when I said we hadn't seen a horse like Arrogate since Secretariat. I think Arrogate and American Pharoah were as good as any horse that has ever stepped on a track. And we can argue about it all you want.

But I feel like someone watching racing one hundred years from now will look back and think that Bob Baffert had some pretty great horses.

Part II

Women of the Thoroughbred World

WITHOUT A DOUBT, HORSE RACING HAS EMBRACED THE PARTICIPATION OF WOMEN MORE THAN ANY OTHER SPORT, WITHOUT THE NEED TO CREATE SEPARATE LEAGUES FOR the genders. Going back to the mid-twentieth century, it was not at all unusual for women to head up major racing stables or run top Thoroughbred farms.

Elizabeth Kane managed August Belmont's Nursery Stud and raised the great Man o' War in the early part of the last century. Elizabeth Daingerfield was the stud manager for Sam Riddle's Riddle Farm, and managed Man o' War's stud career.

Charlie Whittingham owed his success as a trainer to the initial support of women owners such as Mary Florsheim Jones, Mary Elizabeth Altemus, and Greer Garson. Other women in charge of major racing stables included Eve Arden, Gladys Mills Phipps, Helen Hay Whitney, Martha Geery, and Marylou Whitney.

The modern era has seen little drop-off in this phenomenon. While women jockeys and trainers no longer represent the novelty they once did, their participation still lags behind that of their male counterparts. Nobody bats an eye, however, when considering that major breeding operations such as Mill Ridge Farm, Summer Wind Farm, Stonestreet, Pin Oak, Middlebrook, Sequel, Paul's Mill, and Live Oak Plantation are, or have been, helmed by women.

Tampa Bay Downs is owned by Stella Thayer. Belinda Stronach operates the Stronach Group, owner of major racetracks from coast to coast. Shannon Bishop Arvin was named president and CEO of Keeneland in 2020. Women sit on executive and regulatory boards throughout the racing world. Many run their own racing stables or participate as full partners with their spouses or other relatives.

It seems horse racing does not receive the credit it is due for its early embrace of equal opportunity. For many of my generation, Penny Chenery set the pace for others to follow, and it was not the least bit unusual for a reporter covering the sport from the mid-twentieth century forward to find that his interview subject was a strong woman.

8

Helen Alexander

LIKE HER EQUINE FAMILIES, excellence has been a hallmark for generations of **Helen Alexander**'s human connections. She is a granddaughter of Robert Kleberg, whose King Ranch dominated racing from his Texas base, winning the Kentucky Derby in 1946 with Assault and again four years later courtesy of Middleground. Alexander, busting through the gender line, began managing King Ranch very early in life and then moved to Kentucky to helm a division of that operation in the center of the Thoroughbred world. She eventually established Middlebrook Farm in the heart of the Bluegrass. Often in partnership with her mother, Helen Groves, and sisters Dorothy Matz and Emory Hamilton, Alexander has built and furthered generations of the most desirable families in the American Stud Book.

Beginning with her fortuitous purchase of the blue hen mare Courtly Dee, Alexander, while almost invariably naming her horses with the first letter *A*, has maintained her status as one of the most respected breeders in the world. A top success came when Bayern, a horse she bred out of her mare Alittlebitearly, won the Breeders' Cup Classic.

2005

Interviewed at Middlebrook Farm in Lexington

Lenny Shulman: *Did you grow up on your family's legendary King Ranch in Texas?*
Helen Alexander: My mother had a cattle operation in Pennsylvania where I grew up. We moved cattle for Mom, but horses were my passion. Once I got the bridle on, it was all over. I was on the loose. I'd catch my pony in the morning and go riding. I was eight or nine. It was very rural back then, and we used our ponies for transportation.

LS: *Did your grandfather Robert Kleberg, who established such a successful Thoroughbred operation, encourage you with the horses?*
HA: I was the oldest sibling, and every one of us became involved in horses in one way or another. I did a lot of traveling with my grandfather, and he did foster my interest in the horse business. He got me thinking about matings, and we'd talk

Helen Alexander (Keeneland Library Featherston Collection)

about what mares were going to be bred to which stallions and the attributes of different mares and families and stallions. I'd help name the horses and see the babies train at the ranch.

I remember going with my parents to South Carolina to the training center to see Max Hirsch, the King Ranch trainer. We were just little kids, but I remember it so well. Max and Buddy Hirsch were amazing. They always had sugar they gave us to feed the horses, and they'd lead out every single horse for my grandfather to see. I sat there like a sponge soaking up everything they said.

LS: *When you were in your early twenties, you took over the Thoroughbred operation of King Ranch after your grandfather died. That had to be trying for a young woman at that time.*

HA: To be honest, I wasn't aware of any pressure taking over the operation, even though I was young and a woman. That was mostly because I was so involved in the job. I was more concerned with getting the work done, and I was blissfully unaware of any issues that might have been facing me. I came through it without recognizing any of that. I just kept my head down and did my job and made the best out of what I could.

When you're young, you don't notice that you're working constantly. I was so happy doing it. You love horses, you love being out in the country, you love going to races—it was all a good thing.

LS: *King Ranch was a large, diversified operation involved in many different businesses.*

HA: Yes, there was a board of directors made up of family members down in Texas, and I was already in Kentucky. We had different cost centers, with the farm and racing. Costs were going up, and we were selling a lot of international properties owned by King Ranch, and eventually there wasn't enough interest within the family to keep going with the racing. The plan was to consolidate everything back to Texas and concentrate on a few primary areas of business, so the Thoroughbred operation was closed down.

LS: *And you started your current farm, Middlebrook.*

HA: I actually bought Middlebrook before the dispersal of King Ranch stock. I was looking for an older house; I wasn't looking to buy a farm. But the real estate agent pulled in here, and I said, "My God, this is it. This is the place I want." So instead of a small place, I got 350 acres. It's a beautiful setting and isolated back off the road, so it makes you feel like you're farther away.

LS: *You barely missed a beat.*

HA: Well, we still had some King Ranch horses, though most were dispersed. My mother [Helen Groves] had a few, and my sister Emory Hamilton was getting more into it. We found that the King Ranch mares had been bred for stamina for a really long time, and when we started putting a little more speed in those pedigrees, boy, it gave them a new lease on life. It was unbelievable.

We have horses now that are fifth and sixth generation from when we started with the families. So you have to look and see what you've got, and see what's worked and what hasn't, and then think about where you're trying to go with a particular mare. That's one of the most interesting parts of the jigsaw puzzle—figuring out what you need to do to get the best baby you can.

LS: *And in 1980 you spent $900,000 at auction to buy Courtly Dee, which started one of the great families in the pedigree book.*

HA: That was nervous time, buying one for that kind of money. My mother, David Aykroyd, and I partnered on her. We had great success breeding her to Alydar, getting [grade 1 winner] Althea, [grade 2 winner] Aishah, and [grade 2 winner] Aquilegia. And then they all became producers. Ten of Courtly Dee's eleven daughters are stakes producers. And then Althea had two daughters who became grade 1 producers. Aurora produced grade 1 winners Acoma and Arch.

LS: *Do you have to think about more than just the commercial market when you're cultivating generations of families?*

HA: For some people, it's strictly a business. They're not going to build a broodmare band, and they're just going to keep turning things over. You can make money doing that. But if you have families of horses and you want to keep those families and make them successful, you need to be thinking about what's the best thing in terms of racing performance for them. Because if you don't get the racing performance over time, that family is going to shrivel up or lay dormant for a while until somebody picks it up and does something with it again.

LS: *You famously give your horses names beginning with the letter A. What's the story behind that?*

HA: It just started by happenchance. It wasn't really designed, but people expected us to come up with names starting with A after a while. It's getting to be more of a challenge. It's also a challenge for people on the farm and at the track to keep them straight. We've got a whole bunch of them here. We've gotten some grief from the sales companies also. We have sixteen mares on the farm right now whose names start with A, thirteen of them from the Courtly Dee family.

LS: *You have been outspoken in criticizing medication's effect on the breed.*

HA: Unfortunately, I think it distorts everything. It's going to show up over time in every pedigree, and nobody is going to know whether they're buying the real thing, or whether it needs to be hopped up to perform. That goes for stallions and female families. If you've kept your families clean, it might be to your detriment because they might be grade 1–placed instead of being grade 1 winners.

Back in the thirties and forties there was a lot of talk about people using heroin and all these other drugs in horses. Whether they did or not, I don't know. I do feel if we want to keep this business going, it behooves us to make sure that it's run on a level playing field for everybody—breeders, owners, and fans.

It enters into your thinking about what stallions to breed to. You don't know; you can only surmise, and that's not a really good way of making selections.

LS: *You have been a leader in preserving farmland around Lexington.*
HA: I think the Purchase of Development Rights (PDR) program in Fayette County has been a great success, and it's being looked at by a lot of other counties and states as a model. Tobacco is being phased out, and there is a lot of fragmentation of the agricultural area in the county, so it is something that needed to be addressed. We've gotten federal money to help, and we currently have fourteen thousand acres under easement in PDR. The target is fifty thousand. It's expensive and it takes time, but we've been blown away by the reception we've had from the agricultural community.

It takes five or ten years to get people comfortable with the idea of selling easements. But we got thirty-three farms in our first round, where we thought we'd get five, so it's been pretty incredible. The agricultural areas around Lexington are so important for the whole quality of life here. It's what has attracted a lot of people and businesses to relocate here. Without that, it's not the same place.

LS: *You've made a number of commitments to serving the industry.*
HA: When you really love something that's given a lot to you, it's important to give back. Generally, that's time. It's important to be involved and try to come to solutions that benefit everybody. Sometimes you're successful, and sometimes you're not, but if you don't try, how are you going to find out?

I don't think of this as competing against the next person. When we go to the sales, we're all trying to do well. At the races, we're all trying to win, but we're all in this together, so we might as well be having fun doing it. You lose a heck of a lot more than you win. That's a fact. You work hard, do the best you can, and whatever happens, happens. When times are bad, you regroup and get with the community and figure out how to make it better.

9

Charlsie Cantey

IT IS COMMONPLACE TODAY when watching just about any sporting event on TV to see a female reporter relaying information from the sidelines or hear a woman analyst or announcer calling the action. Each one owes a debt of gratitude to **Charlsie Cantey**. A lifelong love of horses, her hands-on experience, and her easy southern charm merged to make Cantey a knowledgeable, effective, and likable presence in television coverage of major races beginning in the 1970s, and a pioneer for women in the field.

Cantey's marriage to trainer Joe Cantey brought her even closer to the action, especially when trying to cover the 1980 Belmont Stakes when the trainer's Temperence Hill came steaming down the stretch, chased along the rail by Charlsie, who was using every piece of body English available to get him home.

Everyone is a critic when it comes to TV, because we all deem ourselves experts as users of the medium. We have never, however, heard a single criticism of Charlsie Cantey during her time on the microphone.

2005

Interviewed as she prepared to retire from TV work

Charlsie Cantey: I'm not very good at talking.

Lenny Shulman: *That's an unusual thing for a TV commentator to say. How did you start with horses?*
CC: Nobody knows where this love of horses came from. I'm from Raleigh, North Carolina, and there weren't any horses around, but I was always passionate about them. I'd cut out pictures of horses from the comics. A guy would come around to sharpen knives with a mule pulling his cart, and I'd sit on the curb and put my arms around its knees just to pet him.

My older sister would put me on a pony ride at the state fair and give the guy a bunch of change and tell him to keep me going around. I couldn't care if I stayed there all day. I took riding lessons when I was six and lived for them. As a young teenager I went up and down the Eastern Seaboard riding a hunter/jumper until I went away to college.

A friend at college mentioned she was working mornings galloping horses at a training center. I was totally unaware of racehorses. They were getting three dollars to gallop each horse, and before that semester was over, I was cutting classes left and right, getting on ten to fifteen horses a day. It was such a sense of empowerment. It set the tone for my life. To go from that to where I ended up was unforeseen and unexpected, but I'll never forget getting that first paycheck and thinking, "This is what I'm going to do." It was the greatest sensation in the world to sit on a racehorse.

LS: *So, was that the end of school?*
CC: I graduated . . . barely. One professor said he couldn't give me a grade because he'd never seen me. I went to Delaware Park looking for a job. Women were practically forbidden on the backstretch in those days. I thought Delaware was the biggest, grandest, finest racetrack ever. Then I went to Saratoga that summer. A bunch of us shared a house and had so much fun, and that set the course.

I got a job for Bert Firestone's private operation in South Carolina, galloping yearlings and two-year-olds in the mornings and schooling jumpers in the afternoon. Joe [Cantey], who I had known from the showing world, and I got married the next year. [Trainer] Frank Whiteley was at Camden and asked me to work a horse. He must have been desperate for help because supposedly he wouldn't let a woman under his shedrow. I was a nervous wreck but did fine, and I wound up being the queen bee in his barn for nine years. I was around so many good horses. I adored Icecapade, the sire of Wild Again. He was mean as a snake, and I'd call him "Sweetie." Frank would mock me, but he was my baby.

LS: *How did the TV work come about?*
CC: A guy from the New York Racing Association would come around the barn and tell me they were going to put a woman on the NYRA TV show and that I'd be really good for it. And I'd excuse myself and go back to work, because when you worked for Frank Whiteley, you worked; you didn't stand around chit-chatting. He kept coming around, and finally I said I'd go talk to the people if he'd leave me alone. I went for an interview, and they asked why I was qualified for the job, and I said, "I'm not. Can I go now?" We chatted for a while, and I never gave it another thought.

A week later [TV reporter] Frank Wright left to do a race for CBS, and I get a phone call to come fill in for him the next day. I called my sister and asked her if I should do this. She said, "Yes. Just wear something quietly colored and smile a lot." So off I went. We were covering the Vosburgh, and No Bias, who had run the day before, was wheeled right back into the race, so I knew what to talk about.

I just started talking, and it all went from there. They called and said to come back every week. I got $100 a show, huge money. I worked seven days a week for Whiteley and barely cleared $125. I thought, "Wow, I'm in the chips."

LS: *So you were talking about people you still worked with.*
CC: I was breezing horses next to jockeys in the morning and interviewing them in the afternoon. I think working at the track gave me credibility, which is what it's all about. I can't say I've ever been 100 percent comfortable doing television, but I do love the sport, and I'm so grateful for what television has done for me. I was always more comfortable and happier around the barn, though.

LS: *You have worked for every national TV network, but you're probably most famous for Temperence Hill's Belmont Stakes in 1980.*
CC: That was one of the greatest days of my life. It started early in the morning in the dark listening to the rain fall and worrying about the track because we thought he had a big chance. He was Joe's horse, and Joe was a great horse trainer. I was four months pregnant with my son, and I was the perfect pregnant person; I would never do anything I wasn't supposed to.

So I did some interviews in the paddock before the race and then walked to the end of the grandstand near the quarter pole. My heart was pounding. Temperence Hill was right there up the backstretch, and then he starts picking horses up on the turn, and when he came by me, he's almost head and head for the lead. I had one of the unprofessional moments of my life—flung all the equipment off me and yelled to the technician, "See ya later." And I start running down the culvert after the horse. People are at the rail screaming, "Hey Charlsie, Go Charlsie." I get to the eighth pole and I can't breathe. I stood for a minute, panting. And I go racing up to the winner's circle as the horse is coming in.

The CBS guys lift me up on the platform and put me down between Jack Whitaker and Frank Wright, and they're asking me questions, and I can hardly breathe. Our producer maintained I finished second in the race. That night we celebrated with Champagne, and I wasn't the perfect pregnant mom. The next morning the barn was filled with flowers and balloons. It was one of the greatest experiences you could have on the racetrack.

LS: *You also trained for a while.*
CC: When Shug [McGaughey] and I worked for Frank Whiteley, we'd always talk about, "Would you do this or that?" I always wanted to try my hand. I went to Laurel Park with a few horses that didn't sell, and figured I'd run them a couple of times, break their maidens, and that would be it in a couple months. But they started doing some good, and I was having fun.

John Franks sent me four. Soon, I had a whole side of the stakes barn at Pimlico—eighteen horses. I kept it up for three or four years, working hard and loving it. I had three stakes winners and some graded-placed, and I was very proud. The single most gratifying and validating thing in my life other than my son.

LS: *Is it tough to give up the TV job?*
CC: Not really. I don't want to do any more on-camera work. Now that I'm doing each show for the last time there are pangs, but I don't want to do any more live TV. Breeders' Cup will be the last one. It's been thirty years exactly, and it's at the place where my TV career started—Belmont Park. The fans in New York are the greatest people. I have a real connection to them. It's the perfect place to go out.

10

Barbara Banke

A FEW YEARS AGO, while out with the team of experts scouting yearlings for the Keeneland September yearling auction, one of the evaluators took me aside and said, "This farm year in and year out raises the best crop of horses." We were at Stonestreet Farm, which has been headed by **Barbara Banke** since 2011.

Although she came into the horse business later in life than many, Banke has determinedly carried on the legacy of Stonestreet that was started by her husband, Jess Jackson, who most famously campaigned superstars Rachel Alexandra and Curlin. While both of those runners came to Jackson via private purchase, he had also begun a breeding operation in Kentucky that, since his death, has blossomed under Banke's leadership. In addition to running the famous Kendall-Jackson Winery, Banke has also helmed Stonestreet and enjoyed great success.

Stonestreet has bred, raced, and sold a wide variety of top-level, stakes-winning racehorses, including recent two-year-old champion Good Magic, and Stonestreet today has several divisions around the Bluegrass, each of showplace quality.

Banke, a ubiquitous presence at major races, has also involved herself in various industry organizations seeking to better the welfare of the sport.

2012

Interviewed at Stonestreet Farm in Lexington

Lenny Shulman: *We know of Jess Jackson's interest in horses, but did you have prior contact with the equine world?*
Barbara Banke: I rode occasionally but not often, having grown up in Palos Verdes, a suburb outside Los Angeles. I was bookish, and it's not something I had exposure to. I wasn't the horse-crazy young girl. I went to law school in San Francisco and practiced there, so I was urban.

Jess and I met in 1984, two years after he started the [Kendall-Jackson] winery, and we practiced law together for a time. In 1990, I'd had enough of practicing law and went into the wine business. We moved to Sonoma and had three children, and it was a nice change, living up there. I became less urban at that point. Now I live on a ranch in Sonoma, and the closest neighbor is a mile away. But I had no exposure to the horse business.

LS: *What are your impressions of it now?*
BB: It's been exciting from the beginning. There's always hope, of course, when you buy a horse at the sale. The first few years were very up and down because we didn't have the best advisers. Jess started in the horse business because he was such a micromanager with the winery that he was driving everyone crazy, so I suggested he get a hobby. He'd been involved in breeding horses with his uncle, so he decided that's what he wanted to do. He bought half a horse at a sale, then more horses, then a farm in Kentucky. We were having problems with our advisers, so I felt I needed to get up to speed, and started learning about the horse business in 2005. That was my first exposure to the horse world.

LS: *The operation really began clicking.*
BB: We became involved with a new bloodstock agent, John Moynihan, and started having success. That's when it became exciting. And that's when I got hooked. The racetrack is an exciting atmosphere, and we were buying really good horses. Our first stakes winner with John was Forest Music, who won the Honorable Miss Stakes. She's a broodmare here now.

Jess was interested in breeding and handicapping. He found a real intellectual satisfaction from those aspects; racing wasn't his first interest. He liked the farm aspect more. He was a farmer. But traveling to the big races became an important thing for us, and it was something our children enjoyed as well. It became a good family activity.

LS: *And it grew on you.*
BB: Jess acknowledged in his last couple of years that I was liking the horse business more than he did. He had to bring lawsuits against some of his advisers, because when you're a successful businessman, it's embarrassing to be defrauded. [One adviser accused of collaborating to defraud Jackson paid Jackson $3.5 million to settle a lawsuit.] Rather than hide, he decided he was going to change it and make it better. That's the type of person he was.

He liked the idea that our children would be involved in the breeding and farming aspects, and at one point he said, "It's yours. Just don't go crazy" (*laughs*). And I take that to heart. Our son Christopher has always been interested and has a good sense of humor about it. He's able to roll with the punches. He's going to help me decide what we're doing with all our yearlings. We have a number of broodmares that are aging and are going to be retired, so we're going to try and bring in a few new ones.

LS: *How much time are you able to devote to the horses?*
BB: The wine business takes up a fair amount of time. I try to get back here to the farm [Stonestreet] once or twice a month. Tonight, we're going to Ocala to check in on the two-year-olds. We go to Saratoga. I'd say a quarter of the time I'm dealing with the horse operation.

LS: *Are there similarities between the two businesses?*
BB: The wine and horse businesses both involve land and farming and weather. They're both nature-dependent. Last year we had weather that made the grape harvest a little short, so you adjust. That's given me good training to adjust to some of the situations that come up in the breeding business.

LS: *Rachel Alexandra was a superstar race mare for you who is now back at the farm and is a broodmare. What is it like having her around?*
BB: Rachel has been a fabulous mom. She shares a paddock with Hot Dixie Chick, which is so funny because they've always been friends. They had stalls right next to each other when they were racing. Hot Dixie Chick was away for a while after having a chip removed, and Rachel was so glad to see her when she returned. They've been friends ever since. And they've switched roles. Dixie was the most easygoing mare in the world, and Rachel was the high-strung racing filly. And now, Dixie is a bit of a pill, and Rachel is very laid-back.

LS: *Dixie raced for you as opposed to for Stonestreet.*
BB: Yes. I helped pick her out with Jess and John. Before Rachel, Jess had decided he didn't want to race fillies, only colts. He wanted to retire all the racing fillies. But we had just purchased a bunch of them at the sales, so I said, "What are we doing?" And he said that if I wanted to race them, go ahead. So I started Grace Racing Stable, which stood for "Girls rule and competently endure." And Dixie became a grade 1 winner for Grace Racing Stable.

Jess did change his mind about racing fillies, by the way. Winning the Breeders' Cup last year with My Miss Aurelia was a wonderful time. It was not a good year for us, with Jess passing away. I needed a boost. We bred Miss Aurelia and named her after [partner] George [Bolton]'s mother, so it was great.

LS: *Are the horses a hobby or a business?*
BB: We very much run it as a business. We have been the top breeding operation by revenue on a couple of occasions. We don't have the numbers to be the leader

by gross, and that's fine. We're more trying to stay at the top end of the market with our breeding. Obviously, we can't do that all the time, but we're trying to develop our families while paying attention to the bottom line.

We do still buy at sales. John is an unusual bloodstock agent. He will go to the sales, and he works like no one I've ever seen. He'll look at a horse ten times. He'll look, and he'll look, and if it makes the cut, he'll look at it again. And again. And again. The short list might start at twenty, and it shrinks and shrinks. Sometimes it shrinks to zero. At the July sale we went from twenty to one. And that's what we did. We bought one.

LS: *Do you play an active role in purchases?*
BB: I like to study the pedigrees. My knowledge is not that great, but it's certainly something I enjoy doing, and I'm learning more about it. It's a fun part of it.

LS: *You have made the farm very active on social media and have brought fans out to see the horses.*
BB: Jess was always of the opinion that we have to do something to broaden the fan base. These are athletes who are on the scene for only a year or two or three. There are things we can do to get the word out about these horses. Our asset here is moms and babies, so that's what we're trying to get people interested in. I think that's a wholesome way to get fans to the sport, and we're happy to do it. I'm in the hospitality business with the wine operation. It's been popular here, particularly because of Rachel, and we'll continue to do that. We need more fans.

LS: *You are also giving back as a member of the Breeders' Cup board of directors.*
BB: With its championship series, Breeders' Cup has an opportunity to broaden the fan base and help horse racing in general. That's my motivation in serving, because I'm a big investor in the horse business. Not just money, but psychic energy invested in it. I want it to succeed. I was asked by some people to consider running for the board, and I didn't think anyone would vote for me, but I got elected. I'm going to do what I can to help out. Breeders' Cup is trying to make the experience better for people. It lengthens the season and keeps the sport in people's minds after the Triple Crown races. I think there are some good things going on there. It's evolving and getting better, and I'm glad to serve and see what I can do.

I think the industry has some challenges, but I'm optimistic. We need medication reform, get Thoroughbred retirement off the ground, and broaden the fan base. We need to have positive things and lead by offense, and that's what I want to work on.

11

Josephine Abercrombie

JOSEPHINE ABERCROMBIE IS ANOTHER horsewoman who has stood the test of time. She has owned and operated Pin Oak Stud in the heart of the Kentucky Bluegrass for more than a half century, standing stallions and forging top-shelf female families that boast many generations of black-type stakes winners.

Abercrombie is respected throughout the Thoroughbred world for her uncompromising horsemanship as well as her philanthropy around the Lexington area in the fields of education, health, and animal welfare. She was a championship-caliber rider in her youth who first learned to love horses on her family's ranch in West Texas. She is celebrated for her longevity and, more importantly, the quality that is associated with her and the Pin Oak name.

2007

Interviewed at Pin Oak Farm, Versailles, Kentucky

Lenny Shulman: *You had an interesting beginning to life.*
Josephine Abercrombie: My father was drilling oil wells in Columbia, but they didn't have good hospitals there, so he sent my mother to Kingston, Jamaica, and I was born there. We stayed there a week, and they snuck me onto a boat and back to the US. The Customs man asked where I was born, and my mother said, "Kingston," and they said, "Louisiana?" And she didn't say anything, so I got in. I was illegal. I grew up in a residential area of Houston, where I rode a lot.

LS: *You had an early affinity for horses?*
JA: It was love at first sight. My father had a ranch in West Texas, and I would ride the quarter horses when I was a little girl. I began showing when I was six and showed until I was in my thirties, and loved it. Horses were my passion.

My father and uncle eventually wanted to get into the Thoroughbred business and asked me if I wanted to go to the sales at Saratoga with them. I was nineteen or twenty at the time, and that's how I got started. We bought yearlings and had real good luck at the racetrack. It got bigger and bigger, and we began having broodmares, and here we are.

Josephine Abercrombie (Keeneland Library *Thoroughbred Times* Collection)

LS: *What lessons did your father teach you?*

JA: He wanted me to always try and do my best. That was very important. To work hard and never give up or quit. I was at the University of Texas, and I hated it because the size of the classes was huge, and I wanted to quit. And he said, "Abercrombies are not quitters," and I compromised by going to Rice University and graduated from there.

LS: *Did he instill philanthropy in you?*
JA: Yes. He said to me that "You've been very blessed in this world and you have to give something back. You can't always just take." I came up with the idea of the Lexington School [a high-quality private school]. I started that with his help, and it was a real good experience.

I'm dead set against the slaughtering of horses. I go up to Washington and lobby congressmen and senators. I support the retirement movement and finding places for these horses when they're finished racing. I'm also involved with the Woodford Humane Society and the Center for Aging. My father died of Alzheimer's, so I'm interested in that. We have a foundation that contributes to a significant list of things.

I also believe in service to the horse industry. Anything I can do, I do. It has been so important to me, and it deserves all the help to make it continue and be strong.

LS: *What were your first impressions of Kentucky?*
JA: Oh, I was crazy about it. We came and showed at the Junior League Show at the Red Mile. It was the most beautiful country I'd ever seen. It was exquisite, and so different from Texas. Horses everywhere, rolling countryside, fences. I asked my father if we could buy just a tiny piece of land here, and he bought one thousand acres (*laughs*). He didn't do things in a small way.

LS: *And you helped populate the land with horses?*
JA: I was involved in picking out the first purchases, but it was apples and oranges as far as my show horse experience and picking out Thoroughbreds. The saddle horse has a neck that comes out completely differently, and they have flat quarters, whereas the Thoroughbred has round hips. They're a totally different shape. I had to learn what to look for in them. I didn't have a clue at the beginning.

At the Keeneland sales my uncle would sit on one side of the ring and my father and I on the other, and my uncle would do the bidding so people didn't know who the buyer was. My father had a signal: when he put his hat on, my uncle would stop bidding. He got to the upper limit on one horse and just kept on bidding. I finally had to take my father's hat and put it on my head.

LS: *How did the operation build up?*
JA: We were pretty darn successful from the beginning. Roman Patrol was one of our first good runners and won the Louisiana Derby. We had three or four really good horses the first year. My father always bought good yearlings. Then, we decided to buy broodmares. We bought at auction and also had some of our own

coming off the track, and we built up a band that is forty-two-strong today. We slowly built the band up with fillies that ran well.

We have families from the beginning that are still with us today. Strike a Balance, the dam of Peaks and Valleys, is out of Strike a Pose, who is out of Take a Stand. There's also Wedding Picture. These families go back with us fifty years. Isn't that amazing? When I go see Strike a Balance, I give her a little sugar, and she licks my face. She's so funny.

LS: *Did you get into pedigrees?*
JA: I studied pedigrees in the early days and was very active with it until recently. It's very hard work. I had my dining room table covered with reference books and stallion registers, and I'd sit there hour after hour fooling with these things. It's difficult remembering all the families, and I had plenty of trouble trying to do it. Age has caught up with me a bit.

LS: *You also have stood stallions.*
JA: Yes, but we were never a commercial operation. The first stallions we had were Circle and Cool. Oh, my lord, that was a hundred years ago. The new stallion concept came about with Peaks and Valleys and Sky Classic. Sky Classic was out of one of the best female families in the stud book, and was a champion two-year-old on dirt and turf, and an Eclipse Award winner at four and five. He had the whole package.

Standing stallions was done as an income generator. We've also had a lot of nice racehorses that we didn't stand, horses like Green Means Go and African Dancer. Their appeal here as stallions in Kentucky wasn't quite there, so we sold them. You have to be very selective bringing a stallion in here. You're competing with twenty-five new horses every year that are commercial. Peaks and Valleys' pedigree was very appealing here, and he was the first one we bred that we also stood.

We breed maybe one-third of our mares to our stallions. If we want something else by our stallions, we'll go to the sales. But we breed most of our mares to outside stallions like Storm Cat, Holy Bull, Unbridled; those are the kind of horses we look for. You're hoping to bring back a potential broodmare or stallion. The yearlings we breed are all to race.

LS: *How thrilling was it to have one of your stallions, Maria's Mon, sire a Kentucky Derby winner [Monarchos]?*
JA: Oh wow. Whoo. The excitement was unbelievable. We were beside ourselves. So exciting.

LS: *And [champion] Wait A While is by Maria's Mon. Is that as satisfying for you as if you owned her?*

JA: NO (*laughs*). We sure take pride in one like her, and we're thrilled to death for her and the others that have done so well for our stallions. But it's not the same.

LS: *Is there a story behind the Pin Oak silks?*

JA: I designed them. They're blue and gray, which represents North and South, and they're the colors of Rice University.

LS: *Do you name your horses?*

JA: Yes, I do all the naming based on pedigrees. I'm crazy about that part of it. It's one of my most favorite things to do, and I spend hours doing it. The reason I fool with it so much and like it so much is because when I first came into the business back in the forties, Alfred Vanderbilt, a good friend of mine, said, "Look, you want to be sure you get a good name for them because you never know who you're going to bring over to your barn, and you're going to have to say, 'Here is Joe Blow.' You want a horse with a good name." So I work hard at it.

LS: *What have been your biggest thrills in racing?*

JA: Peaks and Valleys winning the Molson Million was heaven. I floated from the third floor to the winner's circle. I think there's a picture of me floating. Confessional winning the Frizette was wonderful. Broken Vow winning the Iselin was another great day. We'd been to Delaware and won three races there, and then flew to Monmouth with [trainer] Graham Motion to watch Broken Vow, and he topped off the day by winning the Iselin. Also Missed the Storm winning the Test was fabulous.

LS: *Do you ever miss living in big cities?*

JA: Rural living—I don't ever want to live any other way. I've lived in Houston, and the noise factor versus the peace here . . . the beauty of the green and the rolling land and the trees. It's a wonderful joy to have these trees and to see all this. I adore it. I wouldn't want to live anywhere else or in any other atmosphere. I've gotten hooked on it. It's what I do. I was just thinking the other day there's no way I could live in town. I have to live here. It's peace.

LS: *You have other interests.*

JA: I was into ballroom dancing for four or five years. Traveled around the country doing competitions and loved it. Then I just felt, "I've done this, it's time to try something else." I think golf is going to be the next thing.

I've always been fascinated by boxing since my father took me to the fights when I was eleven. There are interesting young people involved and I've tried to help some of them. When you're in the corner, it's electric.

LS: What are your favorite racetracks?
JA: I love Belmont. Always have. That's where we started. I love Chicago, and [Arlington Park chairman] Dick Duchossois is such a nice man. Fair Grounds is fun. I love New Orleans and food. Woodbine is beautiful. And, of course, Keeneland is fabulous. There's no other track as beautiful, and the elegance of the people who go there. Everyone dresses up; they respect the track. It's gorgeous. I always have a good time no matter where we go.

12

Maggi Moss

FIERCELY INDEPENDENT IN THOUGHT and deed, **Maggi Moss** was a long-shot to succeed in the horse business. But longshots do come in, and Moss, an attorney based in Iowa, has headed a prominent racing stable for decades through sheer hard work.

She doesn't breed or buy expensive stock, yet Moss's charges regularly end up in the winner's circle, partly because of her late-night efforts analyzing data and figures. She largely shuns the use of advisers and is quite content to make her own decisions.

Moss is also an active presence on social media and has been devoted for years to the safe aftercare of racehorses around the country. She serves as a role model for anyone seeking to blaze their own trail.

2013

Interviewed from her home in Iowa

Lenny Shulman: *You've been described as a bit of a hermit.*
Maggi Moss: I've lived five or six lives and have had to do all these things with people, and people will continually disappoint you, be it personally, professionally, and any other way. So when people call me a hermit, I say at least I'm a happy hermit.

LS: *And a rebel?*
MM: The first time I went to Keeneland with a horse in a stakes race they wouldn't let me into the dining room because I was wearing leather pants.

LS: *You're very hands-on with your horse business.*
MM: Most people have racing managers. I don't. I do everything myself. Through the years I've discovered that if you have the right trainers who talk to you with honesty and candidness about what you own and what their condition is, that's the key. It's that simple.

LS: *You seem to constantly have good horses even though you don't spend a lot, relative to others.*

MM: As a lawyer, I wasn't the smartest person practicing, and in the horse business I know I can't compete with the biggest spenders. My lesson in life that I learned from my dad is you have to outwork everybody. And to do that you have to put in the hours, and my hours are at night. I run my horses' performances, watch replays, read condition books, study sheet numbers, and study my whole operation. And then I'll talk to my trainers in the morning. I spend three hours every day going through each of my horses.

LS: *How did you start in the horse business?*
MM: My father was the biggest influence in my life. He had no money and tried to go to law school but couldn't. Ultimately, he got into the coin-operated machine business in Chicago and made money. He bought a farm and built it up, and he started me in horses. He was very protective of me, but he was tough. Through high school I was riding hunters and jumpers twice a day, and he would make me come to his office every Friday to show me how many jukeboxes he had to sell so that I could keep my horses.

I finally made it to Madison Square Garden, which was incredible, coming from Iowa. And I won there, and afterward he said, "I really think you could have ridden a little better." He'd always push me to work harder. I think that's why I became a raving lunatic in the courtroom practicing law.

Horses taught me more than people did growing up. Discipline, integrity, and love. I owe all my knowledge of horses to my upbringing. You can't grow up having spent fifteen years of your life with horses every day without having a comprehension of their temperament and how they feel, and I think that's been a huge asset.

My father had been a pilot in the military, and he loved to fly. Had his own plane. He and my brother died in a plane crash. I was young and thought life was a bowl of cherries. Never had anything bad happen to me. I was sitting in the public defender's office and got that phone call. I lost my passion for riding after he died. But I wonder what he'd think if he could see what I've been lucky enough to accomplish, because he loved horses. His goal for me was to go on and live a normal life. That's one thing I don't think I've accomplished.

LS: *How do you acquire most of your stock?*
MM: Up until a year ago I was watching races for claiming purposes. I have three satellite systems and get feeds from all the racetracks. I have the TV on racing all day long. But I think the claiming business has died, so I've switched my operation away from that. But it's still on my TV all day.

The dilemma for me is I don't want to get into breeding. I've spent a great portion of my life trying to shut down puppy mills. It's a product of too much breeding, and I feel the same way about horses—we're breeding too many, and there aren't enough homes for them. So I don't want to do breeding, although I am standing Native Ruler in Iowa right now, and I'm having second thoughts about that.

Buying horses privately isn't good because the prices are so inflated. So I've started buying young horses at sales; that's the road I'm going down now. I've hit a home run finding Jimmy Schenk, an ex-jockey who appraises horses well. He's very low-key, and we've had a lot of success and a lot of fun. I won't stop claiming entirely, but I like the idea of working with Jimmy and buying younger horses. He bought [grade 1 winner] So Many Ways for me.

LS: *How did you get your current stable star, Delaunay?*
MM: I've been with [trainer] Tom Amoss for fifteen years. That's a long time in this business. We've had our fights, but I think he's the best, and I adore him. He's very honest. We discuss possible claims every morning, and if we're not on the same page, we don't make a move. We both agreed 100 percent on the morning we decided to claim Delaunay. Then he called from the paddock and said, "I don't know if I can go for this horse. He's skinny and his color's not good." Nine out of ten times I bank on him, and I'll agree with him. But these days, people don't give horses breaks, and that makes it harder to evaluate them. Delaunay had been in a half-dozen different barns, and he was going to need some time. So I told Tom to go ahead and put the claim in, because I'll give him the time.

But I give Tom all the credit for what has happened subsequent to that. His care program is great. I judged horse shows for years and have a pretty good eye for how a horse looks, and his horses look phenomenal. Happy horses look good. That's the best claim we've made. Indian Chant, who I claimed in California, still holds a track record at Churchill Downs, and that's a big deal. He was one of the fastest horses I've ever owned. But Delaunay has been magical. And he's a wonderful horse to be around at the barn; a cool guy. [Delaunay won twelve stakes races, including two graded stakes, and more than a million dollars after Amoss claimed him for Moss in 2012.]

LS: *You won your first grade 1, with So Many Ways, last year. What was that like for you?*
MM: The mentality in this business is that you have to have a grade 1 horse or you have to have a Derby horse or you have to win at Saratoga and Del Mar. I have had

to reflect very hard on why that is not my cup of tea. I'm an aberration. What is wrong with me that that is not my objective? The answer I've come up with is that I'm so hard on myself, so intent on making the right decisions and being self-sustaining. I grew up with a father who was poor and who really taught me the value of a dollar. He embedded so much into me about work ethic that maybe the pressure is too much for me. It's just not fun to operate under that type of pressure, so it's not my objective.

The best part of winning the grade 1 at Saratoga, the highlight of it, was being back with her at the barn afterward. I'm not that big a social person, so all the accolades were about her, and knowing what a great filly she is. It was a great thrill, and fabulous. But I've won claiming races with some of my old, favorite horses, and that is pretty thrilling too.

LS: *You've involved yourself in the aftercare of horses.*
MM: The number-one thing bothering me now is the great number of horses out there that do not have great lives. I love my horses and love all horses, and I always try to do the right thing with my horses. I love that they're happy and that they look good. I'm not going to say I don't love winning races. I have Posse Cat, an eight-year-old who is a five-thousand-dollar claiming horse and is one of the coolest horses I've ever owned. He drew off and won by ten lengths recently, and that was thrilling. He's gorgeous, an overachiever, and he's so happy that I was just giddy. I was giddy he won, but just as giddy that he didn't get claimed and came back to us.

LS: *You said you don't want to breed, but are you at all supporting your stallion Native Ruler?*
MM: He is really one of my favorite horses. He's from a Darley line and has a great record, so I decided to try and help the Iowa program by standing him here. I bought one mare to breed to him. And she had all kinds of trouble through the delivery process. Finally, she had a beautiful foal at 12:05 a.m. on February 22 last year. And that is the anniversary of my father's and brother's deaths.

That was my first foal, and I named it Timeless.

13

Charlotte Weber

CHARLOTTE WEBER HAS BEEN a horsewoman her entire life. An heir to the Campbell Soup company, she has operated a top racing stable for more than a half century and recently celebrated the fiftieth anniversary of her Live Oak Stud near Ocala. Weber has tasted success at the highest levels, winning multiple Breeders' Cup races as an owner/breeder, and just as importantly, gives top consideration to the health and welfare of her equines.

A philanthropist and supporter of the arts, Weber has also been instrumental in contributing to the upgrading of the National Museum of Racing and Hall of Fame in Saratoga Springs. We spoke for stories on two occasions more than a decade apart, including as she pondered fifty years of success at Live Oak and what her farm has meant to her entire family.

2005

Interviewed from Live Oak Stud in Ocala before her
High Fly ran in the Kentucky Derby

Lenny Shulman: *What first brought you to racing?*
Charlotte Weber: I always thought racing had attractive people. I had studied art in Paris and had a job curating at the Philadelphia Museum of Art. I had always loved to ride and loved horses, and my family had been involved in racing and steeplechasing. So it was a focus to broaden my interests.

My husband at the time was interested in farming cattle, and I wanted to farm horses, and we thought a farm would be a nice way to raise a family, a nice influence in a nice environment. So we purchased the P. A. B. Widener III property near Ocala to raise cattle, horses, and our family.

LS: *Can you compare art and horses?*
CW: I think they are similar passions. I've never looked at art as an investment. I've only bought art that I've personally liked. I think the aesthetics of art is very

rewarding, and I think of animals in the same way. Art falls off the wall occasionally but doesn't get injured as frequently as horses.

LS: *You had Laser Light run second in the Kentucky Derby in 1982. Is there anything you can take from that as you prepare to return with High Fly?*
CW: I think it's a real honor and privilege to be in it. And as exciting today as it was back then. I had a little different temperament then because I was in the process of raising children. Now I can really enjoy it. I have learned not to drink so many mint juleps (*laughs*). I think what I learned is you have to be extremely well-organized. It's a task trying to get through it. I'm trying to enjoy the process and the race without letting all the hype distract me. Of course, you feel pressure, but I feel pressure when any horse is running.

LS: *You ran second to Gato Del Sol in '82.*
CW: It was breathtaking during the race. I was so focused on, "Get up there, get up there." You're not looking at anyone else in the field. Laser Light had a style of running from behind, and when he hit the top of the stretch and exploded, I was trying to push him to the front of the pack.

LS: *You've gotten some heat for switching trainers for High Fly.*
CW: I respect all my trainers and feel very fortunate I have horses and good relationships with them. But I'm trying to put horses with the person who can maximize their potential. Sometimes that means changing trainers, changing locations. It's not necessarily a criticism of them, but there is no doubt disappointment. But I feel I have to do what's best for the horse and what's best for Live Oak.

Nick Zito having the experience certainly played a role in the change. Everyone is going to try and Monday-morning quarterback me, and I try to take it with a grain of salt. If he hadn't won after he moved to Nick, I'd have looked like the biggest dummy in town. But it worked out well, with him winning the Florida Derby. I think Bill White is disappointed and hurt, but it's not something I did to hurt him. I'm trying to take my best shot.

LS: *Talk about your involvement with the arts and philanthropy. You established the Charlotte C. Weber Galleries for the Arts of Ancient China at the Metropolitan Museum of Art in New York.*
CW: Yes, I'm still with the Metropolitan Museum. I support the New York Women's Foundation, a grassroots organization to strengthen and build up women in

low-income families. I was involved with New York City Parents in Action, a drug-prevention program in schools.

LS: *Is there a downside to wealth?*
CW: I think some people believe that if you have wealth, you have no responsibility. People say, "Gosh, she's rich. She has no problems." Hello! It creates a real challenge and responsibility. You have stewardship of the land, the horses, and trying to live a clean life. I'm not saying not to have fun, but you have to try to be a good citizen and make this a better place than when we got here.

2017

Interviewed on the occasion of her fiftieth year owning and operating Live Oak Stud

Lenny Shulman: *Over the past twenty-five years, at least one Live Oak–bred horse has won a stakes race in every year except one.*
Charlotte Weber: Wow, I didn't realize that. But winning the Triple Crown is still out there.

LS: *You just had a pretty good double, with World Approval winning the Breeders' Cup Mile eleven years after his half brother Miesque's Approval won it. Both home-breds for you.*
CW: I try not to breed a grass horse; I really do. But somehow it happens.

LS: *You've bred four millionaires out of Win Approval, and you've had the family for forty-five years.*
CW: And the whole family is around on the farm. I might have to name the road going up to the barn "Approval Lane." Win Approval is tenacious; she won't have anybody in the paddock with her. Not a pony. Nothing. That is her territory.

LS: *You bring each of your racehorses home for R&R after a while.*
CW: I'm a big believer in everything coming home once a year. That's the bottom line: Come home and get a break. That goes back to the old-fashioned model where you'd race in New York, and everything was sent to Florida for the winter. That model doesn't exist anymore, but I don't think any horse can run all year long.

I also insist on my employees taking their vacations in blocks of time of at least two weeks because it gives you a change of scenery and a different perspective.

LS: *What are your thoughts on fifty years at Live Oak?*
CW: First, it's been a great environment in which to raise my four children. It's all gone according to a plan for which I didn't really have a role model. It's the essence of a dream come true. It's been a long road but a very rewarding and satisfying one. I've learned a lot, and I'm still having fun. And it's not completed; it's still evolving.

14

Marylou Whitney

ALTHOUGH WE DIDN'T GET a lot of time to visit with **Marylou Whitney,** each moment was special. Her life was a whirlwind of admirers and well-wishers seeking a few moments in her spotlight. Such was the nature of her charisma and the aura that surrounded her.

Few have had the impact of Whitney within the racing world—and beyond. A radio DJ during World War II, Whitney became an actress and then the wife of C. V. "Sonny" Whitney, whose family maintained one of the prestigious stables of Thoroughbreds at a time when family operations dominated the sport.

Marylou took over the stable upon her husband's death and ended up campaigning classic winner Birdstone. But her greatest contribution came in leading the effort that reinvigorated her adopted hometown of Saratoga Springs, New York, which was a fading village before Whitney resuscitated it with an influx of celebrities and philanthropy. Today, Saratoga is a mecca of horse racing and a jewel of a resort town. Whitney's contributions can be seen around the racetrack, in a program for backstretch workers, and in the town's parks, dance museum, performing arts center, and hospitals.

Her widower, John Hendrickson, has led the campaign to modernize the National Museum of Racing and Hall of Fame, an institution started in part by Sonny Whitney.

2011

Interviewed at Belmont Park, New York

Lenny Shulman: *When did you first get interested in horses?*
Marylou Whitney: I was born on a horse. My mother showed five-gaited saddlehorses in Kansas City, and we rode every single weekend. We had to, or else we wouldn't get breakfast. They cooked a big breakfast out at the stable. It was wonderful.

Ever since I was big enough to get on a horse, I had a horse. Mother felt we all should learn how to ride at an early age. I started at three or four. Always had a love for them.

LS: *During World War II, you were a popular disc jockey.*
MW: Yes, I did radio and some theater in the Midwest, and I wanted to pursue a show-business career, so I moved to New York but struggled. When I gathered any spare money, I would rent a horse and ride around Central Park. That was my recreation. I so wanted to go on and do acting. But as it turned out, I went on and got married (*laughs*).

LS: *Your second marriage was to "Sonny" Whitney, whose ancestors built the race-track at Saratoga and were so prominent in horse racing.*
MW: After marrying Sonny and going to the races, I fell in love with the sport. Sonny didn't do much socially, but I did. I loved the people in racing, and they became my good friends. I found that I liked the races better than anything. After Sonny died [in 1992], I tried the jet set, but that didn't work. So I went back to the thing I liked best—horses.

Sonny didn't leave me his horses. He sold them just before he died. And I went out and bought the Whitney blood back. I knew what to put together and what clicked. Today it's easy—you can get all the information you want. I did it on paper. I went back four and five generations on each horse and saw what stallions would work with the mares. I did it in different colors to match the things that were good. And it worked.

LS: *And you've maintained a boutique operation ever since.*
MW: I have around fifteen horses in training, thirteen combined foals and year-lings, and twenty-three broodmares. When I started out on my own, I had a wonderful trainer in Tommy Kelly. Tommy was the best; I adored him, and he was very helpful. And we had a good time. It wasn't a big stable; in fact, it was tiny, but we had fun. Tommy said to me, "Marylou, you're the first client I have ever had who gets excited when your horse finishes fourth." And I said, "That means you at least get money. Sonny used to say if you're in the first five, you've got a good horse. Don't worry that you didn't get first." So I always thought fourth was great. Of course, I'm thrilled with first.

LS: *You will always be identified with Saratoga, and all your efforts to make it what it is today.*

MW: Sonny and I had been in the Adirondacks at our hunting and fishing camp. It was cold as could be. Sonny went to Saratoga to sign some papers to sell his house there. It was an adorable house, and I told him, "Sonny, you're not going to sell this house." I think the offer was $35,000, and I told him I'd give him $150,000, because I'd just sold my home in California and told him I'd give him the proceeds from that.

He was stunned. I told him I loved the house, and he said, "You can have it." So that's how I got Cady Hill [a twenty-one-room estate with tennis courts, gardens, and acres of beautiful pasture].

The town was so dead except for the Gideon Putnam Hotel, because the Round Table from New York was taking place there that weekend. Can you imagine sitting with all those men? All the cream of the crop. And Sonny said we were going to spend the weekend there. So we stayed for a while, and I had a lovely time and loved the town, except every store was closed but for the drugstore. I didn't have any clothes with me, and I had a heck of a time finding a store. Finally, I found one the Skidmore students went to. Thank God they had my size, so I bought some of those clothes and went to the drugstore and bought some fake pearls that I still have because I'm so in love with them.

LS: *Saratoga wasn't the bustling town then that it is today.*
MW: Sonny told me how his ancestors literally helped build Saratoga, and created interest in people to travel there. He told me I needed to bring it back up, and how his ancestors had given great parties in the park there. And I said, "With your money and my imagination, I can do anything."

So we set out to completely redo the Canfield Casino in Congress Park, where we now have the Whitney Gala every year. And then we brought in movie stars from Hollywood and had them do interviews that went out nationwide with the motto, "Saratoga is the summer place to be." We had Kirk Douglas, Fred Astaire, Ginger Rogers, Frank Sinatra, Walter Cronkite. Everyone was there. I actually irritated people at the racetrack because back then all the television cameras and equipment were quite bulky.

LS: *You used your speech earlier this year while receiving the Eclipse Award of Merit to recognize the plight of backstretch workers.*
MW: They are the sport's unsung heroes. They work long hours in dangerous situations and live in poor conditions, and all of us should try to improve their lives.

LS: *You started the Backstretch Appreciation Program at Saratoga, providing meals and entertainment on a daily basis.*

MW: The people who have volunteered to help the backstretch program are great and [husband] John [Hendrickson] has done a great job putting the programs together. It's been very gratifying.

I'm still working on saving horses. I'm trying every way possible. I wish they'd put on the ownership papers that the horse be sent back to you if anything happens, so it doesn't get sent to a slaughterhouse. I have all these horses back at the farm that belonged to Sonny, and I love them. I look out my window and see all the beautiful horses having such a good time in their old age.

LS: *What did you think about Birdplay winning the Brooklyn Handicap yesterday?*
MW: That's our breeding.

Part III

Celebrities

HORSE RACING HAS A LONG HISTORY OF ATTRACTING NOTED
PERSONALITIES AS PARTICIPANTS AND FANS, PARTICULARLY
IN THE MID-TWENTIETH CENTURY WHEN THE SPORT WAS
one of the dominant American pastimes and fully intertwined in the
popular culture, in stark contrast to its current marginalization.

When author John Gregory Dunne adapted his novel *True Confessions* into a film of the same name, the noir classic, set in 1940s Los
Angeles, had hard-boiled police detective Tom Spellacy ask a down-on-
her-luck madame of a house of ill repute, "How are you, Brenda?" She
replied caustically, "I'm in the pink. I have a box at Santa Anita."

Hollywood was immersed in horse racing at the time. The popular
crooner Bing Crosby founded Del Mar in 1937 along with actor Pat
O'Brien (both still have stakes named after them there). Hordes of celebrities made the one-hundred-mile journey from Hollywood to Del Mar
to spend their summers at the seaside palace for horse racing. Barbara
Stanwyck and Zeppo Marx built and operated a large breeding and stallion farm called Marwyk for years in Van Nuys, just north of Hollywood. The upscale clubhouse section of Hollywood Park was named the
Cary Grant Pavilion.

While East Coast racing was populated more by titans of business
and industry, celebrities such as Frank Sinatra and Kirk Douglas were

instrumental in popularizing Saratoga and making it an attractive tourist destination, as documented by Marylou Whitney in her interview in this volume.

Today, horse racing is not nearly the mainstream phenomenon it once was, and celebrity participation comes on an individual basis rather than an industry-wide one. Of course, it can also be argued that celebrities aren't what they once were, either. Nevertheless, popular figures who earned recognition in endeavors far afield from horse racing do populate the equine industry as either owners, gamblers, or fans. I've had the opportunity to speak with a wide cross-section of them over the years.

15

Jenny Craig

THE NAME **JENNY CRAIG** is synonymous with the weight-management business she started with her husband, Sid, in the early 1980s, which quickly grew to include more than seven hundred centers worldwide. The Craigs also maintained a substantial racing stable in California through the years from their home in Rancho Santa Fe near Del Mar, enjoying success with Hall of Fame trainer Ron McAnally. The stable's best horses were Argentinian champion imports Paseana and Candy Ride, the latter of whom the Craigs brought to the States and realized a dream by campaigning him to victory in the Pacific Classic, Del Mar's flagship race. Today, he is a leading sire of top runners, several of whom Jenny Craig has raced in the Kentucky Derby.

2009

Interviewed from her home in California

Lenny Shulman: *What got you involved in horses?*
Jenny Craig: I grew up in New Orleans, and my brother had an avocation to train horses. He had a business, but he liked to train in his spare time. He actually trained our first horse, JJ's Star, who bowed a tendon and didn't do very much. I loved going to the races at Fair Grounds, especially opening day on Thanksgiving; it was a social event. So I always had an interest in horses, but I didn't own any until I met [husband] Sid.

When I met Sid, he had two horses that he had claimed, and they both won in their first races for him, and he thought this was a really easy game. So he continued claiming more horses after we got married. He claimed Exchange for fifty thousand dollars, and she went on to win more than a million. Then Paseana came along, and she was a winning machine. So we had Paseana and Exchange, and then I gave Dr Devious to Sid for his sixtieth birthday, and among those three horses in 1992 alone I think we won eight grade 1 races.

LS: *What is it about the horses or the game that attracts you?*
JC: I think the social aspect. Going to the track is a fun day with friends. And, of course, watching the horses. They are so graceful. It's a phenomenon that those

spindly legs can support one thousand pounds and run that fast. It's amazing. There's also the betting aspect. You like to win. I don't care if you have two dollars on a horse. It's the idea that you won. We love the thrill of winning. That's true in both our lives. Sid [who died in 2008] was very competitive at everything.

LS: *What is it like to own great horses?*
JC: I don't think there are words to accurately describe it. It's such a thrill but also anxiety. Every time one of those horses ran, I would say a prayer just to let them be safe. There is so much danger and risk in racing, you're hoping the horse will come out of it well. So it's a combination of anxiety and the thrill and excitement. We've had so many great races and rides when you feel, "Gee, the horse isn't going to make it today," and they come and win.

LS: *Can you compare a racing stable to your other business?*
JC: I think in business you feel like you have control over the outcome, that you have control and can influence the outcome. In racing, I don't think that's true. Even with talented horses, there is so much luck in how the race sets up. It's not just about your horse; it's about all the others too. The parallel I would make is the risk in business and the risk in owning and running horses.

LS: *How hands-on are you with the horses?*
JC: I don't know that I've been greatly involved. We've been owners who rely on the advice of our trainers. If the trainer thinks a horse should run in a certain race, we respect his opinion. I know there are owners who want to direct the operation, but we feel if you hire a professional, you should take the professional's advice.

But we have looked at the bottom line through the years, because it involves a lot of money, and you have to see if you're in a dream world or you're in reality. It can get to be very expensive. That's why they call it the Sport of Kings. You almost have to have a king's ransom to afford it.

LS: *Candy Ride is off to a great start as a stallion.*
JC: His offspring have been doing terrific, and I think he's leading the country this year as a sire. I'm thrilled with his success. And he's been doing so well without getting top mares. Who knows what he can do with top-grade mares?

LS: *You have Chocolate Candy perhaps heading for the Kentucky Derby.*
JC: We have the distinction of being the only people whose horses have finished last in every Kentucky Derby we've been in (*laughs*). Actually, Dr Devious was seventh; at least he finished ahead of the star of that show, Arazi.

The Derby is unbelievable. It's unlike anything else I've ever attended. It's an unusual and wonderful experience to go as an owner. When Dr Devious ran they put a microphone on Sid so that if the horse won, they can hear your comments. As soon as the race was over, the guy came and grabbed the mic off Sid's lapel, and Sid said, "Boy, they don't waste any time." It was, "Good-bye and God bless you."

But being there, I never fail to get tears in my eyes when they play "My Old Kentucky Home." It is so emotional and magical. Watching on TV doesn't come close to being there and feeling the excitement and the electricity in the spectators. It gets to you. Even the horses seem like they know, and can feel the pride and the history behind it as they're walking out there proudly.

LS: *Has anyone pointed out the irony of you naming a horse Chocolate Candy?*
JC: Every woman at the Derby will be carrying a chocolate candy if we get there, I'll tell you that. It's off the diet for a day. Everyone comments about what a great name it is, but so far nobody has teased me about being in the business I'm in. Just because you name a horse that doesn't mean you eat that. [Chocolate Candy finished fifth in the Kentucky Derby.]

LS: *Do you have a favorite race?*
JC: Probably the Epsom Derby, because when I bought Dr Devious for Sid, all the people were saying, "What a dumb broad, she doesn't know what she's doing, she paid too much money for that horse, blah, blah, blah." So I felt redemption after Dr Devious won the race by four lengths. The announcer came up to me and asked how I felt, and I said, "I feel like I just went from a dumb broad to a genius." And it was true.

The irony is that Hal King, who was managing our operation, had been looking for a Derby horse to buy, and he called and said he couldn't find anything, but that he had a filly who looked promising. This was a week before Dr Devious came to my attention, and I was desperate to get Sid a birthday present, so I bought the filly. And that was Crownette, who is Chocolate Candy's dam. How strong is that? It gives me goosebumps to think about it.

LS: *What are the reasons behind your success in business?*
JC: Someone once said, "The harder I work, the luckier I get." My work ethic is that you never give up on anything. So I have that plus enthusiasm, vision, and determination. That's the way I was raised. My dad always told me I could do anything and be anything if I was willing to work hard enough and really want it. And that's been my philosophy my whole life. I've never been afraid to work for

what I wanted. I'm glad he didn't tell me I could fly, because I'm liable to have tried it.

LS: *How do you handle the fame?*
JC: There are times when people come up to me and tell me stories about how they or a relative have lost weight on the program and how it changed their life, and I would really and truly enjoy hearing that. Other times Sid and I would be enjoying a quiet dinner and somebody would come and slide into the booth and start talking to me. I do love people and love talking to people and never feel they're intruding unless they do something like that.

LS: *You have been very strong in advancing women in your company.*
JC: You have to know your market. Eighty-five percent of our clientele were women, and it makes sense that women relate to women's challenges. I think men, when they gain weight, worry about their health. Women, when they gain weight, worry about their appearance and how their clothes aren't going to fit. Different mentalities. So 98 percent of our executives were women. Most of our advertising appealed to women. Nutrisystem has focused on the male market. Now the baby boomers are of an age where their weight is beginning to affect their health. It's amazing how much obesity there is today. It's shocking.

I'm not active in the business anymore. I do go to conferences occasionally and make presentations for the company. But I'm not involved in the day-to-day operation. However, the woman who is the CEO today started in a center as a counselor and worked her way up through the company, so that's gratifying.

LS: *Do you have hobbies?*
JC: I love to play poker. Sid had a group of guys that played—Bob Strauss, the ambassador; [baseball executive] Buzzy Bavasi; [horse owner and breeder] Leonard Lavin. They'd all come in a couple of times a year to play poker. Once, they were a player short, so I stepped in and of course won, so they've been inviting me to play ever since to get their money back. I have a women's group that plays every week. And I try to play golf, too.

2010

(Jenny Craig was back in the Kentucky Derby the following year with Sidney's Candy.)

Lenny Shulman: *Two years in a row you're going to the Derby with a son of Candy Ride.*

Jenny Craig: Just having a horse in the Derby is exciting in itself. I'd like to tell you I named the horse after Sid because I felt he was a special horse. But the truth is I had twelve babies to name, and I had no idea what their talent was, and I selected this one to name "Sidney's Candy" not even looking at the horse. They're all Candy Rides, but picking that name for this one—I know that was divine intervention. It's really amazing. When I saw his talent as he was coming along, I just knew there was more to it than coincidence. He's the only one I've ever named "Sidney."

My whole family—kids and grandkids old enough, will be there. We have fourteen grandkids. To be able to share it with all the people you love makes it more exciting.

There's a lot of speed in the race, so we'll see how it sets up and hope he gets a good post position. Each time you go to the Derby you say, "I don't think I'll do this again," and then you get a great horse and say, "How can you not?"

[Sidney's Candy sat second early in the Derby before fading to finish seventeenth.]

16

Sam Shepard

IT WOULD BE DIFFICULT to come up with a more versatile talent than **Sam Shepard,** who excelled as a playwright, author, actor, and musician. Much of his work was set in the romantic cowboy era of the West and encompassed his affinity for horses. Although his talents as a Thoroughbred breeder did not reach the heights of his fame in other fields, he was immersed in his Kentucky farm, from which he did achieve a measure of success.

2007

Interviewed in Midway, Kentucky

Lenny Shulman: *The American West has had a great influence on your work.*
Sam Shepard: I grew up in it, out near Chino, California. There were a lot of lay-up farms around, and I worked at those places as a kid. I worked at Rex Ellsworth's farm out there for a while. Worked at Santa Anita as a hotwalker. I never had any money to even dream about getting into the game as a breeder or owner.

But I noticed that every good horse at Santa Anita was bred in Kentucky, so I thought, "One day . . ." But I never in a million years thought I'd have the money to buy a broodmare. I was working on a Woody Allen film in 1987, and I got fired from it, but I had the per diem cash. I went to a California-bred sale at Hollywood Park with $3,500 in my pocket. I saw a mare by Upper Nile out of a mare named Light Verse. At that time, there was one piece of black type underneath Light Verse, and I bought her mare for $3,200.

That was River Chant, who is the third dam of High Heels [a grade 2 winner], who just ran third in the Kentucky Oaks. I bred the first two dams of High Heels [stakes winner Ornate and Nile Chant, bred under the name of Shepard's Totier Creek Farm]. After twenty years it's great to see you have a little bit of influence on the breed.

LS: *You've had some other success.*
SS: I brought River Chant to Virginia, where I had a place named Totier Creek Farm. The creek ran right through the farm, and I've kept the name through the

years. I bred her to Key to the Kingdom on a $2,500 stud fee and sold that filly for $40,000 to Jimmy Gladwell, who turned her over to Mike Pegram and Bob Baffert when he was just coming up from the quarter horses, and she [Common Threads] made about $250,000 and was stakes-placed.

I bred a filly named Two Trail Sioux [by Indian Charlie], a grade 2 winner of $664,960; and I bred Zophie, the dam of Appealing Zophie, who won the [grade 1] Spinaway.

LS: *Eventually you bought a farm here in Midway.*
SS: I've known [Saxony Farm owner] Bruce Hundley for a long time, and I was looking for a place here. Bruce has a great eye for land, and he's bought some beautiful places. He told me he had this little place that was tucked away. I went to look at it and fell in love with it. I bought it in 2000. It has an old brick house on it we refurbished that was in Jesse James's mother's family. It fronts on Elkhorn Creek.

I just keep cutting horses and cattle there. I keep the mares with Nuckols Farm. I don't have the expertise for foaling, and I don't want to have a staff. I couldn't afford it anyway, and they do a great job.

LS: *How big is your broodmare band?*
SS: I have a half dozen mares. I decided I was only going to keep as many mares as I could hold in my head. I know each and every one of them, and for the most part they're all homebreds—four of them are from the same family as River Chant. I have a half sister to Ornate, and I have a half sister to Two Trail Sioux by Maria's Mon who is still on the track. I don't buy mares anymore. I breed them. They're like gold.

People ask me why do I want to keep mares from the same family. Well, because one of these days . . . (*laughs*). And it's turned out.

LS: *So you actively study pedigrees?*
SS: I plan all the matings. I never talk to bloodstock agents (*laughs*). They only get you in trouble. It's a bogus occupation to begin with. Who needs any more bullshit?

I absolutely get involved in pedigree study. I can't count the hours I've spent poring over pedigrees. But some of the best horses I've bred came more out of instinct than anything else, know what I mean? I bred Quiet Trail, a Quiet American mare that I raced, to Indian Charlie because he was a gorgeous horse physically. I didn't study the pedigree much. That was Two Trail Sioux. Later I found out Indian Charlie traces back to the family of In Reality, and Quiet American is loaded with In Reality and Dr. Fager. So it turned out I'm a genius.

This year I did a radical thing. I bred all but one mare to Littlexpectations. When [Millennium Farm manager] Bobby Miller walked that horse out, I just loved him. Gorgeous, fantastic temperament, speed to beat the band. He's already got a grade 2 horse, King of the Roxy, who's going to the Preakness. First time I've ever sent them to one stallion. People think I'm nuts.

A million years ago Walter Merrick, who bred more great quarter horses than anyone in history, bred them that way. He'd back the mares up like cattle and breed them to the same horse. It does work, sometimes, and the percentages are probably better than shopping them around.

LS: *Have you learned anything about horses here in Kentucky you didn't know?*
SS: I've learned a lot here about spotting a good horse. Mainly by the way a horse should walk. Jimmy Gladwell taught me more about that than anybody, what to look for in pastures.

I keep the fillies and sell the colts as a rule. A couple, like Ornate, have slipped through the cracks. I couldn't afford to keep her. She's by Gilded Time, who was red hot then. So I sold her as a weanling. Sold Two Trail Sioux too because she was offset in the knees and I didn't think she was going to train. There you go . . .

My accountant would disagree if you said I was breaking even, but I'm doing all right. Racing is tough because it's so expensive. You've got to have a good one. [John] Nerud said once that $3 billion was earned by racehorses last year, except it cost $6 billion to train them (*laughs*). And you wonder why we don't breed to race.

LS: *Do you enjoy the racing aspect?*
SS: The sport is so incredible. It's unfortunate that now it's being marketed as an entertainment venue connected to gambling, because the horse has kinda taken a backseat. It's too bad, because the public would like to know more about the horse, and it's very little about the horse now as opposed to gambling. I don't understand the marketing notion that skips the horse, and the breeder, for that matter. On Breeders' Cup day, how many interviews do you have with the breeder? Not one. It's called the Breeders' Cup. I just don't get it. But I think racing is a tremendous sport.

LS: *So you breed to get a racehorse?*
SS: The thing is, if you breed to get a racehorse, you're going to be able to sell it. People know what a racehorse looks like. I don't think you need to have a fancy pedigree anymore; you need a good-looking horse that looks like he's gonna get the job done. I don't see that discrepancy between breeding to race and breeding

to sell, unless you have a horse by an absolutely unheard-of stallion in New Mexico or something. And people in New Mexico have bred some good horses too.

LS: *You portrayed trainer Frank Whiteley in the* Ruffian *movie. What was that like?*
SS: I didn't talk to Whiteley beforehand because I heard he was sick, and I didn't want to bother him. And I also heard he was cantankerous, and I didn't want to mess around and bust into his private life. There's such a wealth of information about the man from all the people I talked to who've met him, and I've seen several TV interviews with him that were quite revealing, I thought. I got a lot of information out of that.

LS: *You played him with a definite slice of playfulness.*
SS: From what I understand he had a sense of humor. All these reporters and photographers came around to see Ruffian, and he sent them down the shedrow to photograph what turned out to be a gelding. That's funny. And he'd spray reporters with the hose he'd be using to cool down horses' legs.

LS: *What attracted you to the project?*
SS: You can pay me all day long to sit on a horse and go around a racetrack, or do a Western.

I grew up with the American West and the cowboy way. In the fifties, real horsemen I was around weren't that forthcoming. They were tight-lipped. To get any information out of them at all you had to watch. Simultaneously there was Hopalong Cassidy, Roy Rogers, Gene Autry, *The Rifleman,* and Steve McQueen on TV, so you grew up in this kind of aura of the imagination while at the same time I was around guys who were actually working with horses. I was saturated with it. I remember watching the Rose Bowl Parade with Roy Rogers coming down the street on horseback with silver trappings—very impressive when you were a kid. I rodeo'd a little bit, team-roped, rode some bareback, and grew up in it.

LS: *Does the West represent something of a vanishing America?*
SS: I'm not as interested in the symbology of it as I am the land itself, know what I mean? When you cross the river and get into Big Country—South Dakota, Wyoming, Montana, parts of Colorado—something changes. You feel different. You have a different respect for the land. That's what it's always been for me. Just that feeling. The symbology is promotional. Even in the early days, the East Coast was writing fantasies about the West with all these dime novels, and hardly any of them had anything to do with reality.

LS: *What are you working on now?*

SS: I just premiered a play at the national theater in Dublin called *Kicking a Dead Horse* about a guy in the latter part of his life who decides he's going to take one last fling and takes off on his horse to go venture out in the Badlands. The horse dies on him, and he spends the rest of the play kicking the horse. It's coming to New York in the fall.

We still have the band, now called the Velocity Ramblers, and have been playing at clubs in New York. Same guys as the Holy Modal Rounders.

I cut hay and grass, and love to fish. Going out to Montana in August. The brown fishing is spectacular in August. I'm in Mexico a lot, New York out of necessity, here, and in Montana. New York is too damn many people. I do love Saratoga. Great track. Raced a couple of horses there that didn't do any good.

I have a Jesse James film with Brad Pitt coming up that the studio has cast a spell on by calling it an art movie. It looked like a beautiful movie when we were shooting it. I hope it gets out there, but who knows? Everyone wants a cut-and-burn movie.

I work when I have to, and when they'll have me (*laughs*).

17

Bo Derek

A UBIQUITOUS PRESENCE AT Breeders' Cup World Championships, **Bo Derek** to this day brings out a visceral reaction from fans when she's spotted at the racetrack. A lifelong lover of animals and an equestrian, Derek lives on a ranch north of Los Angeles and served a stint as a commissioner on the California Horse Racing Board, where she emphasized safety and aftercare. She has embraced being an ambassador for the horse racing industry.

2012

Interviewed from Los Angeles

Lenny Shulman: *You have an affinity for horses.*
Bo Derek: I was brought up in the Los Angeles suburbs near the beach, but I always—my mom says from the time I was able to walk, I was crawling up on my rocking horse. If we were driving as a family and we passed a horse, I screamed and yelled and wanted to look at it. I think some people are born with that.

I rode some on vacations, then one summer my father got my brother and me an old, retired riding horse. You can learn a lot on those, especially the ones that want to run back to the barn.

LS: *And when you began to achieve success in your acting career?*
BD: As soon as I made some money after making the movie *10*, I bought a place up in Santa Ynez first thing, and got some horses—Arabians and quarter horses. I first went to Spain in 1982 and got to ride my first Andalusian, and that was it. That's the horse that hit my genetic brain, the one I'd been dreaming about. They are hot-blooded horses, and they are the first saddle horses used through wars and bullfighting. Perhaps they are more attuned to humans.

So much around my life is horses—friendships around the world.

LS: *You wrote a book entitled* Riding Lessons: Everything That Matters in Life I Learned from Horses.
BD: That was a gimmick. I didn't set out to write that. I got a great offer to write a book, and it was one of the worst experiences of my life. I had the hardest time.

I went through ghostwriters who tried to make me nauseatingly nice, so I ended up writing it myself, and it took on a life of its own.

But in general, animals teach you a lot about instinctive base behaviors and inclinations. Horses especially, because you don't win them over by just feeding them. It takes something else to get a real relationship. To get them to leave their friends out in a grass pasture and come see you is a huge, huge compliment.

LS: *What about racehorses?*
BD: What fascinates me most about racehorses and horsemen—I'm constantly explaining or defending the sport—I think there's something magical about a horseman getting a racehorse ready for the races; to love what they do. You can only get so much out of a horse through pressure. To get real brilliance, they have to want to do it. I find it so interesting compared to other disciplines and the things we ask of horses. I think asking them to run is the most natural thing we ask of them.

LS: *You have been appointed to the California Horse Racing Board [CHRB]. What do you hope to concentrate on in that role?*
BD: I don't know how anyone thought of me. It came from out of the blue. Someone from the governor's office called me as I was just getting off the Kennedy Center board and some other things I'd gotten involved with, and the last thing I wanted to do was get involved with any other boards.

I had put a lot of time into getting horse slaughter banned in the US, but that doesn't mean I'm a member of PETA. I concentrated my efforts on the horse slaughter bill. So on horse welfare issues, I think I've gotten a lot of credit that I'm not sure I've earned. I am a special envoy to the secretary of state on wildlife trafficking. People assume you're all-encompassing and very broad into welfare issues, but I really am not. I can only take on what I really understand.

It was a difficult decision to say "yes" to the CHRB. I was a fan of racing but knew very little about it. Sure, I was a horsewoman, and they said they wanted a woman and someone to represent the horse welfare and safety issues, and they wanted someone to represent the fan. They told me to try it, and that I could always say "no."

The background check and confirmation happened so quickly it was hilarious. Like one week. The first meeting was a lot about race dates and wagering issues, and I sat there for six hours concerned because they hadn't mentioned the horse once, so I figured this wasn't for me. I took the Clarence Thomas posture on the board, just sitting there and learning for the first couple of years. Now I feel

I'm just starting to, after four years, be able to take on a couple of issues I feel passionate about.

LS: *What are those?*
BD: The drug issues in California get a lot of attention. It is a sport run by humans, so there will always be people trying to get an edge, especially with so much to gain. People cheat in horse shows where all you get is a ribbon. With millions of dollars at stake . . .

Lasix is something the industry will work out. There are arguments on both sides, and I think it's been proven to be both performance-enhancing and therapeutic. People with a lot more expertise than I have will pursue that.

I'm very interested in reforming the claiming rules, which I think will be beneficial to the safety and welfare of the horses and riders. The hot-potato aspect of it gives too much incentive to enter a compromised horse. I know it's been 150 years and it's the way it's always been, but that doesn't make it right.

Voiding claims of injured horses is something I feel strongly about, and that change would encourage people to rest horses longer and take away the incentive of running a compromised horse. If an owner still wants to buy the horse after it gets put on the vet list after a race, they can still do so privately.

LS: *You seem to pop up with regularity at big races.*
BD: I go to main-event races around the world. I've led the post parade a couple of times at Hollywood Park. I love the sport. It's wonderful, and I always have a good time out there, but it's a very complicated sport.

LS: *What has surprised you about horse racing?*
BD: I've been around long enough that not much shocks me. Sometimes, sitting on the board, I find myself getting upset about something, but then you realize how crazy and defensive everyone gets. It's racing. What has impressed me most is the people I'm involved with. It's like running off and joining the circus. I've enjoyed it very much, which surprises me, even though it's a lot more work than I expected.

LS: *Can you compare racing here with international races you've attended?*
BD: I treasure every moment I get to talk about horses, be it with Bob Baffert and John Shirreffs here, or at the Arc, or in Australia. There's nothing like going out to morning workouts in Europe and seeing the Aidan O'Brien horses come out together and go so freely without the pony horses and restraints. How different everything is and yet the same.

You go to the Melbourne Cup, and the city shuts down and it's a national holiday. But we have the same thing with the Kentucky Derby. We just need to bridge the gap between the normal race days and the big events. But that takes work and education. I think the sport could be more mainstream here. When we do the big events, people come. But if you look at Breeders' Cup, the brand awareness doesn't exist among the public. Nobody in California knows what it is, and it's the best horse racing there is on an international level.

Our society is such that you can't make it popular without celebrities. It's sad.

LS: *You haven't felt the need to own racehorses?*
BD: I have a hard-enough time feeding my riding horses. So, no. I get my fix being on the board and spending so much time at the track. I live vicariously through so many friends when their horses win.

I've got two more years to go on the CHRB, and that will have been a great chapter in my life. I would never leave being around racing, but when my term is up, I'll be ready to move on from the board. I have gotten so much out of it, though.

18

David Milch

IF I WERE TO pick the most unforgettable interview I've conducted over twenty years at *Bloodhorse,* it would be my session with the brilliant TV and film writer **David Milch.** He is the most obvious genius I've encountered, and his honesty and willingness to share painful aspects of his life is breathtaking. Milch owned Breeders' Cup winners Gilded Time and Val Royal, but his addictive personality, which helped bring forth culture-changing shows such as *NYPD Blue,* also made him, at different points in his life, a heroin and gambling addict, and he lost millions at the racetrack.

2002

Interviewed at Paramount Studios, Hollywood, California

Lenny Shulman: What was your first experience with horse racing?
David Milch: One of my great-uncles worked for Meyer Lansky when he had gambling clubs in Saratoga Springs. My father worked as a busboy in one of the casinos, and he was always drawn to the races. We lived in Buffalo, and every August, as far back as I can remember, he would go to Saratoga, and that was a big deal. My brother and I would go to camp in the Adirondack Mountains, and we'd spend a week at Saratoga when camp was over.

My father was a doctor, and I think he took care of Lansky. In the fifties, when the Kefauver Commission began hearings into the Mob, we had an awful lot of people living with us who had suddenly come up with hernia conditions, and my dad would operate on them, and so therefore they couldn't testify before the committee.

My father was given a racehorse named Lord Mike, and there was a Lady Mike as well. I didn't understand what the hell was going on, but it was a lot of fun, and there were all these tips and countertips and beards going to the windows to mislead people. It never occurred to me that it might be a square deal (*laughs*). The idea that the best horse won was about twelfth on the list of potential outcomes.

I remember getting to sit with Sunny Jim Fitzsimmons, who had Nashua at the time. He was all stooped over; he looked like a question mark. But for some reason, I amused him, and I'd sit with him in the mornings. To a young mind like mine, the environment was so overwhelming. I wish I could say I developed some affinity for the animals. But the horses were so much the pawns of forces and processes that were at once incomprehensible and compelling. They were the mystery at the eye of the storm.

LS: *How did you get into ownership?*
DM: There are two streams that feed into that river of my involvement with horses. One is my obsession with gambling, which is not a constructive obsession. I always gambled but was never in a position to pursue the ownership of horses until I had been a teacher at Yale and then came out here in 1983. The first thing I wrote [a script for the TV show *L.A. Law*] won a bunch of prizes, an Emmy, and, more importantly, a Humanitas Prize given by the Catholic Church that was fifteen thousand dollars—tax free. They were holding a gun to my head—I had to use that to buy a horse.

LS: *Do you get any satisfaction from owning horses?*
DM: It's very difficult to disentangle all the different threads that make up the fabric of a person's life. On one level, I think the process of a life is trying to find benign accommodations for the inevitable paths we take. In the scheme of things, it was a given I was going to be involved with gambling and horses—it's just part of my family background. Here was my dad, who was fascinated by horses but forbidden to be involved with them because he was supposed to be an upstanding guy. And I was his dutiful son, and it was a given I would pursue these interests. And that isn't a prescription either for success or happiness—living someone else's dreams.

The process of trying to make that something positive and loving and constructive is a challenge. For me, horse racing is a very complicated, cutthroat affair. An abyss is waiting on either side of a very narrow path. And the abyss is painted in very pleasant colors and populated by very charming people. Risk-taking has a perverse appeal to it. For me, at least, it's not a pretty process.

LS: *What was it like for you when your Val Royal won the Breeders' Cup Mile last year?*
DM: I was relieved for a little piece of time, because that was a horse with such terrible problems for whom I'd paid an awful lot of money. He came here from Europe, won one race, and bowed a tendon. It took us eighteen months to bring

him back. The part of it I enjoy is to come to know a little bit about what it takes to get a horse ready, and so on. I check up on my horses every day, and that was about 550 days of difficult news with that horse, so when he exploded the way he did, we had always thought he was that good a horse. So that was good.

LS: *Having researched you, I'm going to say you have a bit of an addictive personality . . .*
DM: I think you're on safe ground there.

LS: *So your involvement is just an act of feeding this addictive personality through gambling?*
DM: As I said, I'm trying to find benign accommodations for the obsessions of my nature. To own a horse is a benign accommodation for what is otherwise to me a purely addictive process. When you gamble, or engage in any addictive process, the content of the behavior becomes increasingly fixated on the addictive act. Let's say you and I are carrying on a civil conversation, and I'm perfectly content to do that. If at a certain point you get between me and the object of my addiction, I'm going to fuck you up. Whatever respect I have for you as a human being, whatever civility I'd like to maintain, is subordinate, as my disease progresses, to the satisfaction of the addiction. That's not a very human way to live. It's the opposite of human. And so it's been my dream for some time to be able to somehow civilize that process in some way.

LS: *Is writing the same kind of benign accommodation for you?*
DM: Writing is a genuinely benign outlet. It's obsessive in some of its impulses, but it can transmute itself. The trouble with addiction is that it doesn't let God's light in. It needs to conduct itself in the darkness. Whereas there are other kinds of behavior which allow . . . writing is an opening up to other souls, so it's a healing process.

LS: *Getting back to horses, what kind of success were you having before Gilded Time came along?*
DM: I originally got involved as a minority participant and that wasn't much fun, so I started to claim horses and did pretty well. I started buying horses out of Europe in the mid-1980s. Then I bought Ria Jessie, who won the Santa Ana Handicap, and I had a few other horses do well. Marvin's Policy won a stakes at Monmouth. I was doing OK. I bought Gilded Time [for eighty thousand dollars] out of a two-year-old sale, and [trainer] Darrell [Vienna] said he was the fastest horse he'd ever had.

The first time he ran he stayed in the gate and was last by twenty lengths. Gary Stevens rode him and said he was just trying to get him close enough after that to get some dirt in his face so he'd get something out of the race. He was ten-wide in the far turn, and by the time they reached the head of the stretch he was still ten-wide, but five lengths in front. It was an amazing performance. His second race he ran the fastest six furlongs any two-year-old ever ran: 1:07 $\frac{4}{5}$ at Monmouth. And then he started developing problems, and we nursed him along.

LS: *What was the experience like when he won the Breeders' Cup Juvenile that year?*
DM: It was great. I flew fifty people down to Florida. My business manager called me and said, "If your horse doesn't win, you're not going to be able to fly the people back." So I took a job fixing a movie script while I was there. The producer was a real jerk who would call me at three in the morning complaining about the pages I was sending him. The project got green-lighted after I'd rewritten the first fifty pages. Then the horse won the race, so I didn't need the work. So he calls me to finish the script, and I told him, "You're wasting the next two minutes of your life."

LS: *Do you look for something specific when buying horses?*
DM: For a while you could do well bringing horses over from Europe. Then it reached a point where you had to overpay so wildly. I finally came to a point where if I thought the horse had upside, I was willing to pay much more than what the horse was worth. Val Royal, for example, I paid almost a million for even though his demonstrated form, having won a couple of group 2s, made him worth maybe $300,000.

The economics of horse racing don't make sense, anyway. I've never quite understood why people think there's a difference between spending $240,000 and $270,000 if they shouldn't be spending the first $240,000 anyway. If I feel a horse has got it . . . we were interested in a filly named Above Perfection, but the only way we could buy her was if we bought a package of horses. But we felt she had upside. You know the old story, "If you want to hear God laugh, tell Him your plans?" Disturbingthepeace (four-time grade 2 winner) was part of that package. If I think a horse has a chance, I won't let an extra $50,000 dissuade me, and I'm perfectly OK to hear the seller say he got more than top dollar.

LS: *Have you come close to breaking even over the years in this business?*
DM: As an owner, I've made a lot of money. I sold Tuzla, Caffe Latte, Gilded Time . . . I've sold four or five horses for more than a million bucks apiece.

LS: *Are there any comparisons you can draw between horse ownership and scriptwriting?*
DM: Well, they're both exercises in humility. I used to think scriptwriting ... that the exercise of the imagination was predicated on the self. What I've come to understand is the exercise of the imagination comes from the sublimation of the self. Getting out of the way. So in that sense, humility is of the essence of being a good owner and being a good writer.

LS: *So it's not difficult as an owner to relinquish that control to others?*
DM: No. I'm about forty-four kinds of fool, but that's one kind I'm not.

LS: *Many of your stakes horses have been geldings.*
DM: We cut Disturbingthepeace. Plants that are trimmed in the shape of animals are called topiary. In his first race for us, he tried to have carnal relations with some topiary in the shape of a horse in the paddock.

LS: *Are there people in Hollywood you can talk to about horses?*
DM: No.

LS: *Does the mathematical stimulation of trying to figure out who is going to win a race do anything for you?*
DM: No, because I know it's a lie. I know what's being done with horse racing. If you think you can quantify the likelihood of a horse's success based on past performance, it's more likely it's based on which trainer has which illegal drug in which state. And the way to make money is to wait until the given trainer goes from one state where he can't get to the stuff to another where he can get to the stuff. And then his horse, which has been beaten thirty-five lengths in some race, suddenly runs second in a classic. Without mentioning any names.

LS: *In articles I have read about you, it stuns me how open you are about what goes on in your life.*
DM: Just to turn over all my cards, the thing about any disease is it always gets worse. One of the things that's said about another addiction is, "While I'm not using, my disease is doing push-ups in the parking lot." I would say over the past year my disease has progressed exponentially—the act of gambling.

With the approach of a race, I start to engage in ritualized behavior a couple of days out. When Disturbingthepeace was running at Hollywood Park on a Saturday, on Thursday I went out and began losing money, about $275,000. The next day is given to remorse and thoughts of self-annihilation. The day of the race I went out, and by the time Disturbingthepeace is about to run I was behind

$400,000 for the day. My family was with me, and we went down to saddle the horse, and my sole focus was not throwing myself off the second story. Just trying to get through it.

The horse won, and because of the way I bet, I had every possible combination—the trifectas, triples, Pick 4s, Pick 6s. So I won about $750,000. Afterwards, I gathered the family together and told them what utter despair the process was, how dangerous, the danger I felt we were all in.

Through processes of trying to find a way to live with other obsessions, I've been blessed to come to a belief in God. But this was a part of my life I was not willing to forgive. As it turned out, when I was a kid, I was being sexually abused on a protracted basis by someone at the racetrack, and the way a child tries to deal with that sort of thing is to redirect attention to persuade yourself that you're having a good time. And the tremendous amount of energy I devoted to trying to idealize that was a way of holding on to . . . of not facing, living through, forgiving, and moving on with the rest of my life.

So that was my choice. What happened fifty years ago happened fifty years ago, but what God gives me to deal with is how I'm going to live today. I guess if I were trying to put a nice color on this conversation, mine is not a typical experience of horse racing, and so I suppose some of the anger I express about the process of gambling is fueled by some kind of continued resentment that comes from other sources. I have no axes to grind. I've never talked about any of this in regard to horse racing. I have a lot of happy memories; we can say that for the purposes of this discussion. I'm not trying to beat anything up. All I can do is give my own testimony.

Maybe we can just leave it that I'm not a good guy to talk to about it. Maybe you want to sell the article to somebody else.

LS: *I don't want to write anything that you're uncomfortable about me writing.*
DM: I'm not uncomfortable with any of it.

LS: *What in life gives you joy?*
DM: My family gives me joy, my work gives me great joy. I'm a happy guy.

LS: *Are you?*
DM: Yeah. I'm a grateful guy.

LS: *Are there any shows coming up I should write about?*
DM: Yeah, I'm doing a series for HBO, a Western called *Deadwood*. We're going to start to shoot in six weeks. A real Western. Kinda tough. And it's all about gambling.

19

Michael Imperioli

SPEAKING WITH THE NEW YORK actor **Michael Imperioli** is not much different from watching the characters he's created on-screen that are ingrained into our consciousness. A fan of horse racing, Imperioli first came to our attention in the film *Goodfellas,* when his character, Spider, was shot by the gangster played by Joe Pesci. Imperioli is best known for playing Christopher Moltisanti, the nephew of mob boss Tony Soprano, in the epic HBO show *The Sopranos.*

2001

Interviewed at Belmont Park, New York

Lenny Shulman: *You look comfortable here at the track.*
Michael Imperioli: I grew up a few miles away from Yonkers Raceway in Mount Vernon, so I went to Yonkers a lot as a kid. My dad took me, and we had some friends across the street who were into it. It's always something that's fascinated me back since I was a kid—the energy and excitement.

I got busy trying to be an actor and didn't focus on anything but that for a while. Then, about four or five years ago, I started getting into it again. Two years ago, I began learning how to handicap; I'd been winging it before that. I started asking, "What is it about this sport?" because there's a lot to it; a lot to look at and a science to it, and with that I gained more of an appreciation for the sport and for what goes into the breeding and training of the Thoroughbred. Now I love it. It's an awesome sport, an exciting sport. To me, horses are the ultimate athletes because that's all they do. They're bred and trained and they live for that race. They're wonders of nature.

LS: *What clicked that got you back into it?*
MI: I was living close to an OTB in Manhattan, and I started going there because I liked the energy. Then I started going out to the tracks again—Aqueduct and Belmont. It's a great game and a beautiful sport. What goes into these animals is a lot of expertise, hopes, care, love, and expectations, and it's exciting, especially when the stakes are high like today [Belmont Stakes].

I went to my first Kentucky Derby this year, and it was amazing. When those horses hit the turn at the top of the stretch, that roar from the crowd; there's so much focused on this tiny block of time. It's beautiful.

LS: *Have you considered buying horses?*
MI: I need to learn a lot more before I would do that. I would consider it eventually but want to learn more about the game.

LS: *Since you write in addition to acting, is there a romantic aspect to the sport for you?*
MI: Of course. There are so many dreams that are broken or fulfilled, so many stories, and the other thing is that everyone can have a share of that dream. You can go and bet two dollars and you've got a share of the dream. You don't have to be the big owner or the great trainer. It's available to everybody to have a stake in. There are dreams that work on all levels of society, and it absolutely is about that.

The rarity of having a horse that actually gets into the Derby . . . it's extremely tough, and I'm sure the Oxleys this year when their horse [Monarchos] won that race, I can't imagine what that must have felt like for people like them and [trainer] John Ward and [jockey Jorge] Chavez, who have all been in the game a long time.

The great thing about this to me is that ultimately, it's not about the people. In the end, it's about a horse. And you don't know what that horse is thinking and you don't know what that horse is gonna feel like that day. You may think it's the greatest horse, but he has a bad day. You may feel a horse has no chance, and he upsets you. Ultimately, we don't have the control. It's the horse. It's beautiful.

LS: *Are you a history buff about racing? Have you gone back and read about Secretariat?*
MI: Yeah, a bit. That's a story, Secretariat, Jesus. They did an autopsy on him, and his heart was gigantic. Which, also metaphorically, his heart was huge. Can you imagine winning this race by thirty-one lengths, what that must have felt like? I saw a clip of it today on the news, and people were going mad. He was like a rock star.

LS: *Tell me about the experience of being in Kentucky in comparison to the New York feel here.*
MI: Kentucky is horse country, and it's a big deal there. When you're there and you turn on the TV it's "Derby, Derby, Derby" all day long. It's great tradition and a sense of that legacy. It has an importance. New York, because it has so many

other things going on, it's not as big a deal to New York. But you have all the characters here and all the different types of people who are into racing, and the people who are into racing here are *really* into it. I was just down in the paddock, and there are people arguing back and forth. New York's a big town, and there are a lot of racing fans here. This is a beautiful park, so we have our place in racing.

LS: *You're writing some episodes of* The Sopranos. *Will there be a track scene?*
MI: I'd love to get one in there. There will be a track scene in something that I write. I don't know if it will be *The Sopranos,* but it will be something.

LS: *Do you get tired of being shot so many times in shows and films?*
MI: I've been shot or killed at least a half dozen times, *Goodfellas* being the first and most famous. But if I'm still alive, I'll be back here for the Breeders' Cup this fall.

20

Rick Pitino

LOVE HIM OR HATE him—and there are plenty of Kentuckians on both sides of that equation—**Rick Pitino** is a legend in the world of basketball, having led both the University of Kentucky and Louisville to national collegiate championships. The bitter rivalry between those two schools and his jumping from one to the other explains the raw feelings toward him from fans. But Pitino, who also coached the NBA's New York Knicks and Boston Celtics, and is currently the coach of Iona College, is also a longtime owner of Thoroughbreds who in 2013 was driving Louisville toward a title while his Goldencents was burning up the racetrack.

2013

Interviewed from Louisville, Kentucky

Lenny Shulman: *Thanks for taking the time to talk so soon after the [NCAA] tournament.*
Rick Pitino: It's a nice change to talk horses and not basketball.

LS: *Did you go to the tracks in New York when you were growing up?*
RP: Even though I lived close to Belmont Park, I never went to the Thoroughbreds. I did go to Roosevelt Raceway because I went to school at St. Dominic's in Oyster Bay. When I was coaching the Knicks and also at Providence College, I met the trainer John Parisella, who was a big fan of both those teams, and he started naming horses Full Court Press and Friar Magic. [Providence's nickname is the Friars.] I found out about Thoroughbreds through him.

When I worked as an assistant at Syracuse I went to Saratoga, and that was my first real introduction to the sport. I've been vacationing in Saratoga for thirty years, and if you learn the sport at places like Keeneland and Saratoga, you fall in love with it. They are pretty special places.

Then I really got to know it when I moved to Kentucky and became friends with Seth Hancock at Claiborne Farm. I would regularly take every recruit and their family to see Secretariat. It worked for the kids, and for me especially.

LS: *You own horses exclusively in partnerships?*
RP: That's the only way I can go. I'll tell you my favorite story. I run a golf tournament at Saratoga every year for charity. I had Celtic Pride Stable, a small stable with six horses. So I'm at the yearling sale up there talking to people from the golf tournament in the bar, and my wife comes back and tells me to go to the arena—our friend Will Farish has a horse going through the ring, a son of A. P. Indy out of a Secretariat mare, and it's going to go for a million dollars. And I said, "I'm not doing that, I'm not getting involved in bidding on a horse like that." And she says to come in, [trainer] Nick [Zito] is there, and I said, "You're going to make me raise my hand, and I'm not doing that."

So of course I go inside, and I'm sitting there with Nick, and Bill and Will Farish, and they tell me he's going to sell for well over a million dollars, and why don't I make a bid. I figure they've got a reserve on it for at least $750,000, so I say "OK" and raise my hand at $450,000. And all of a sudden, it's "450 once, 450 twice. Sold."

I grab my wife's leg and tell her, "I'll never speak to you for as long as I live. Where am I going to get that kind of money? I'm going to have to go get a loan from a bank."

So I go back to the bar and start telling everyone this story about this royally bred horse, and everyone thought I got a tremendous discount, and they're like, "I'll take 10 percent." "I'll take 20 percent." And in no time, I had 80 percent of the horse sold at the bar.

So that was A P Valentine. He wins the Champagne Stakes, and I end up selling him for $15 million against the wishes of my partners. They were begging me not to sell, but as general partner, I was selling. I grew up a modest man; my father was a truck driver, my mother was a nurse's assistant, and I was selling. By the end of that year he wasn't worth one-third of that, and then Lloyd's of London got stuck because it turned out he was sterile.

LS: *You went to the Kentucky Derby in 1998 with Halory Hunter.*
RP: He was really special because he wasn't a well-bred horse; he was a fighter. My wife and I loved that horse. Indian Charlie nosed us out for third in the Derby. A P Valentine was a terrific horse, but Halory Hunter . . . The difference was A P Valentine was like the championship I won at Kentucky—we had eight future pros on the team, and everyone knew we were great, and we just had to come through. Halory Hunter is more like this Louisville team. In the middle of the year no one expected us to win a championship, but we went ahead and did it,

and it was great. [Louisville won the National Championship in 2013, but the title was eventually vacated by the NCAA because of recruiting violations.]

LS: *Talk about your current star Goldencents, who will be running in the Derby soon.*

RP: He was breezing at Del Mar last summer alongside a horse I own, and they went head-to-head the entire breeze, and I told his owners I was really impressed with their horse. Dave Kenney, who owned him, asked if I wanted a piece. I didn't know these guys, and the New Yorker came out in me. I thought, "Uh-oh, what's this about?" I whispered to someone asking if these were good guys, and she told me they were the best, so I said, "Sure, I'd love to be part of it. What do you value him at?"

Dave said they paid sixty [thousand] for him, but his value now is about one hundred. So I took 5 percent and wrote him a check right there. I got to know them as the week went on, and they are great guys who I really enjoy, and I'm really happy to be partners with them. Doug O'Neill trains him, and Doug and his brother Dennis are like a West Coast bunch of New Yorkers—great guys who love to have a good time and make it fun.

So on Santa Anita Derby day we're playing Wichita State in the tournament, and we were in a flat-out war, and I'm walking off the court at halftime and I'm absolutely miserable, but you have to do these interviews as you're leaving the court. The TV announcer Jim Gray, who is a horse enthusiast, asks me the two basketball questions on the air, then off the air says, "By the way, your horse won."

That's the last thing I wanted to know about at that moment. I'm dying a thousand deaths being down at halftime, and I'm in a war. After the game, now I'm happy, and I mentioned to my associate, Jordan, about the horse winning. And he said, "Not only that, but you bet on it." I had told him a week before to put 50/50 on it, and he was 6–1. I knew I'd be tied up, and I forgot I'd told him to bet it for me. [Goldencents ran unplaced in the Kentucky Derby but won consecutive editions of the Breeders' Cup Dirt Mile in 2013 and 2014.]

LS: *Is it frustrating not to be in control of a horse race like you are when you're coaching?*

RP: The only frustrating thing about the sport is how infrequently they run and how often the horses get hurt. The fun part are the social aspects of it, and the hope that you may have a champion, but you have no idea whether you do or you don't. It's a great hobby. I love the people I've met in horse racing. They're real characters, and I enjoy that. I've met a lot of Damon Runyon characters.

It's the people who gamble on the horses that I get a kick out of. I can sit there with a bag of popcorn and listen to them all day. The excuses and the "What ifs?" I'll ask somebody why he's betting a horse, and he'll tell me he's got the best jockey in the game who knows exactly what to do. Then, after the race, the guy's the worst jockey ever, he set too fast of a pace, what was he thinking, he's an idiot. And I'm sitting there laughing because five minutes ago he was the best. I'd hate to have these guys critique my coaching.

LS: *Can you compare the thrills you get from the two sports?*
RP: For me, the Final Four and the championship, there's nothing close to it. For a horse trainer, they'd get that kind of thrill from a big race. As an owner, all we do is put up our money; we have no skill and no talents as far as the race. I'm like a cheerleader on the sideline.

LS: *You're on quite a roll. Inducted into the basketball Hall of Fame. Won a championship. And the Santa Anita Derby.*
RP: When you're lucky you feel like you're blessed. But you realize there's going to come a time when somebody else makes the buzzer shot or beats you by a nose.

21

Tom Hammond

TOM HAMMOND COULD BECOME the mayor of Lexington, Kentucky, anytime he wishes to run for the office. Hammond can't go two strides in public without being stopped by an admirer who shares a mutual friend or a memory from having watched and listened to the broadcaster. Hammond began his career as a local radio and TV sports reporter and ended up as the voice of the Olympic Games on NBC and of Notre Dame football, among many other assignments in virtually all sports. That of course included his hosting many years of Triple Crown and Breeders' Cup races, to which he brought a thorough knowledge of the sport couched in a silky-smooth delivery. Hammond is also a horse owner and loves all aspects of the horse world.

2001

Interviewed in Lexington, Kentucky

Lenny Shulman: *Having grown up in Lexington, it's not surprising you were bitten by the horse bug.*

Tom Hammond: I fell in love with the whole picture with a trip to Keeneland as a teenager—the beauty of the horses and the excitement of the sport. In high school I worked summer jobs at Spendthrift Farm building fences, and then working with broodmares. While I was in college, I worked as a hotwalker and groom, and then worked for [trainer] Sherrill Ward in New York three years just before he had Forego.

I studied equine genetics and animal sciences at the University of Kentucky. I started helping Tom Gentry look up pedigrees before the sales. During graduate school, I began working at WVLK radio doing a nightly race results show. I didn't have the slightest idea what I was doing, but nobody else wanted to do it, and I made thirty-five dollars a week. Then they needed somebody to do a nightly sports show. Then a news director. Then a program director. I kept volunteering.

I quit graduate school and in 1970 got the job as Channel 18's sports director, which was my start in TV.

Tom Hammond (Keeneland Association by Bill Straus)

LS: *How did you go from local to national TV?*
TH: The normal progression is to keep moving to bigger markets, but I didn't want to leave Lexington. I got a job as sales announcer at Keeneland, which led me to working the sales in Ocala, and then working sales in a dozen states.

My big break came with the first Breeders' Cup in 1984. NBC was televising it, and I had worked at an NBC affiliate for ten years and had a reputation as a horse expert. So they hired me to do the backstretch beat at Breeders' Cup at Hollywood Park, which I considered to be the bottom man on the totem pole. But things started happening.

John Henry was stabled back there, and even though he wasn't running in the Breeders' Cup, he was going to be Horse of the Year depending on the result of the Breeders' Cup Classic. So I had a little TV placed outside his stall so I could do a live report of him supposedly watching the race. Well, as I'm doing the report, he sticks his head out of the stall as if he really *is* watching it. A fan had sent him a dozen roses, which I was holding, and he starts eating them on live TV. It was a big hit.

Then I interviewed Wild Again's owner, Bill Allen, before the race, and I asked him why he paid fifty thousand dollars to supplement a 30–1 shot into the

Classic. And he said, "Not only do we have a good chance to win, we're gonna bet our money on it." And the horse is behind me nodding his head. And then he goes out and wins the race, which ends in an inquiry, and I'm standing there in the winner's circle not even working, but the jockeys, especially Pat Day, come up to me and start talking, so I ended up doing interviews there. Everything just worked out. And NBC's lead producer, Michael Weisman, hires me on the spot to do football.

LS: *And just about every other sport.*
TH: It started with lower-level AFC games, then I began to get better games with a permanent partner, Joe Namath. NBC then got the NBA games, and I had a role in that. Dick Ebersol, then the president of NBC Sports, asked me to do track and field. I added the Notre Dame football games. And called basketball and track and field in the Olympics.

LS: *Can you compare covering horse racing to other sports?*
TH: Racing is very specialized knowledge, so it scares most sportscasters. They don't like to venture into the unknown too much because they don't want to look bad. You tend to hold back so you don't get exposed for not knowing enough. I had that with figure skating and track and field. I overprepared because I didn't want to look like I didn't know anything, even if I didn't. You have to know when to shut up, too. Horses helped me with track and field because a race is a race. It has a certain dynamic that applies.

LS: *Outside of horse racing, can you point to one moment that stood out to you while announcing?*
TH: Michael Johnson winning in Atlanta in 1996, when he did what no man had ever done before in the Olympics. He'd already won the 400 and now he's lining up for the 200, and it's almost as if the world had come to a stop. There's an electric feeling in the stadium, and as he's coming around flashbulbs are following him, and not only does he win it, he sets a world record in the process. It was so exciting that, without even knowing it, I went from sitting down to standing up to call it. Just a tremendous moment.

Another was at the Olympics in Sydney when the Aboriginal Australian Cathy Freeman, who had lit the Olympic flame at the Opening Ceremonies, was in the blocks, and the hopes of the continent were riding on her. The pressure's almost unbearable; you can see the tension on her. And she gets to the top of the stretch and she's not going to win . . . and then suddenly she wills herself to victory. Emotion just flows off her, and the pressure flies away. And in moments like that you try and come up with something to say that will match the moment. After all, these things are going to last a hundred years.

LS: *What is the best horse race you ever saw?*

TH: I wasn't covering it, but I think Affirmed and Alydar in the [1978] Belmont [Stakes] is the greatest race I ever saw. Their rivalry was so compelling, and I had done the radio broadcast of Alydar winning the Blue Grass Stakes. Chic Anderson, the race-caller in New York, was a friend, and he said I could stand with him for the Belmont. I stayed with Doug Flynn, who was playing for the New York Mets at the time, who I knew from his days playing in Cincinnati. I asked him the night before the race if he wanted to go get a drink and he said, "No, I'm playing a day game tomorrow so I better not." Then he thought about it a second and said, "You know what, Juan Marichal is pitching and I'm not going to get a hit anyway, so let's go out."

He dropped me off at Belmont the next day. and I watched the race with Chic and listened to him call it, with the two of them battling head-to-head and Affirmed winning the Triple Crown. After the race, the phone rang, and it was Doug Flynn saying he got two hits, was the star of the game, and was doing the postgame show so he'd be late picking me up.

LS: *And you eventually did get to call a Triple Crown.*

TH: I've been in lots of stadiums with more than one hundred thousand fans, but I've never heard anything as loud as that ninety thousand at Belmont when American Pharoah turned for home and it became obvious he was going to win. It was pandemonium. People standing on tables, on chairs, throwing drinks in the air. It was deafening. And when they pulled up and [jockey Victor] Espinoza paraded him the length of that long grandstand, it was special, a nice touch.

I had told my producer that if he won, I was just going to let it play. Nothing I could say would equal what that was going to be like. What could you say? Anything that was said could detract from the moment. So I just shut up for a minute, which is an hour or so in TV time, until I finally said, "He did it." It was an unforgettable moment. It sent a chill down your spine.

LS: *You got to do your first Kentucky Derby in 2001 when NBC got the rights. What was that like?*

TH: Well, I'm a Kentuckian. I've lived in Lexington my whole life. To be able to broadcast the Kentucky Derby was the best. For all the thirteen Olympics I've done, all the football and basketball I've done through the years, to do the Derby was special. Ironically, I had gotten ill and was in the hospital for ten days beforehand. Here I'd waited my whole life to do the Derby, and I used that as my goal to be able to get well enough in time. That made it doubly satisfying to be there and not miss it.

You can't cram for it overnight, so I followed the prep races, and I also went back into the history of the Derby for items I could bring up. There was lots of preparation. And it was ironic that [trainer] John Ward, who had been a friend of mine in high school and college, and for whose uncle I'd worked in the summers, won that Derby with Monarchos. That was pretty special and interesting. He said, "If you're a Kentuckian, they paint it on you and it never wears off." He had taken me into Monarchos's stall before the race and showed me he was thriving. You'd have thought I'd go bet on him, but I didn't.

2019

After Hammond's retirement from broadcasting

LS: *You're being inducted this summer into the Racing Hall of Fame's Joe Hirsch Media Roll of Honor.*
TH: Wow. It's mind-boggling to be in the company of all those great journalists in the Hall of Fame. It's pretty exclusive company. I'm flabbergasted to be included in that, and it means even more because Joe Hirsch encouraged me early in my career when I was with WVLK radio and working in the press box at Keeneland. He would be working on his "Derby Doings" columns, and he encouraged me to get involved in horse racing.

If you think about how improbable this whole thing is: I never took a journalism course and thought I was going to end up managing a horse farm or something, and here I am going into the Hall of Fame with all these great journalists. It's pretty special. Jack Whitaker and Jim McKay are in there.

LS: *Everybody in Lexington feels like they know you, from your TV and radio work and the many commercials you do. Do you get a kick out of knowing people trust you?*
TH: It's a source of pride. I've been around a long time, which has something to do with it. Strangers will come up and say, "You make us proud." These are people from my hometown, so what better endorsement could you have? Any money or fame or celebrity is nonsense, but for someone to say that, gosh, how lucky have I been to do all these events in a field I never dreamt I'd be involved in? It's been magical. What a great ride. But that's the ultimate compliment, a stranger saying, "You make us proud."

22

Joe Torre

IN MORE THAN A decade-long run as manager of the New York Yankees, **Joe Torre** was known to steal away with coach Don Zimmer and relieve the tension of the job with an afternoon at whatever local racetrack or simulcasting parlor was available on the road. Torre, who won four World Series managing the Yankees, became fast friends with fellow Brooklyn native Bobby Frankel and often hosted the Hall of Fame trainer as his guest at Yankees games. Torre also entered the ownership side of racing with a stake in Game On Dude, one of the top handicap horses of the early twenty-first century.

2012

Interviewed at Santa Anita Park, California

Lenny Shulman: *I know you're from Brooklyn. Did you go to the races in New York growing up?*
Joe Torre: My older brother Frank would take me to the track every once in a while. He's eight years older than I am, and he'd let me string along. Jamaica Racetrack, Aqueduct, Belmont, and the harness races at night. I would watch on television and go every once in a while, but I never really got into it on a regular basis until I started managing the Yankees.

The thing that hooked me was [coach] Don Zimmer telling me he was going to Pimlico one day when we were in Baltimore. He asked me if I wanted to go, and I said, "No, but here, take a couple hundred bucks and bet what you bet." He brings me back a bunch of money that we won, and I knew at that point I was hooked. And I wound up for the rest of our eight years together losing a lot of sleep, especially traveling from East to West, and going to a simulcast every day.

We talked racing all the time, but the one thing I couldn't do that he did was bet four tracks at the same time. I always kid him that I could have retired from baseball a long time ago, but I had to continue to manage so I could afford to live.

LS: *Managing games nearly every day, your schedule must have been tight.*
JT: Every once in a while we'd be able to go to the races, but a lot of the simulcasts were at racetracks, and we'd do that more frequently. We'd go to Golden Gate Fields when we were in Oakland and to Arlington when we were in Chicago. New York is a little easier because you could stay in the city and bet. Our most consistent stop was Pimlico.

LS: *You became very good friends with another native of Brooklyn, Bobby Frankel.*
JT: You meet a lot of people who come to the ball games, and I realized there was a lot of crossover between people who had horses and were also interested in baseball. Zim knew [trainer] Richard Dutrow, and through Dutrow I met Bobby Frankel, and we became very close. He was a special guy. You realize he didn't let many people in. I really treasured our relationship even though it didn't last long enough. [Frankel died in 2009.] He was down-to-earth. I'd prod him all the time about how somebody from Brooklyn could become a Hall of Fame trainer. And he gave me a little history of how he started hotwalking the horses, and on up. It was in his blood, and he could hear the horses. He could read their minds.

I appreciate what trainers do a lot more after hanging around with him. A lot of it is feel, which is something I realized too when I was managing. Just knowing your craft and relying on your sensitivities and what you sense.

LS: *I used to get jealous when Bobby would tell me he was hanging out in the dugout with you before games, because he wasn't even a Yankee fan, and I am.*
JT: Us both being from Brooklyn, it was a very close relationship. I'd get a call from him after a tough game, and he'd tell me who let me down; it was never my fault in Bobby's opinion. I treasure that and have a lot of memories and mementos in my home from Bobby. He donated his baseball card collection to me in his will, so I could auction it off to benefit my Safe At Home Foundation. He was very proud of that, no question about it.

LS: *How did you get into owning horses?*
JT: The first horse I owned was with Bernie Schiappa. It was a European horse who won a race, but that was about it. Then in 2009 Bernie called me and said they were going to buy a horse and asked if I was interested. I said, "Yeah, with you, sure." I had gotten to know him. And that was Game On Dude. We've certainly had a lot of fun with that horse [three-time winner of the Santa Anita Handicap].

Vineyard Haven was an interesting story. Bernie was thinking of buying him, and I said I'd take a piece, but then Bernie decided to pass on him.

Meantime, I had asked Bobby to try to find us a horse who could run in the Derby. And he ends up buying Vineyard Haven for us. We ended up selling him after he won the Champagne Stakes in 2008, and we did very well on that deal. The funny part of that day was we had beaten the Cubs to clinch a divisional championship, so it was Champagne on top of Champagne for me.

LS: *You also had part of grade 1 winner Sis City.*
JT: Yeah, at the time, and it was stupid, really, I kept saying "yes" to everything Dutrow would bring to me. I had 10 percent of this, 5 percent of that, and soon you wind up with eighteen horses. And they all eat. I finally said, "This is silly," and I basically phased out and now have a workable number.

LS: *They can't all be Game On Dude.*
JT: I'd call Zim when my horses ran. There was a race a couple of years ago, when Game On Dude ran and survived an objection and paid thirty-one dollars. And I had forgotten to call Zim. He called and said, "Thanks a lot." So now I make sure to call him when the horse goes off at 3–5.

I treasure the times when I was there to see Dude win. But even the races he's lost, he's competed. That's what I admire most about this horse. If he gets a chance to look you in the eye, he's going to give you a battle.

And that's all I've ever asked my players to do, is the best they can. There are no guarantees in life that you're supposed to win. You come to work every day, and this horse has certainly done that.

LS: *Can you compare participating in horse racing to playing or managing baseball games?*
JT: This sport is a heart-pounder, no question. When it comes close to race time, you get yourself geared up. I'd compare it to baseball in the sense that it's like fast-forwarding to the ninth inning. Go right to the ninth inning with Mariano [Rivera] on the mound. You know you've got a heck of a chance even though there's a chance something will not go your way. I've always said that winning the World Series is the greatest feeling in the world, but losing it has to be the second-greatest, because you had a chance to do it.

When they come down the stretch here, I know it's tempting just to watch the TV screen, but I like it much better being outdoors and watching them come down. Hearing it, feeling it, it's really an emotional rush. It's like two outs in the ninth. The thing about it is, it has the same helpless feeling to it. Once I decide to bring in my closer, that's the last decision I have to make. Now it's about being a spectator, and it's the same thing here. It's pretty cool.

LS: *After the New York intensity with Frankel, you have Game On Dude with Mr. California Cool.*

JT: Yeah, with Game On Dude I've gotten close to Bob Baffert. I've at least gotten behind the sunglasses. It's sort of like Bobby. He's mysterious in some ways, but once you get to know him, you like what you see and feel. Once you get a feel for their sense of humor, you're more comfortable around those people. You want to make sure when you say something and you're trying to joke with somebody that they take it the way you mean it. Bob is a lot of fun.

LS: *What is it like now working in the commissioner of baseball's office?*

JT: I enjoy my new job. The best part of it is, it's still baseball, but there's no stress. The most stressful part of it is determining when to call off a game in the post-season because of rain. The fact I played and I managed helps me have a sense of perspective. I may not make a decision that they agree with, but at least they know I'm trying to be fair.

The commissioner will pick up the phone and scream at me every once in a while, but that's fine. That's what I'm paid for.

Part **IV**

Kentucky Hardboots

TECHNICALLY SPEAKING, THE DEFINITION OF A "HARDBOOT"
IS "A WELL-TRAVELED HORSEMAN WHOSE BOOTS ARE CAKED
WITH MUD AND THEREFORE HARD. FURTHER, A BREEDER OR
trainer whose methods are characterized as old-fashioned."

That's as good a starting point as any. But the Kentucky hardboot is
a specialized breed. He needn't be "well-traveled," in fact, he may rarely
leave the area in which he was born and raised. The term means many
things to many people, and in the Kentucky Bluegrass, it is willingly
applied to certain knowledgeable and accomplished people who have
worked with and around horses most of their lives. In Supreme Court
Justice Potter Stewart's famous opinion in 1964 as to whether a certain
motion picture was obscene, he wrote, "I know it when I see it." Likewise,
you know a hardboot when you see one. And certainly, as you talk to one.

By the time I came to start interviewing horse industry participants
in 2000, the Kentucky hardboots of the latter half of the twentieth century were graying but still active. Although not as physically spry as
they once were, they had a lifetime of experience to call on when making
daily judgments about acquiring or culling racing and breeding stock,
and about how to raise the best horse they possibly could.

Some owned large horse farms; others managed them for wealthy
clients; some worked exclusively on the racetrack. I got to interview more
than a dozen of this breed, the folks who kept the Thoroughbred industry

churning for decades. The best of those interviews are included below. As might be inferred from the name, some of these hardboots were gruff as sandpaper. Others had a sense of humor and a knack for storytelling that drew audiences from near and far whenever they ventured out to a horse sale or racetrack. All, in their time, knew what a good horse looked like and relentlessly pursued breeding them and lovingly raising them with whatever knowledge and methods they had in their toolbox.

And they had the ability to surprise. When I was new and still green on the job, an editor who thrived on conflict chuckled as he assigned me to go interview Charles Nuckols Jr. Nuckols was a second-generation horseman who drove a horse and buggy to school in the 1930s and was the definition of old school. He also had a reputation in his earlier years as a brawler, earned in action in concert with his two brothers. Eyeing my beard and ponytail and knowing my politics, the editor said, sarcastically, "He's really going to love you."

I sat with Mr. Nuckols at his Midway, Kentucky, farm, and listened to him recite generations of pedigrees of his horse families. I was astonished that a man pushing eighty could recall name after name of pedigree after pedigree. I wrote a cover story on Charlie Nuckols in the July 8, 2000, *Bloodhorse* with the cover line "Midway Marvel." We became fast friends, going out to dinner several times in Midway.

One Christmas week, I was in the kitchen of a mutual friend pouring Mr. Nuckols a predinner bourbon. As I put down the bottle, his gravelly voice growled out from the living room, "What's the matter, boy, your arm broken?" I commenced immediately to lengthen the pour.

A couple of years later, a horse he bred and raised, War Emblem, won the Kentucky Derby, fulfilling the dream of a lifetime for a Kentucky hardboot.

That magazine with his cover story was on the table, propped up in a stand, next to his casket at his memorial celebration at Keeneland in 2005. It was probably the greatest honor I've ever received.

23

Robert Courtney

OUT ON QUIET ROYSTER Road east of Lexington—which used to be a lot quieter before Interstate 75 ripped through the property—you once could gain an education of the horse business sitting with **Robert Courtney** in his homey office. Behind his desk, decades-old clippings and photos and pedigree pages of his equine successes hung on the walls. His Crestfield Farm was the definition of a family operation, and Courtney, eighty-four at the time of our interview, never met a stranger in his life. You would be hard-pressed to find any horseman around Kentucky who didn't get a helping hand or piece of solid advice from him. He not only raised, bred, and/or sold horses such as Fit to Fight, Meadowlake, Action This Day, and Dollar Bill, but he was also key to the establishment of the Fasig-Tipton sale company in Lexington.

2005

Interviewed at Crestfield Farm in Lexington

Robert Courtney: My first story in the *Bloodhorse* was written by Ed Bowen way back in the past. I don't know why he picked me.

Lenny Shulman: *I'm sure he had a good reason. What have been the major changes in breeding since then?*
RC: The small breeder like myself is a dying breed. When I got into the business the Paris Pike was the Wall Street of the horse industry, with the Whitneys and the Wideners. The other people who raised horses were basically farmers. There were very few sales because most of them raced their own horses.

This thing has grown from there. The American public seems to believe bigger is better, but I don't think so. I'm proud this is a family operation. I'm not a rich man, but I've made a nice living. My philosophies don't really work in today's environment, where you have to take mares to untried stallions. When I came up, you took a young mare to a made horse to find out what she was capable of producing. It's all flipped over now.

LS: *You also race some horses.*
RC: I love to race horses. If I can't sell one, I race it, and I've had a lot of luck doing it. It's expensive, but if you get one or two that can run a little bit, you cover the expenses. I bought Bluffing Girl back for eleven thousand dollars, and she's made $250,000 racing.

LS: *Who is that photo of behind your desk?*
RC: Mighty Story. When I syndicated him, the contract was two pages. Now you got to get UPS to deliver the contract because the post office won't deliver something that heavy.

Going back to Bluffing Girl, she's a perfect example of how hard it is to sell a horse today. Used to be when the hammer fell, the horse was sold. Now the saying is, "When the hammer falls, the negotiations begin." With the X-rays and the scopes, we have so many minor things that become major in people's minds. When I tried to sell her, she had a small piece broken off her hoof, and people tried to make a big issue out of nothing. I brought her home and let the hoof grow out. Had nothing to do with how she could run. Mr. [Hal Price] Headley always said, "Don't worry about what you can see; worry about what you can't see." And that's the heart, and you damn well better believe that.

LS: *What was it about this business that made you choose it?*
RC: I just love being out in the country. The day school was over, I'd move out to the farm owned by Mr. Estill, my father's friend who was a director of his bank. He was a hell of a cattleman. I rode all summer all over his farm, and I loved that life. That's the reason I'm in it.

LS: *Who else mentored you?*
RC: When I was young I was a feed man on the racetrack, and I serviced Calumet Farm's stable. One day an exercise boy says, "Feed man, B.A. wants to see ya." That would be Ben Jones, who would run a horse on Tuesday to win the Derby Trial and come back Saturday and win the Kentucky Derby with him. I went to see him and he said, "You got any hay better than that?" I knew he was a clover/hay man, and I said, "Mr. Jones, yes sir, I do." And I replaced that hay, and he never said another word to me. Those kind of men were better basic horsemen than you see today.

John Nerud—all the good ones came up from the Midwest, where horses were part of life. Back then people had a chicken yard and a milk cow in the backyard. Today they got an automobile. Instead of taking care of animals they got to take care of the car. That's just a philosophy on my part.

Robert Courtney

LS: *Is there a secret to raising horses?*
RC: I just try to raise mine outdoors. Today they fill 'em so full of steroids their ears are popping, and they're going to fall apart before long. Somebody came out with drops you were supposed to put down their throats as a supplement. I said, "You can get that for free. All you have to do is let the horse stay out in the sun." Funny thing about a horse: You turn him out in the sun and he'll be laying at the high point in the field with the sun beating down. They love it. The rest of this stuff are fads.

They talk about these limestone lands here, but go out there and dig and see how far down you have to go to get to limestone. It's ten foot down. Maybe the land's been laying here long enough where the lime comes up, but I think you have to add to it. No fertilizer man believes that because they don't sell lime. But I preach that. John Marr used to raise nice horses around here. I asked him how he got such beautiful grass, and he said he put lime on the ground.

LS: *Is the breed the same today as in years past?*
RC: I don't think the breed is any weaker or less sound. When I started, Old Man [Bud] Greeley would come down here after Churchill Downs ended in the fall, and he'd turn all his horses out. Said he was going to go home and clean the gutters on his house. And around the first of February he'd take the horses back to the track. Now they got twelve months of racing because it's so expensive they feel like they gotta race them all year. And they wonder why they don't last.

LS: *What do you look for when you're buying mares?*
RC: Used to be unraced daughters of stakes producers, but they're harder to find today because more people are onto that. I bought Hasty Queen for eleven thousand dollars and sold about a million dollars' worth of yearlings out of her and raced a few stakes winners out of her. Now you need more race record than you used to. It used to be pedigree was everything. I try to buy as much race record as I can afford. I was just at the sale bidding on a mare and it reached seventy-five thousand dollars, and I said to myself, "Why am I bidding this much on this mare right now? At eighty-four, I don't like to buy green bananas."

LS: *Do you have a favorite horse?*
RC: Fit to Fight always stands out. Bob Congleton and I bred him and raised him for the sales. [Trainer] Mack Miller looked at him at Saratoga, but he didn't like buying horses from friends. We were at Mack's house for dinner, and he never said a word to me about the horse. I was shocked when he bought him. We had a lot of fun with Fearless Day, a beautiful chestnut who broke her maiden first start at 50–1. I won a stake with Bluffing Girl the third time I ran her.

I bred a Pine Bluff colt named Tinseltown who just won a stake up in New York. Sold him for ninety thousand dollars on a ten-thousand-dollar stud fee. That's how you make your money, son. Nothing wrong with that. That's how you make a living.

LS: *In 1972, you helped establish the Kentucky branch of the Fasig-Tipton sales company. Talk about that.*
RC: Keeneland was the only place in town to sell. Business was booming, they weren't expanding to meet it, and there was a lot of discontent in town. The higher a monkey climbs a tree, the more of his ass he shows. There was an arrogance associated with the existing sale company. People were complaining all the time about not getting a fair shake there. That's what got me thinking. Dr. Jim Griggs and I were talking about how many churches there were in town and how many banks, and he said if I got ten people to kick in one hundred thousand dollars apiece, he'd lend me my share, and we'd start a horse sale with that million dollars.

A lot of people thought it was a good idea but didn't want to take the risk. I didn't blame them. I went to see Warner Jones, who was on the board at Keeneland, and he said, "Something needs to be done." We got a bunch of consignors together, and it was the right thing that was needed at that time.

Most of the Fasig-Tipton investors owned horses and had a real interest in it succeeding. People really responded to it, good businesspeople who saw there was a need. A few people got upset and said they'd never sell horses there, but you started seeing their names in the catalogue.

It gave me a great deal of pleasure watching it develop. I'm just a little country boy, and I thought the only place where my name would be is on a tombstone out here, not on a brass plaque at Fasig-Tipton.

LS: *You have a remarkable reputation among other horsemen in Kentucky.*
RC: I had a client who approached Bull Hancock about Bull taking his mares, and Bull asked who had them now, and the man said that I did. Bull said, "He takes as good care of a horse as I do, why the hell you want to bring 'em over here?"

Bill Landes, who managed Hermitage for Warner Jones, said that Warner told him there were three honest people in the horse business, and I was one of them. That means a lot when a man like Warner Jones says that about you.

My problem is I got more friends out on West Main Street [Lexington Cemetery] than I do on East Main Street. Once in a while people approach me for advice because I'm old. I tell 'em my advice is free, and most of the time it ain't worth any more than that.

This has been a great life, and I've loved every minute of it, especially being able to work for yourself. People forget about you when you're gone. The only thing you leave behind is your reputation, and I've got my integrity. The most you can ask for is people remembering you and saying, "He was all right."

24

Charles Nuckols Jr.

CHARLES NUCKOLS JR. WAS built as strong as the horses he raised. He bred more than a dozen champions and north of three hundred stakes winners. He planned the matings that produced top sire Distorted Humor and champion Smart Deb. He bred and raised champions Typecast, Decathlon, White Skies, Broadway Dancer, and Habitat. He also came of age riding the train from Midway, Kentucky, to Saratoga, accompanying his family's sale yearlings, until World War II begat gasoline rationing and the Kentucky sales. He became a trustee at Keeneland, and his era spanned the Roaring Twenties clear through to the Internet. At his heart, he was a proud farmer.

2000

Interviewed at Nuckols Farm, Midway, Kentucky

Lenny Shulman: *This farm has been in your family more than one hundred years. What important lessons did you learn from your father?*
Charles Nuckols Jr.: My father taught my brothers and me responsibility. Certain chores on the farm were up to us, and we had to do a first-class job. You didn't cut corners with my dad. It was done right and in the proper manner.

He believed the land came first. Whatever you took off the land, you'd better put back in. Raise a crop, and you're taking elements out of the soil. You must put them back for that land to produce again as good. Same with horses. A little foal comes into this world weighing 70–75 pounds. Where does he get his muscle and bone marrow from? From the ground. So when he leaves here weighing 800–900 pounds, you better check your soil and find out what elements are gone, and replace them. My father did that, and we still do it today.

LS: *Talk about breeding a racehorse as opposed to a sale horse.*
CN: Very few horses are being bred just to race. They're being bred because they're popular and they're gonna bring a lot of money at sale. And if you win a big race, you make more money out of it that way [breeding], by gone it, than you can from

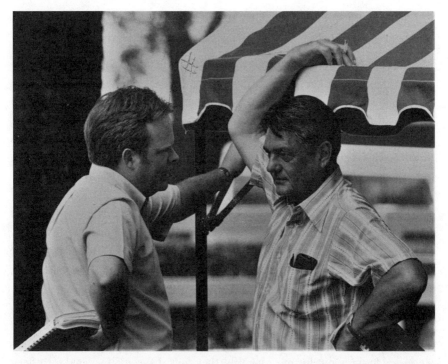

Hal Price Headley Jr. (*left*) and Charles Nuckols Jr. (Keeneland Association by John Wyatt)

the purse money. Today you take a good, solid stud horse who's sound and has a good pedigree, and it's hard to fill a book of mares.

Popularity, by God, changes every year, like women's clothes. Who knows what's going to be popular three years from now? You breed them this year, don't foal them until next year, and you get them to the racetrack two years after that. So you may be lucky or unlucky depending on what is popular at that time. I'd rather make my own luck.

LS: *Who is that in the picture on the wall?*
CN: A mare named Anna Horton, who belonged to Mr. B. B. Jones. She was a little bitty thing but could really run. She'd be in a group of horses, and you couldn't tell if she was in the race. Neither Mr. Jones nor my father could get her in foal, so Mr. Jones sold her to me for five dollars. We got her in foal—I think she ended up with twelve or thirteen foals. And that family, by God, if you look at the whole tree since then, I bet they've won $12 million.

I believe the most fun I get out of this is planning a mating, raising a foal, and having it turn out to be a good one. That's the biggest pleasure in life.

LS: *Can you talk about taking the yearlings up to the sale in Saratoga before Kentucky began holding sales?*
CN: We'd lead them over from the farm to the train station at Midway and put them on the horse cars, and then wait for the cars to come in from Warner Jones near Louisville and Mr. Thresled in Pleasureville and Mr. John Morris's horses from Bosque Bonita [the present-day Lane's End] and Mr. Charley Black from Silver Lake in Frankfort. Then we'd push the cars to Lexington, where we'd meet up with Carter Thornton, then go to Paris to pick up Claiborne.

All the help would go along. It was a big thing in those days—getting your cars ready and cleaned and getting your clothes packed and food taken. We'd stay right on the cars all the way to Saratoga and lead 'em off to the barns. All the farms would be together and help each other out. It wasn't work, but enjoyment. Almost a vacation.

In 1937 my father was having surgery, and I was in charge of the show. I was seventeen and too scared to have fun that year. My only instructions from Dad were, "Don't bring any of 'em home." The auctioneers were friends of my father's and were looking out for me. One filly, they must have auctioneered for fifteen minutes and never got a bid on her. Finally, I found a guy from Canada who agreed to split the filly with us and not send us any bills. I called my dad, who said, "Give him 50 percent of the horse and, by God, give him the halter and shank too and make sure she's gone." Turns out she could run a little, and the guy calls my dad and says he could sell her for ten thousand dollars. My dad said, "Fine, send me five thousand." Well, he never saw the five or the filly again.

LS: *This game is full of characters.*
CN: My brother Alfred and I were lookin' the hair off this one yearling at the sale, going over him from the tip of his nose to his a-hole, and we finally bought him and gave him to John Ward to start breaking him. The next day John calls up and says, "Charlie, did you know you bought a horse with no front teeth?" So I went to see Henry McDaniel, who sold me the horse, to see what he was gonna do about this.

I said, "Did you know that horse didn't have any front teeth?" and he said, "Yes." I said, "Was he a cribber?" And he said, "Yeah, but he don't crib no more. I just wanted to teach you two whippersnappers what this game's all about." And he turns and walks off. Well, I kept the horse in training and named him

Dadgumit, and it turned out he could run a little bit. He didn't need no teeth to run. We got out and made a little money, and the next people who bought him didn't know he had no teeth, either.

LS: *Has picking out a yearling changed?*
CN: When I started, the pedigrees were done by hand. You knew a sibling had won three races and made a certain amount of money, but you didn't know where he ran, and you'd have to look up each chart to see if it was an allowance or claiming race or whatever. You can grade twenty times more horses now.

But one thing hasn't changed much: We still pick them on pedigree, by sire; or if it's a good first-year sire who was an excellent racehorse, sure we want those. With good female families, the more black type the better. And then you look for a good individual after that. I've been over pedigrees my whole life, studying them by family: "This is the Whitney family, this is the Widener family, this is Claiborne." It's easier for me to remember them that way.

LS: *Nobody in this business has a bad word to say about you.*
CN: Well, I don't know about that. I'm sure somebody calls me a SOB now and then. But I do know my word is my bond. Whatever I say is what I'm gonna do. When I was growing up around my dad, we didn't have all the lawyers. When you did a handshake, by God, that was it.

LS: *Is there a story behind that statue [a two-foot-long statuette in his office of a comical-looking jockey aboard a buck-tooth horse who's draped in a blanket of roses]?*
CN: (*laughing*) Fella who gave me that said, "That's the closest you're gonna come to raising a Derby winner."

2003

After the Nuckols-bred and -raised War Emblem
won the Kentucky Derby

LS: *How did it feel to win the Derby?*
CN: I think you're very fortunate, out of hundreds of thousands of breeders who want to breed a horse to win the Kentucky Derby, and we were lucky to do it. After so many years, you still always think it's going to happen. I was hoping it would. You realize a lot of it is sheer luck. I've been through too much of it to get nervous.

When he hit the wire, I almost swallowed my tongue. I didn't have the bourbon in hand; I had to walk from the den to the kitchen to get it. It was relief and joy, and I was there with my oldest daughter and couldn't have been happier.

LS: *Talk about the mating.*

CN: I had bred to Miner's Mark, who is Our Emblem's full brother. It's one of the greatest pedigrees in the stud book, and I was disappointed in the horses that I got from Miner's Mark, so I went and bred to his full brother, who had a lot of speed. Crossed with a Lord at War mare, I thought it would be a good cross, and it turned out to be that way.

I'm ready for another.

25

Arthur Hancock III

ARTHUR HANCOCK III SPIT out the silver spoon with which he was born and made it to the top using his own utensils. Scion of the most famous family in Kentucky breeding, the elder son of industry giant "Bull" Hancock marched to his own drummer right off jump street and built his Stone Farm five miles down the road from his family's legendary Claiborne Farm. There, Hancock co-bred and co-owned Kentucky Derby winner Gato Del Sol and raised and co-owned the great Sunday Silence, who became one of the most significant runners and stallions in Thoroughbred history. Hancock, also an accomplished musician and great storyteller, continues to turn out top runners, aligning himself with various omens that he uses to point himself to success.

2005

Interviewed at Stone Farm, Paris, Kentucky

Lenny Shulman: *Your father [Arthur B. "Bull" Hancock Jr.] is always talked about as a larger-than-life figure in the Thoroughbred industry. What was he like as a father?*
Arthur Hancock III: Well, he was a hardworking, serious man. But he also had a big sense of humor and loved to have a couple of drinks and tell great stories. He was strict as a father, a stickler for hard work and being on time. He was an Army captain in World War II, and he was a tough man, about as tough as I've ever seen.

He was a really good horseman who'd get in a stall with a horse and get down on his knees if he needed to. A horseman's horseman. He knew a lot about every aspect of horses. That was his life. And he was honest.

LS: *Growing up in an idyllic farm environment at Claiborne Farm, how did that affect you?*
AH: It gave me a love of the land. I always wanted to farm. As a little boy we'd play down at the creek and hunt and fish a lot. If you're in this business, you have to have that love of the land, because you're out on it. Also being around horses, I've always loved the animals. So my childhood laid the foundation.

Arthur Hancock III (*left*) and Hal Price Headley Jr. (Keeneland Association by John Wyatt)

LS: *Legend has it that you were pretty wild when young. Is that true, and was it a rebellious wildness?*
AH: I was headstrong. Anything I learned, I had to learn the hard way. I was always a rebel. My father once told me when I grew up, I should go into politics because I was the god-damnedest agitator he'd ever seen. I also used to drink too much, and that added fuel to the fire.

LS: *Was your rebelliousness a reaction to your father?*
AH: I think so. We were sitting around cooking steaks one time when Sputnik had just gone up, and I said it was amazing it could go 5,000 mph. And he said it only went 3,000 mph. And we started arguing back and forth, and he said, "Goddamn it, don't contradict your father." And I made a couple of fists in a mocking way behind his back, and he turned around and knocked me twenty feet back and down and said, "Never double up your fists behind a man's back, bud." That's the way it was.

He was a good man, but you didn't want to cross him. He had a bad temper, and, being the oldest, I got the brunt of it. And I probably deserved it. I got into music and dyed my hair black to look like Ricky Nelson, and he hated that. Called me the canary. So I think you're right—my rebelliousness was a reaction to all that.

LS: *But you learned horsemanship from him?*
AH: Yeah. I worked doing everything. In fact, when Gato Del Sol won the Kentucky Derby, I dedicated it to my father, who taught me everything I know.

LS: *How did you come to own your own farm?*
AH: After I graduated from Vanderbilt, I worked at the racetrack for trainer Eddie Neloy in New York for a year to learn that side of the game. Then I worked for Dad until about 1970. When he was a young man, his father sent him to Virginia to run Ellerslie, the family farm there. Told him, "If you make a profit, I'll hire you back. If you don't, I don't need you." So Daddy thought that would be a good thing for me. I leased one hundred acres from Claiborne that became Stone Farm. He charged me three thousand dollars to lease it for a year and sent me three or four mares to board. I kept the books, paid the bills, and ran the place for two years before he died.

I went back to Claiborne and worked there, thinking I'd run it. But Daddy's will said the executors should follow the advice of the advisory board, and they decided that [younger brother] Seth should be the captain. I saw the writing on the wall, and I resigned. Going back to Ricky Nelson, he had a song called "Garden Party" with the lyric, "It's all right now, I learned my lesson well, you can't please everyone, so you've got to please yourself."

I figured I'd just go back to Stone Farm and do my best. I played hard, but I've always worked hard too. I was there at six o'clock every morning. Like with Eddie Neloy: John Campo was the foreman, and it was tough—they'd give us afternoons off but never a day off. After six months there, I went to the city and had a date and stayed up late, and slept through the alarm the next morning. I called Neloy and told him I'd be there at six thirty. He says, "Hitchcock"—that was my nickname— "You got somebody there with you?" And I said, "Yes sir, I do." And he said, "Hitchcock, if you come in today, you're fired. I'll see you tomorrow." That was my day off—the only day I missed in a year. I wanted to prove what I could do.

LS: *In those couple of years before your father died, did you feel you proved yourself to him?*
AH: I think so. He and I were getting along a lot better. He respected the fact I'd done a good job for Mr. Neloy, and we just sort of started to get back together. I had dinner with him at Saratoga the last four or five nights before he went to

Europe, where he got sick and died three weeks later. I've had a lot of people tell me I am a lot like him. I've knocked the hell out of a few people in my life, but I don't have the temper he did. And after having a couple of car wrecks, I gave up drinking.

LS: *As a father now, what do you try to teach your children?*
AH: Be on time for work and put in an honest day's work. Don't beat your brains out, but do what has to be done, treat people right, and try and learn something. Do what you say you're gonna do. And do the best you can at whatever you do. If you work hard and are nice to people, you'll be OK.

LS: *How did you build up Stone Farm after you left Claiborne?*
AH: First thing I did was buy the one hundred acres I'd been leasing from Claiborne. I had bought the mare Punctilious based on Daddy's advice, and soon after, she threw The Pruner, who won the American Derby Handicap. Then I had a Forli colt out of Punctilious who had a bump on his leg and I couldn't sell him. Vincent O'Brien, the great European trainer, came to look at him and liked him and said he had a lucky guy back in Europe named Charles St. George who would buy half. I remember asking Vincent about luck, and he said, "It means everything. I've seen people put millions into this game and not win a race. This guy is lucky." And that horse was Dapper, the first horse I ever named. He won the Gladness and Tetriarch Stakes. I sold pieces of him for a lot of money, enough to expand the farm.

I bought some mares out of the sales, sold some yearlings, and worked hard seven days a week. That's how it all got started. Leone Peters came in and put thirty mares here. Aaron Jones was a huge help. Mary Bradley. Charlie Whittingham had people who sent horses. Tom Tatham sent Halo here. If you see a turtle on a fencepost, he didn't get there by himself. I had help, worked hard, and did my best. And like Vincent said, I've been lucky.

You learn over time not so much what to buy, but what not to buy. You know what you like in mares. We bought Anne Campbell and Bottle Top. Bought Angel Fever with Bob McNair. Those good mares carry the farm. My trouble is I've always kept some and tried to make chicken salad out of chicken shit with cheap mares. They become pets; you get attached to them. My father warned me about that. He said, "Never fall in love with a whore or a horse, 'cause they'll both break you."

LS: *What was it like winning the Kentucky Derby in 1982 with Gato Del Sol, a horse you co-bred and co-owned?*

AH: I didn't believe it until it was official. I kept thinking they would take it away. When we were out there getting the trophy, I felt like I could walk on air, like an out-of-body experience. It was just unbelievable that we could win the Derby. I've never had a feeling like that before.

LS: *And then came Sunday Silence in 1989, who you credit for saving the farm.*
AH: I think God sent him. I'd gotten into heavy debt and had six children, and it was pretty bad. I used to walk down this road in the middle of the night wondering what I was going to do. I was paying three thousand dollars a day in interest, and the rates were going up, and it looked bad.

When Sunday Silence won the Derby, a lot of what I felt was relief. I thanked God that there was at least hope now. He won the Preakness by a nose, and one of the bankers was there with us, and he said, "This could save Arthur." And then he won the Breeders' Cup Classic and Horse of the Year and three-year-old champion. I felt gratitude and relief. He basically saved the farm and my family. Everything. I have no doubt he was sent . . . those kinds of horses don't come along very often to anybody.

LS: *And you defeated Easy Goer in the Derby, Preakness, and Classic, to boot.*
AH: That was ironic, because Easy Goer was owned by Mr. [Ogden] Phipps, who was on that advisory board that wanted me out at Claiborne. The truth is I'd always liked Mr. Phipps. He was like Daddy—a tough, quiet man, and I appreciated the fact he gave me a job for a year at his stable [under Neloy]. I walked Buckpasser. Their family has meant so much to my family. Mr. Phipps wrote me a letter after Gato won the Derby telling me it was a job well done. And I appreciated that. So I never gloated about Sunday Silence defeating Easy Goer. But I had a sense of vindication.

LS: *Was the business aspect of running the farm harder than you imagined?*
AH: For me, I love the land, and then you have to do the business part. Daddy helped me there too. He brought Herbager to stand at Claiborne and was breeding Delta, a real good mare, to him. I asked him why, and he said, "If I don't send a good mare to him, I can't expect anyone else to." And that produced Dahlia.

He showed me the financial statements. I thought Claiborne was making all this money, but after taxes and depreciation and all that . . . it was a good living and steady. But not what I'd thought. You have to like what you're doing, and I believe if you're good to the land, the land will be good to you. Take care of the land, take care of your horses. What goes around comes around. I believe in destiny, and that there's more than meets the eye in this existence.

LS: *Are you a religious man?*

AH: I'm spiritual. I thank God every day for all the blessings, but I'm not a churchgoer. I go out in the woods and listen to the birds and to nature. That's where I get my peace of mind.

LS: *You also believe in omens.*

AH: Well, you see things, and they make you wonder. Before Sunday Silence's Derby we came out of the track kitchen and there was a penny on the ground. And a friend said, "Wouldn't it be something if it was a 1982, because that was the year Gato won." I picked it up, and it was a 1982. And I said, "Man, this is an omen." When [wife] Staci and I were walking over for the race, I looked down and there was a four-leaf clover on the track.

Four or five days before the Preakness, I was coming out of my house with Eddie Sutton, the basketball coach, and there was a Baltimore oriole sitting up in this little tree, which is unusual around here. And this bluebird lit right over top of it. Bluebirds are good luck, and I thought that was an omen. I didn't invent them. The Romans talked about them way back in history. Before Waterloo, an animal came running out of the bushes, and Napoleon's horse reared up and threw him on his ass, and one of his generals said, "This is a bad omen. Let's not fight today."

I think there are things you better pay attention to out there, because this all isn't just one big accident. If you try to stay attuned to nature you might see things. A few days before the Derby in 1989 there's a rabbit sitting in front of the house. I looked at him and started talking to him and walked toward him, and he just sat there before nonchalantly hopping away. I'd never seen one there in fifteen years, and I figured that was a good omen. And it was. Maybe it was a fluke. I don't know. But it was weird because I never saw another one there after that, either.

LS: *Sunday Silence was a horse nobody wanted, both when he was a young horse and again when he went to stud. Any regrets about selling him overseas?*

AH: I know everybody in the horse business, and I had people helping me try to syndicate him. Nobody wanted to breed to him. Nobody. Believe me. We called everyone in the horse business. Three people said they'd take a share—Dick Duchossois, Josephine Abercrombie, and Tom Tatham, who bred him.

People thought he was a freak. The business was down at the time; the real estate market had collapsed. Halo was not known as a sire of sires. So I guess there was some justification for people not wanting to commit. But I don't have any remorse, because I don't feel like I sold Sunday Silence. The breeders sold him. I had no other choice. Mr. Yoshida offered $11 million for him.

As Daddy said, and it's my philosophy now: "For a deal to be a good deal, it's got to be good for both parties." And that was good for both parties. It was a great sale for us and turned out to be a great buy for them. It had to be done. I wish it didn't, but it did, and I never had any regrets. I'm glad he did so well for the Yoshida family. If I could have syndicated him over here for the same amount of money I sold him for, I'd go kick myself all the way to wherever it is I'm going to be buried. But that wasn't the case.

26

E. S. Clark Jr.

IN AN ERA WHEN African Americans played influential roles as jockeys, trainers, and horsemen, men like **E. S. Clark Jr.** made the Thoroughbred industry go. He came of age at the racetrack and early on hooked on with legendary trainer Ben "B.A." Jones, who guided the careers of the great Calumet Farm horses of the mid-1900s. Jones still holds the record for training the most Kentucky Derby winners (now shared by Bob Baffert). Clark was right there for the great Citation-Coaltown controversy at the 1948 Run for the Roses and was also the groom of Ponder a year before that colt won the Derby. Clark became the first African American judge on the Standardbred circuit and also served as an athletics coach in schools around Kentucky. It was a huge thrill when, in 2003, we were able to bring Clark onto Calumet Farm and hear his stories as he walked through the equine cemetery, remembering the great horses enshrined there.

2003

Interviewed in Lexington

Lenny Shulman: *You came up in a time when most of the racetrack workers were African American.*
E. S. Clark: My father was riding races in Louisville when I was born there. That's how come I got involved, and it's been in my blood all my life. According to my mother, I was at the racetrack at a very young age. My father and uncles on both sides of the family were all in horse racing, so I had no other choice.

I was ten or eleven when I started working on a farm. The first thing I learned to do was fill up the kerosene lanterns and set the wood out for the boilers and keep the fire and hot water going all day long for however many cents they felt like paying me.

LS: *You said you made it to the racetrack early on?*
ESC: I learned to gallop horses early on, galloped horses for Phil Chin at the old fairgrounds, where the Red Mile harness track is now in Lexington. Did that for free to learn how; then you could get hired for fifty cents a head. My uncle Henry

Clark taught me some. He worked for Ben Jones, and as a kid I hung around him. I was around the barn when Whirlaway won the [Kentucky] Derby in '41 and when Pensive won it in '44. In '45 I went to work for Ivan Parke when he was training for Fred Hooper, and they won the Derby with Hoop Jr.

I left school early in '45 and went to Chicago, where Ivan was. There was a fight in the shed, and one guy was sticking a pitchfork into another. I got a broom and knocked the fork away from him, and Ivan gave me a job taking care of some two-year-olds. I was only fifteen and carrying on, and Ivan took the horses away from me and gave me two goats and a dog to take care of. I was walking horses for him that summer. It was the year the Derby wasn't until June because of the war.

LS: *How did you start working for Ben Jones?*
ESC: I hooked up with Calumet just looking for a job. I was around all their exercise boys all the time, around the barn all the time before I got a salary. I always worked in Kentucky or Chicago with B.A. [Ben Jones]. I never worked for [Ben's son] Jimmy at all.

LS: *This was around the time of Citation?*
ESC: I first laid eyes on Citation in '47 when he was a two-year-old in Chicago. He was tall, like a wide receiver, tall and thin. His eyes were totally different. He had big black eyes, but he was always looking somewhere else, never at what was going on. It was like he was looking off in the distance somewhere. He was different, kind of quiet. But he was tough to gallop.

In '48, he went to Maryland from Florida, didn't come to Kentucky until a week or so before the Derby. Jimmy had him in Maryland, and he got beat in the Chesapeake Trial, and Ben got on the phone with Jimmy and said, "If you get that horse beat again, he's coming to Chicago to stay."

When he got to Kentucky at three, he had matured a bit. Same build. We got him at the train station and vanned him over to Churchill Downs. When you have a horse like that, everything comes with him. The best of everything. The best groom, the best exercise rider, the best night watchman, hotwalker, everything.

LS: *And Jones also had Coaltown, who had just won the Blue Grass Stakes.*
ESC: He set a record at every pole he passed in that race. And I was the only idiot in the barn. I bet the night watchman one hundred dollars that Citation couldn't beat Coaltown. I hadn't seen Citation run since the year before, and Coaltown was so impressive in the Blue Grass. I didn't believe Citation could be that much better. But there was no doubt about it. He gave me part of the money back.

LS: *There remains a controversy over whether Jones told Coaltown's rider to allow Citation to win the Derby.*

ESC: Let me tell you about that day. We came out of the chute onto the track for the walkover, and people were calling out, "Who's that? Who's that?" And finally, I said, "This is Citation." And like wildfire, it spread all down that fence, people saying, "Citation's coming." People were climbing the fence. I'm full of chills; never in my life have I experienced that sensation, before or since. It was like a wave running in front of you down that fence line all the way to the tunnel and the paddock: "Citation's coming." People running to see him.

Now, people say what they want to say about that race, but I was standing right there when Ben Jones was talking to Eddie Arcaro [Citation's jockey] and Leroy Pierson, who rode Coaltown. Jones said to Pierson, "Leroy, I want Citation to win, but if he can't, you go ahead and win it." He wasn't concerned about the other four horses in the race.

Coaltown was a free-running horse; he would just take off. So in the Derby Leroy is just sitting on him, and Coaltown opens up by six lengths. Turning for home he's still in front by a length, and he's looking for Eddie. When Eddie came with Citation they just blew right by. There is no doubt Coaltown was not the horse Citation was. Citation was the best horse in the world and the greatest horse I've ever seen. There's a possibility Coaltown was sharp enough that day to have beat him. But no. I just feel fortunate to have been around Citation and have my hands on him.

LS: *And you had your hands on another Derby winner as well.*

ESC: At the time of Citation's Derby, I was rubbing Ponder, who won the Derby the following year, except by then I had gone off to college at Kentucky State to play football. Anyway, around the time of Citation's Derby, I was rubbing Ponder, and one afternoon I had some hay on a pitchfork and was throwing it into Ponder's stall. He was standing in the back, but he turned just as I threw the hay and he ran up on my fork. I could feel him hit it, but there was no blood or anything, and it looked all right.

I came in the next morning and one side of his chest was hanging down. I ran looking for Doc Harthill. I told him what happened, and he asked if B.A. had seen this, and I said, "No." And he said, "Don't say anything. I'll take care of it."

So when B.A. came back from the track, Doc brought him over to Ponder's stall and told B.A. he thought a scorpion had bit him, and he wanted to try a new drug to treat him with. That was penicillin. Ponder was the first horse ever to be treated with penicillin. Within three or four days he was back to the racetrack, but it scared the living daylights out of me.

I think Harthill helped me because I had rubbed a horse who had hock trouble, and Harthill had made up some salve to rub on the horse's hock, and it went straight through to the bone. Harthill told me not to tell B.A., so we kept that quiet. If it hadn't been for Harthill, Ponder wouldn't have been around to win the Derby the next year. He saved his life, no doubt about it. And B.A. never knew.

LS: *And you moved on to train yourself?*
ESC: Yeah, I raced around Chicago and Canada. I was a beer drinker reaching for Champagne, shooting for the moon with cheap horses. I had a horse named Supreme Chief who made seventy-seven thousand dollars for me. My best horse was probably Road Man, who won some stakes races in Michigan and more than two hundred thousand dollars. But I survived, and that's the main thing.

I became the first Black associate pari-mutuel judge in America. I was also teaching school and coaching sports in Lexington. I became an assistant paddock judge on the harness circuit around Chicago for seven or eight years.

LS: *Who were some of the characters on the backstretch?*
ESC: There was a guy named Slow and Easy who rubbed Bewitch and Coaltown. His real name was Charlie Martin, and he was with Ben Jones back in the thirties, when he won the Derby with Lawrin for Woolford Farm in 1938. When [Calumet owner] Warren Wright was hiring Ben Jones, only white people worked for Calumet. Ben told him that Slow and Easy's been with him since the beginning, and if he comes aboard, Slow and Easy has to come. And that's the first time a Black man worked for Calumet Farm.

Charlie went everywhere B.A. went. They had a safe in the office, and that safe had all Charlie's money in it. He hardly ever cashed a check. He got his nickname because—can you imagine training Bewitch and Coaltown and you got a groom who has a muck sack out and is cleaning out stalls at one or two o'clock in the afternoon? You'd fire him in a second. But nobody bothered Charlie. He never was in a hurry, but he knew how to take care of a horse. He came out of Missouri with B.A. and went to Mexico with him when B.A. raced down there and Pancho Villa was running people out of there.

I worked for a man named Frank Shelton at C. V. Whitney Farm in New York. He knew more about a racehorse than any man I ever knew. He could tell you from the nail in a horse's shoe to the dandruff in his bridle path about him. I learned a lot from Frank about a horse. Guys like him and Marshall Lilly never got the credit. Lilly worked for Greentree, and he chose every good horse Greentree had. Every good horse Greentree had, he sent from the farm to the racetrack. He picked each one—Guillotine, Straight Face, all them good horses.

Lucien Laurin was the only trainer I ever saw give a groom credit in print. Eddie Sweat was rubbing Secretariat. Laurin came around the barn, and Secretariat was laying down, and Laurin asked, "What's wrong with him? Is he sick?" And Sweat said, "No, he does this every day. Lays down and takes a nap." You live with horses twenty-four hours a day, you know what he eats, and every pimple that comes out on him.

When I started, Black guys were all the help. Those guys were men when I was a boy. Black guys who had been outstanding riders were old men then, still around galloping horses and grooming. They were legends. I was shocked when I turned around and I was the man; I'd been the young one for so long. Most all those guys are gone now.

27

Gov. Brereton Jones

NOBODY ELSE CAN MATCH the career arc traveled by **Brereton Jones**, who had a dream as a youngster growing up in West Virginia to raise great Thoroughbreds in Kentucky. Jones has not only lived his dream, he made a unique stopover as the governor of the Commonwealth along the way, during which he aided the horse industry by instituting awards for Kentucky breeders and also turned a statewide financial deficit into a surplus. Jones has built up his family's Airdrie Stud into an enduring Thoroughbred institution, breeding (to date) three Kentucky Oaks winners and standing stallions such as Silver Hawk, Harlan's Holiday, Indian Charlie, and Proud Citizen. Few have made a more indelible mark on the industry.

2004

Interviewed at Airdrie Stud, Midway, Kentucky

Lenny Shulman: *When did horses become a part of your life?*
Brereton Jones: I grew up on a cattle and dairy farm in Point Pleasant, West Virginia. I always had a pony or a horse I rode, and showed Western. I liked the cowboy stuff. Horses were always involved in my life. When I was seven years old and people would ask me what I wanted to do when I grew up, I'd say I was going to raise horses in Kentucky. And they'd be, "Where did that boy get that crazy idea?" It was something I was born with, I guess, and I knew Kentucky was the horse capital of the world. Maybe that's why I feel so fiercely competitive about not allowing other states to steal that away from us.

LS: *And so eventually you made your way to Kentucky?*
BJ: I did well in the construction business in West Virginia. I served in the state legislature as a Republican and had a leadership position. My father had been a state senator, and we always talked about issues and responsibility to make a contribution—that if you leave politics to the crooks and misfits, you get what you deserve—bad government.

Anyway, the Republican nominee for governor, I knew he was a crook, and I wasn't going to serve if he got elected. So I decided it was time to follow my dream

Brereton Jones (Keeneland Association by John Wyatt)

and go to Kentucky. Libby and I got married in 1970 and then started the horse operation. I leased some acreage from her father. Then, the male ego being what it is, I didn't want to be living on her farm, so I began to buy land that adjoined it, and then other land in the vicinity until we had three thousand acres.

LS: *But you got back into politics.*
BJ: In 1987 I ran for lieutenant governor as a Democrat on a platform of integrity and hard work. Political experts didn't think I had a chance. I went to every county and looked people in the eye and said we can do better than we're doing. I never said a negative word about my opponents, never threw any mud. People know one party doesn't have all the answers—one is all good and the other's all bad. They're tired of all that baloney and want somebody who will respect their opinion and talk to them.

LS: *When you got elected, what was the relationship between the Thoroughbred industry and the government?*
BJ: I realized the horse lobby in Frankfort [the capital] is one of the weakest lobbies in the state, which is sad. The various breeds never joined together to find strength

and unity. Thoroughbred people stood alone. Standardbred people. Quarter horse people. And even within the Thoroughbred industry you had the racetracks on one side and the breeders on the other side lobbying for different things.

LS: *What did you do to fix that when you were elected governor in 1991?*
BJ: I started a breeder award program. In my first speech to the General Assembly, I said, "Everybody knows I'm from the horse industry, and I'm going to fight as hard as I can to help it." At the time, the industry provided more than eighty thousand jobs, directly and indirectly, in the state. And any governor who won't fight to save eighty thousand jobs ought to be impeached. Horse jobs are just as important as any other jobs, and I was going to stand up for the horse industry.

Of course, I got criticism because they thought that was a conflict of interest. But I saw the need for a breeders' award program and a stallion awards program. Other states had just begun them, and I knew it was going to catch on, and I'd seen what had happened when New Jersey moved aggressively to take the Standardbred industry away from Kentucky. Nobody did anything about it.

So we got a modest breeders' award program going. We couldn't take money from education or health care, so we set up new off-track betting facilities and used those to fund the program. So that was a major reform. Then, because there was so much waste in government, I combined the two racing commissions we had into one. When I took office, the state was $400 million in the red. Four years later, I left a $300 million surplus, the biggest in history. Just using common sense, and I think that's why people respected my administration.

LS: *What do you suggest to make the government more responsive to the needs of the industry?*
BJ: Go to the local level and educate as to why the horse industry is important to them. One thing I figured out is that legislators will eat your shrimp and drink your whiskey and then vote to perpetuate themselves in office every single time. That's just human nature. But if you win over their constituents, then when we have legislation we need to get passed, instead of going to Frankfort and feeding politicians shrimp and whiskey, we call the people who elected them and say, "We need your help. We need five hundred emails and one thousand phone calls to tell Senator So-and-So to get right on this bill." And then all of a sudden, like magic, you get legislators saying, "Sure, I'm for that bill. Where's the shrimp and whiskey?"

LS: *Let's move on to your horse operation. How do you decide which stallions to bring in to stand stud at Airdrie?*

BJ: It's very tough. You have to analyze each horse according to your standards, and then you've got to determine what a proper stud fee for that stallion would be. Then you make your offer based on being able to get your money back from that acquisition by the time his two-year-olds get to the racetrack. And if you can do that, then it's a good deal. And you can never lose sight of the fact that 95 percent of all stallions fail from the standpoint of being a viable commercial product that will give you a reasonable return on investment. Many stallions will give you one or two good horses, but overall, they'll move their mares down instead of moving them up.

LS: *I covered the race when Mazel Trick, who you co-owned, won the San Diego Handicap, and you said he showed a brilliance you don't see often, and that's what you need to look for in a stallion prospect.*
BJ: You try and look for the most desirable total package, and that would be a horse that was brilliant. There's a need in American racing for that brilliance. Just because a horse won a race at a mile and a half doesn't guarantee he's going to be well-received. They need brilliance, they need conformation, and they need pedigree. If you've got all three at the highest level, you've got a horse that's going to be worth a ton of money. And that's not the level I've ever felt comfortable at. I've never gone after a $40 million horse.

I feel more comfortable getting a horse who can stand for ten thousand or twenty thousand dollars and can be well-received by the breeders and the buyers so that I can get my investment back. Then, if the horse hits, you're in good shape. And if he doesn't, you move on and find another home for that horse in another state where there's less competition. Just because they can't meet the competition in Kentucky doesn't mean they're a bad sire. They can meet the competition somewhere else.

LS: *Do you have just as much chance at being successful as the guy who does buy a $40 million horse?*
BJ: I think the odds are better at this level. And I feel more comfortable.

LS: *What sire has been the most pleasant surprise for you?*
BJ: Silver Hawk was a dramatically good stallion who we just retired. He's been here his whole life, bred about 10 percent stakes winners, 5 percent graded stakes winners, and 2 percent grade 1 winners. Fabulous statistics. The great thing about this business is you can dream. I had those dreams about Silver Hawk, but at first the market didn't share them with me. Then his first crop didn't run well, and it was a struggle. But from the second crop on, he came up with good horses and became

a truly international sire. The Europeans and the Japanese and the Middle Eastern folks bought the Silver Hawks and won many of the top races all over the world. He's had champions in England, France, Ireland, Japan, Germany, and already this year two of his daughters have produced grade 1 winners in America.

LS: *Who are your up-and-comers?*

BJ: We brought in three new stallions this year—pay your money and take your chances. All three have been exceptionally well-received, and that shows we priced them right, or maybe less than where they should have been. Proud Citizen is by Gone West and out of Northern Dancer's female family. He's an awesome individual who showed tremendous ability at two and three. Harlan's Holiday won more than $3 million and three grade 1 races. And Yankee Gentleman, who is a son of Storm Cat out of a grade 1–winning race mare. He's got that brilliance by Storm Cat, and I think he's a time bomb waiting to explode.

LS: *How have you built your broodmare band?*

BJ: We raise many of them ourselves and then buy some. One of my great pleasures is going to the breeding stock sales and sitting up close and making split-second decisions as they come into the ring. I buy a lot of mares that way. I enjoy playing the numbers game. Economically, you could make the case for having a smaller operation, but I would be bored to tears if I only had ten mares. I have about 175 mares and like to go to the sale and buy some and sell some. I love the free trade and the free enterprise system. It's relaxation and fun for me.

LS: *Do you plan the matings for all those mares?*

BJ: Do them all myself. I don't allow any pedigree experts to mate those mares because it takes all the fun out of it. I tell them, "I know you're more qualified than I am, but I'm going to do it myself." Going up to that foaling barn during foaling season every morning is like a kid at Christmas: "Did Santa Claus come last night? What did he bring?" You just get all excited about the babies and let your dreams run wild.

LS: *Any secrets to how you raise them?*

BJ: We like to raise them like horses. Like athletes. Let them get out and get stressed and participate. I love at the sales when people come up and analyze to make sure every knee is exactly perfect. You have to laugh at them, because that's not the way you pick out a runner. That's not the way you pick out a sound horse. The good horseman gets the overall view of a horse and can decide whether or not he's an athlete. Those are the people you enjoy doing business with.

We mostly end up racing what we don't sell. [Jones has subsequently raced three Kentucky Oaks winners—Proud Spell, 2008; Believe You Can, 2012; and Lovely Maria, 2015.] If there's a filly out of an older mare that you want to keep for the broodmare band, you keep her out of the sale. But the colt you think the most of, we always take it to the sale. And we try to reserve our horses at less than what we think their value is, because people have to know they can get a good value, or there's no reason for them to come back. That's just good merchandising.

LS: *Best horse you've bred?*
BJ: Probably By Land By Sea, a filly whose pedigree inspired nobody at the sale, so I put her into training and had her on the market for thirty thousand dollars. There were no takers, so we ran her at Ellis Park, and she won by seven lengths first out. A guy who had turned her down called and said he'd give us the thirty for her. I said, "I bet you would. I'll take fifty for her." And he said that was too much, so we ran her back in an allowance race and she won by eight. He called back and said he'd give the fifty, and I said, "I bet you would. The price is one hundred." She ended up being a grade 1 winner who earned more than $600,000.

LS: *When you see a filly you bred, Caressing, become a champion, is it as much of a thrill being the breeder as being the owner?*
BJ: I'd say it's more of a thrill if you still owned her. But it is a thrill.

LS: *You and your wife, Libby, are active in land conservation. Why is that so important to you?*
BJ: Not only is the land important to us right now, it will be even more important to future generations as you have more and more population explosion and less available land on which to raise agricultural products. I'm in a position where I can give the conservation easement away and put it on there in perpetuity, and I feel it's the greatest gift I can give to future generations. The conservation mentality started with Libby, and she educated me and brought me along to it.

LS: *Has that childhood dream of yours turned out to meet expectations?*
BJ: Beyond expectations. There's nobody more fortunate or luckier than I am. I give thanks to God every day.

28

Henry White

HENRY WHITE SPENT FORTY-FIVE of his years on Plum Lane Farm raising honest horses he liked to call "bill-payers" for clients such as Preston Burch, Paul Mellon, Ogden Phipps, John Galbreath, Jack Dreyfus, Mary Hecht, and Nelson Bunker Hunt. He had his hands on plenty of headliners such as Cryptoclearance and Temperate Sil, and planned the mating that produced Kentucky Derby winner Sea Hero for Mellon. He also mentored a parade of aspiring horsemen. One, Catherine Parke of Valkyre Stud, said, "The right thing is his only choice. He does it for his clients, his horses, and his pastures without even thinking about it."

2002

Interviewed at Plum Lane Farm, Lexington

Lenny Shulman: *You're known for having developed a lot of people in this business.*
Henry White: I've started out a couple of dozen people, everyone from veterinarians to stall shakers [grooms]. One year I had nineteen mares in the November sale, and I hired five men from Dr. Baker at the University of Kentucky to groom the mares every night for six weeks. I set them up like a production line. Fast as they'd get one curried, they'd vacuum 'em in another stall, brush them, do their feet, manes, tales, and on to the next one. Those nineteen mares came out of there spotless. Those guys worked at the sale, too. That was a real good crew, and all were working on their masters or doctorates.

LS: *What were the most important lessons you imparted to people?*
HW: Tell me if you're scared of horses before I find it out and tell you. I liked to have people who were willing to learn my system. You know, all us farm managers think we're geniuses because our system is the only system that works. I don't like to rush people much, but I want to know where you want to go, whether you're staying in the business or looking for pocket change.

LS: *What makes your system different from the next guy's?*
HW: I've always liked sheds. Always used a lot of them. I used to have a barn up here on the hill with fourteen stalls, and I'd run twenty horses through it, putting

Nick Nicholson (*left*) and Henry White (Keeneland Library Featherston Collection)

two weanlings to a stall. Put them up every day, groom them, walk them a little bit, treat their cuts, and make sure they don't have a temperature. Usually, horses in sheds don't get pneumonia.

I never put many horses up in the winter. I had a big shed, and you'd go back there on a cold, blustery night and you wouldn't find them in the shed. They'd be over the hill bedded down in the snow, sprawled out. I just put them up to check on the cuts. Some of these people have built beautiful barns, and the ventilation stinks and they get sick horses. The best barn in the world to raise horses in is a tobacco barn with stalls in it. Plenty of ventilation. Except you can't hang your feed tub on the back wall 'cause it'll rain in it, and the water might freeze in the water bucket.

I have a lot of hedges on the farm, and those old mares will find where the wind's blowing, and they'll get up along that hedge. Horses outside, their feet don't dry out. They just do better. They're grazing animals. A horseman could care less if they get a scratch on them. In fact, they like to see them like that because they know they haven't been put in the fattening pens. Some of these places fix yearlings like fat cattle. Exercise is good for both horses and man, but I'm a bad example of that right now.

LS: *Your father managed farms also. Did he have the biggest influence on you?*
HW: I had some awful good mentors. Preston Burch, who was a real good friend of my daddy's, was a big help to me. He'd tell me, "You always try to give a person the best knowledge you can on that day. Now, a week later, it might be wrong, but that's not the point. What happens down the road you have no control over." He was very good on pedigrees. He taught me to look for a mare with a nice eye, a good slope of the shoulder, and that stands up good on its feet. If she toes in or out a little bit, don't let that stop you. And a good hind quarter. And he liked mares to look like mares, not studs.

Mr. [Paul] Mellon was a big help to me along the way. He was a good horseman. When we had the Rokeby horses, you'd call his assistant and say, "We had a little bit of bad luck last night. So-and-so had to go for gut surgery." And he'd ask how she was, and ask about the rest of the mares. And that was the end of it. He didn't give you the third degree. They left you alone to do your job.

LS: *Is there a secret to doing this job?*
HW: If you don't like it, you can't do it. The greatest thing about a horseman is they're doing something they really want to do. And I've been lucky. You can have your computers; I've got all my books and all the knowledge I've accumulated—but just give me luck. Best mare I ever had was this crippled little mare who was a half sister to the dam of Mr. Leader. I bred that mare, and she had me five stakes winners.

I got Mr. Mellon as a client through Mr. Burch. Then Mack Miller kept me on after he started as a trainer, and we accumulated a heckuva good bunch of mares who showed up with runners. It makes you feel good that you had a little something to do with them. Sea Hero's dam was bred to Polish Navy because we couldn't get her in foal to Danzig, and at the time Polish Navy was the best son of Danzig. And what'd we get? A Derby winner. I was so happy for Mack and Mr. Mellon.

LS: *Do you race any yourself?*
HW: If you're in the horse business and you haven't got the guts enough to race them, you should get out of the business. The thing I like about racing claimers is that the vets can't screw them up scoping them and x-raying them. Look at War Emblem. What a blessing he was. Here's a horse with chips in both knees winning the Derby and Preakness. There's an awful lot of nice horses that go through the

last five days of the September yearling sale. Bill-payers. Give me the bill-payer. They're not world-beaters. They're racehorses. Bill-payers. They make somebody happy, and that's part of it.

I Are Sharp might be the best one I kept and raced. I bred a nice filly named Moment to Buy who went to California and won seven in a row. She won the grade 1 Hollywood Oaks and made more than $400,000.

LS: *What are your thoughts on doing matings?*

HW: One of the things on breeding is we're getting too much into this damn breeding paper [pedigree] to paper, and I think we need to get back to breeding horses to horses. Joe Estes [former editor of the *Bloodhorse*] was a good friend of my father's, and they used to fight like cats and dogs because Joe thought you could do everything on paper. Daddy would say, "You didn't put conformation in there." He always told Joe Estes that. There's no way to put conformation in a computer. I know they're measuring horses, and all the hustlers will be all over me and I don't care, because you still have to eyeball them.

LS: *After seventy-five years on this corner, you'll be moving off this farm soon. Talk about its history.*

HW: Man o' War stood his first two years at stud here. All the early pictures of him, he had a saddle on him because he was sway-backed. I have a picture of him without. Plum Lane was Hinata Stock Farm back in the twenties. When we took it over, the front was full of black plum trees. Even further back, in 1913, there was a racetrack here, and they had a one-day race meet with pari-mutuel wagering. They raised money for World War I. We called it the Track Field when we took it over. I used that old track for a long time to gallop yearlings. This farm has produced a lot of good horses.

My father used to run the farm across the street, Elsmeade. He raised Bold Venture, who won the Kentucky Derby. Daddy used to turn twelve or fourteen colts out together, take the shoes off, and make sure they got a tad sore. Turned them out and said, "See you boys tomorrow." They'd wrestle and come up scratched and bumped and everything else, and damn good racehorses came out of them bunch of horses. They weren't put into a velvet cell. They were put out there on Dr. Green. You give them horses a lot of Dr. Green, boy, you can solve more damn horse problems. You take care of Dr. Green and Dr. Green will take care of you. You better believe it.

LS: *What is retirement going to look like?*

HW: The horses I'm keeping will go to Catherine Parke at Valkyre Stud. She's a lovely girl, used to work for me. I told everyone when I retire, I'm not going to have anything to do with anything that eats and shits. I started taking care of horses when I was a big, old, fat lazy boy of thirteen. I'm going to work a little as a consultant. I have a man who bought a farm who shouldn't have, so I'm gonna look over his shoulder. I had one person ask me what I could do for him, and I said, "Keep these young SOBs from stealing you blind."

I ran into four guys at a TOBA (Thoroughbred Owners and Breeders Association) dinner who said they weren't gonna have anything to race but stake horses. And I said, "No kidding? Let me know when that happens, because if you do that, you're gonna break up racing." There's never been but one man who almost broke up racing, and that was W. C. Whitney. Nobody has ever locked this business up.

This is the greatest business in the world. I think about all the fine people who've come through here, and all the damn hustlers who've come through here. And both kinds are still in the business. You can tell when the business is improving because you see some of the same hustlers from the past show up again. But to be able to go out to dinner with men like Paul Mellon, George Widener, John Galbreath, Ogden Phipps . . .

Old Doc Charlie Hagyard had the best line when they asked how he was doing. "I'm doin' good. I'm on the green side looking down."

It's been a good life. I don't have any regrets.

29

Ted Carr

OF THE HUNDREDS OF farm managers who have plied their trade in the Kentucky Bluegrass, none has been more respected by his peers than **Ted Carr.** The son of a horseman, Carr grew up riding and taking care of studs and mares and selling yearlings while still in his teens. Right out of high school he was helping his father manage three operations. When his father's health failed, Carr stepped up and never had to look for a job thereafter; major owners and breeders came to him. He is most known for his work building and managing Allen Paulson's Brookside Farm and raising the great Cigar, which came right around the time Carr left cancer in the dust.

2001

Interviewed at Diamond A Farm (formerly Brookside),
Versailles, Kentucky

Lenny Shulman: *Growing up, how did you learn about horses?*
Ted Carr: I grew up with horses on a little farm about two miles from Calumet on Parkers Mill Road. My dad was in the horse business and farmed too. He was running three farms. He'd put me on a horse every morning starting when I was five and send me out to ride. He taught me, and then I've learned from others and on my own. I've always tried to study people who I felt I could learn from.

My dad's health was bad, so right out of high school I was running his farm and Doc Mundy's farm. I stayed with Mundy nine years, then the trainer Henry Forrester talked me into going out to Man o' War Farm. They were looking for a farm manager, and I took that job in 1962. A few years later J. R. Cowdin bought the place, and I stayed on. His son was a good friend of mine. We grew up neighbors. It's a small world.

Then we bought Poplar Hill Farm and added it to Man o' War. One parcel had the statue and the old Man o' War stud barn and everything. That was our headquarters where we had the stallions: John's Joy, Federal Hill, Mito. Eventually W. B. Terry bought out Cowdin and also owned Domino, and I ended up running Poplar Hill and Domino for him until 1980.

Ted Carr (Keeneland Library *Thoroughbred Times* Collection)

LS: *How did you meet up with Allen Paulson?*
TC: I worked for Mrs. Payson from 1980 until 1984. This man called me from his jet airplane, introduced himself, and asked if I'd be interested in talking about a job. I'd seen him active out there at Keeneland buying yearlings for a lot of money. I didn't know him but figured I best go and meet him and see what he's got to say.

I could tell he was serious and was going to spend a lot of money in the horse business. So before that day was done, he and my wife and I had dinner at Columbia Steak House, and he had me hired before he left that night. I gave Mrs. Payson sixty days' notice and came down here to work the first of August, 1984.

LS: *And that was Brookside, now Diamond A. Was there anything on the farm when you started?*
TC: No. I had to start cleaning and clearing this land and get ready to start building a horse farm. I laid the whole thing out and designed it. We went around and looked at barns to see what kind of look he wanted. He liked the old Greentree look; the old Kentucky look with the cupolas and dormers and all that kind of stuff.

I've always adjusted to different owners. You see what makes them happy and try and please them. But I always had a big say-so. I've thought about going out on my own from time to time, but it seemed like I just felt better working for the millionaire. Worst I could do was get fired. And I never have looked for a job. They always found me. So I was fortunate there.

LS: *What are the most important considerations in building a farm from scratch?*
TC: Laying your barns out so they're all on higher spots—you don't want water running down into them. Set them up so you can develop paddocks and fields around them. You don't want any long leads getting from the barns to the fields. Everything here runs to the barn. We don't have to walk a mile and a half.

With your stallion area you want all your good ones around you in close proximity. The others are gonna be further away, but you can't help that.

LS: *Is there a story behind the large pond you can see from the road at the front of the property?*
TC: That's a real cavernous area with a lot of rock and old springs. Mr. Paulson said we need to put us a pond out there. The farm is called Brookside, and he wanted water. I said, "Boss, it's a bad place to build one. It won't hold." He said the hell with it, put a liner in it and make it hold. So that's what we did. After we got it built, he wanted a babbling brook. You can see that out there now. After I'd been out to California and seen the botanical gardens he had out there, I could see you can make creeks and brooks and lakes.

The more you had going on, the better he liked it. If you had ten barns going up, he said, "Great, build them. I ain't a kid no more and I don't want to spend my whole life building the damn place. Get it built." And we built it fast. He'd come in, fly in his Gulfstream [Paulson founded the jet company], and we'd show him everything we'd done. He loved to shoot at the groundhogs. This place was eaten alive by groundhogs, and I'd keep a rifle in the truck. He'd get to the farm and the first thing he'd say is, "You got that gun with you?" It'd be dark 'till we'd think about eating. Had a lot of fun.

LS: *How do you learn to have an eye for a horse?*
TC: I guess you just develop that over the years from seein' a lot of nice horses and being around nice horses. You can't really pick out who's gonna be the top horse out of twenty. You can pick out a nice horse who's athletic; that's the main thing. An intelligent, good-looking animal with a good head and eye. It's just something you see about them and like, mainly.

LS: *Is it a sixth sense?*
TC: I don't know. I can't answer that. People like different types. A horse that's well-balanced, got enough leg under him, got enough daylight under him, balanced up front to rear. It's hard to describe. You look at him and you either like him or you don't. I don't like back at the knee if I can avoid it, but we've had some good horses that had a tad of that, or in at the knee. If they're gonna toe one way or the other, I'd rather see them toe out a little bit. Seems to be less of an unsoundness problem. Some of the crooked ones run in spite of it, but they're less likely to.

LS: *You've planned a lot of matings through the years. How much is pedigree and how much is conformation?*
TC: You have to use them together. With conformation, you have to try and breed out your defects if you can. You wouldn't want to breed a crooked, toed-in mare to a horse that produces that. I like to add speed to everything. I think without speed you're dead in this country. We've been lucky here mixing and matching them; we've come up with a lot of good horses. Mr. Paulson wasn't into buying a lot of outside seasons. He'd say, "Hell, let's make our own studs. To hell with these others." And you can see we were pretty lucky. The man had some pretty good horses. Eight Breeders' Cup winners, thirteen Eclipse Awards.

LS: *Stallions like Theatrical, Jade Hunter, and Strawberry Road weren't obvious choices to have the successful stud careers they did. You made those stallions.*
TC: We supported our horses. We had a lot of mares, and this man supported his stud horses, and that was the key. The studs didn't sit here and do nothing. And if the outside world wasn't interested in them that much, it didn't bother him. We went right on breeding to them.

We bought a lot of nice fillies at the sales. More so than colts, although we bought some of them, too. But so many things can happen to the colts, and if they don't become superstars, they're not much for the stud barn. Mr. Paulson bought into Strawberry Road as a racehorse. He bought a half interest in Theatrical from Bert Firestone when the horse was still in Europe. He didn't get good until he came here and wound up with Bill Mott. Bill made that horse what he was. Theatrical was cantankerous, and Bill is a great horseman who worked through that and got his mind right and made him into a champ. Mr. Paulson bought half of Jade Hunter, who looked like he was going to be one hell of a horse. He won two grade 1 races at Gulfstream and fractured a cannon bone, and we brought him to stud the next year.

You never know with studs. It's a gamble game. It sure is a gamble. You never know who's gonna hit and who isn't. We had faith in them and brought a lot of nice mares to them.

LS: *The operation will always be associated with Cigar. Did you raise him here?*
TC: He was foaled in Maryland. We were breeding mares to Allen's Prospect because the boss owned shares in him. That mare was due later in the season so we let her foal out there and brought them home at the end of breeding season. Early in his life, being by Palace Music, you didn't think of Cigar as a big star. He was a nice colt, but nothing spectacular about him. He'd like to have killed himself as a weanling. He ran through a damn wire fence after some deer scared him early one morning. Cut himself all to hell in the shoulder and forearm. We took him to the clinic, sewed him up, and I wasn't sure we could save him. Mac [Carr's son] healed him up slowly. Hosed him twice daily and gradually got him back together. He still has the scar. But you wouldn't have given a quarter for his life when it happened. He was lucky to be alive.

Mac broke him as a yearling, and he was a lovely yearling. Smart. Mac said if he didn't make it at the races, he could make a good lead pony out of him. It's a great feeling when they turn out like he did. You hope to raise some superstars for these owners. Anytime you raise a good horse you feel great that you played some kind of part.

LS: *Do you notice what other farm managers are doing?*
TC: We kind of do our own things, the things we've learned and developed and figured out with horses over the years, and stick to that. Don't really pay that much attention to what the guy across the fence is doing.

LS: *Have horses changed in your time working around them?*
TC: Probably gotten more fragile, just seems to be. This industry—they never cull anything, just go on and breed. Hell, you're down to only four or five stud

families that're in just about everybody's pedigree now. You got the Northern Dancers, Mr. Prospectors, Raise A Natives, Seattle Slews. It's getting hard to do your matings today without doing some inbreeding. Too much racing is a likely reason for the fragility. We used to turn them all out in the fall. Always.

LS: *How about raising young horses?*
TC: We don't pamper them. Have them up in the morning to feed them inside, groom them, pick their feet, doctor them, keep them stall-civilized. Then turn them back out. Feed them out of a tub at 3:30, check them two or three times a day. They're out. We like them gentle and we like to handle them. It's harder to break a horse that doesn't have confidence in people. We do a lot of ground work. Play with them in the round pen. Work them loose and free, then work them on a twelve-foot rope.

LS: *How satisfying is it that your son has followed you in this?*
TC: He's a great horseman. Anything that comes up, he can do as good or better than I can now. He started at the same age I did, and I'd rank him against anyone in the industry. I don't know what I would have done without him the way the help situation has gotten the last fifteen years.

We don't have any young people who want to come along and work and learn and do. They'd rather be bloodstock agents or something. They don't want to be out here smelling this horseshit and getting beat and thumped on all the time. It's a lot of work, seven days a week. That's been our lifestyle. You get a day off, you're lucky. Local folks don't want to work anymore. Young generation don't want to do this kind of work. You've got Toyota and all these other things that have come in over the years. They work a lot less hours and make a lot more money. I guess you just have to understand that.

30

Dr. Smiser West

IF RAISING HORSES CAN seem as difficult as pulling teeth, then **Dr. Smiser West** had an early advantage. He was a dentist in Lexington before moving to his wife, Kathryn's, Waterford Farm in Midway. With his great friend trainer Mack Miller and Miller's wife, the Wests bred such horses as Chilukki, De La Rose, Lite Light, Tweedside, and Wanda. A spry ninety-two when we spoke, West had lost none of his enthusiasm for a promising yearling and took great pride in the fact that the female families established by the Wests and Millers were perpetuating. He also took pride in that, one year earlier, he had his arm broken while delivering a foal. He was further proof that raising horses makes for a kind person and a pleasant life.

2001

Interviewed at Waterford Farm, Midway, Kentucky

Lenny Shulman: *Not many people use dentistry as their entrance into breeding horses.*

Smiser West: My father wanted me to be a farmer, and I didn't want to because the farm belonged to him, and there wasn't enough for the two of us. I grew up on the farm and actually rode ponies to the country school. I'd ridden horses all my life. He didn't approve of me going to dental school, so I did it on my own. I had taken engineering at the University of Kentucky, but everybody who was graduating in engineering was getting a job pumping gasoline, and I said, "That's not for me." So I decided to take medicine and dentistry.

I thought I had enough money saved up to stay at the Brown Hotel in Louisville and go to dental school, but I found out differently.

I knew Mack Miller from when I was an undergrad at the University of Kentucky. Mack's father was superintendent of maintenance at Greyhound Bus Company in Louisville, and I went to him for a job. So I washed busses at night and went to school days. Mack worked there too. He was on the grease rack, and I was on the wash rack, so we worked together. Later, Mack and I became partners and owned horses together.

Dr. R. Smiser and Kathryn West (Keeneland Association)

I came back to Lexington to practice. I was the first person to go out to the residential section of town to open my office rather than downtown, and it paid off. I practiced around twenty years and loved dentistry. At that time a lot of the owners of the farms around here were absentee; they lived back East. When they came here to visit, they'd have dental problems and were sent to me. I did gold inlay work and bridge work. I'd say by the time I quit 30 percent of my practice was people from back East. I did replacements, prosthetics—removing teeth and making new ones, and we'd take them to the hospital and put them right in. It was a new dentistry at that time.

It was through those people from out of town that I got into the horse business. I had a big practice among them at the time I went into the service. They were very kind to me and helped me, especially Charlie Kenney, probably one of the best horsemen I ever knew. I did quite a bit of work for him, and he helped me when I got into horses. He would help me pick out mares and get breeding seasons. When I got married, Kathryn had some horses too, and we worked together. She's a very good horsewoman and a better judge of horses than I am. We lived on a farm between Harrodsburg Road and Keene, then sold that when she inherited this one, and we fixed it up for horses.

LS: *What were some painful lessons you had to learn at the beginning?*
SW: Some of the more painful lessons I'm having to learn right now. I didn't suffer much because I didn't have the money to go into it in a big way. I had to feel my way. As time went on, we did well. Charlie Kenney told you just the way it was, and that's the only way you're gonna learn anything. Somebody who pats you on the back, that's not gonna do you any good. Charlie Kenney and Bull Hancock were kind to me—Bull always saw to it that I had something to breed to that was good, and that I could afford. I was doing well to stay above water. Back then, stud fees were around ten thousand dollars and you'd get what you could for them as yearlings as far as selling them. But we had nice people who we dealt with. It's been fifty years since I started breeding.

We didn't expect a whole lot, and we didn't get a whole lot. First horse I ever sold was a yearling by a horse named Flare. Everybody told me you got to get him fat and slick. So I sent him up to Saratoga with Carter Thornton, and Carter said the first time he brought him out to show him, someone said, "My God, beef on the hoof." A little too fat and slick.

LS: *You've had some prominent clients through the years.*
SW: The Firestones did so many nice things for us. We used to go with them to Ireland several times a year, and we met a lot of nice people and clients through them. The Aga Khan, for instance. We kept horses for him. We met after the Arc one night. He was a nice man who sent about twenty horses over here, and we'd breed them for him.

LS: *What do you look for when buying mares?*
SW: First thing is pedigree, then you think about the individual. I think that the head on a horse means an awful lot—to have a good, attractive head on them. If you have one with a plain head, people just don't take to them. I can recall one yearling that had such an attractive head and fine muzzle, and he didn't have the best front legs on him, but people couldn't keep their eyes off him, and he sold well. I don't know that an attractive head makes them run, but he did well. I try to stay away from plain heads.

LS: *How can you identify a good one?*
SW: A good-looking horse has something that just catches your eye, and you'll look a second time. The conformation—good legs and so forth. It's hard to say exactly what it is. I buy some sometimes that don't turn out so well, too. It's something that comes natural to you, a horse that catches your eye.

LS: *Was Chilukki [a graded stakes winner bred by West] like that?*
SW: I loved her. I'll never forget, she sold the next-to-last day of the sale. And one of the leading buyers from Europe came to the farm to look at the horses, and I told him I had a nice filly who doesn't sell 'till late, and he said he had another appointment and didn't have time. He came back a year later and said, "Did you show me that filly when I was at the farm?" And I said, "No, you were too busy to look at her." But she would catch your eye every time out in the field. It wouldn't take a good horseman to see she was a standout.

LS: *How do you go about picking sires to match up to?*
SW: I spend a lot of time right here under this little light going over the horses and the ones you can afford. You can overbreed before you know it if you don't watch yourself; pay too high a stud fee. Conformation matches are important.

I've had success with Unbridled's Song and Cherokee Run, Red Ransom, Maria's Mon. I bred quite a few to [Mack Miller's Derby winner] Sea Hero. Eastern Echo is one of the better-looking sires, but he hasn't turned out that well. You have to be careful about picking sires—you can like them so much that you keep right on thinking he's got to produce a good horse. I don't like to go over fifty thousand dollars. In fact, I don't like to go *to* fifty thousand. It doesn't cost me as much to raise a horse as it does a lot of people. Here on this farm I raise my own hay, my own bedding, my own corn. You don't find many people who feed corn, and I don't know why. I always thought it was good feed. We go out in a pickup truck and drop off six or seven piles of cobs, and they eat it right off the cob. You

171

can feed it year-round. We take our own corn to Saratoga for our horses. Gives a horse a good coat.

LS: *What has changed in your time in the business?*
SW: I think we're better horsemen now than we were fifty years ago. Things we take for granted nowadays they wouldn't have years ago. Veterinary is much better now. Years ago, we figured out when to breed mares from a teaser. Nowadays you have a vet to inspect and palpitate them. I don't think the breed is any better today. Everybody is ready to stand a horse if they win a race. They're afraid to leave them out there to race because they might get beat. Too many businessmen and not enough sportsmen. They get a lead at the head of the stretch, and people start thinking about how many mares they can get to them. It's ruining racing.

LS: *How did you build your broodmare band?*
SW: I own sixteen to eighteen myself, and then some with the Millers. Mack and I were fortunate to get some mares from Mr. Charles Engelhard's dispersal. Mrs. Engelhard allowed us to buy some mares without signing notes. She did that for Mack because he trained for them and they loved Mack like a brother. Those mares are great—De La Rose, we bought her dam from Mrs. E. Mack knew those mares, and we bought what we could. Rosetta Stone was in foal carrying De La Rose when we bought her. We couldn't afford [to keep] De La Rose. She was the highest-priced filly ever to be sold at Saratoga at the time, $500,000. That was a lot of money, and we were two happy boys.

LS: *Going back to Chilukki, do you think more people are interested in status—that they'd rather buy a horse that is selling the first day of the sale?*
SW: I think that is true. There's a lot of sellers who say if they can't sell in the first week, they won't sell. Well, you can't do that. The company has to run the sale, and you have to abide by it. But some of the big buyers only stay two or three days, maybe a week, but there's bound to be good horses after that. You get to the point where you know who the good horsemen are. When you're selling a horse, you don't try and tell a person about your horse and how good he is. You don't tell him anything, and I don't think he wants you to tell him anything. I never try to sell anybody.

LS: *How do you feel when one goes on and runs?*
SW: You feel like you've accomplished something. You watch them every time they run. You don't get too many of those like Chilukki. Mack and I talk about this every day. The main thing you want is to have the respect of people. Money

hasn't meant much to us. We need it, we talk about it a lot (*laughs*), but in reality, we want to raise a good horse.

We bred Lite Light, who won the Coaching Club American Oaks and the Kentucky Oaks ten years ago. We bred Tweedside, who won the Coaching Club American Oaks this year. I watched Tweedside on television when she won it. Lite Light, I was there when she won it. We've got a little filly now who won out here last week. She was so mean and tough, she'd bite you. She threw the boy who was trying to break her so many times we named her Don't Ruffle Me. Mack and I race her. We ran her through the sale and the bidding only went to fourteen thousand dollars, so I said to Mack that seven thousand dollars isn't going to do either of us much good, so I bid her in. And we're getting a kick out of her.

LS: *Is it harder to sell a horse today?*
SW: I recall a fella who came out here—one of the big buyers—and I had a dandy colt by Hero's Honor, and he wanted to buy him before the sale, and wanted to know if he could x-ray him. I told him "no," because if he found something wrong, I couldn't in good faith run that horse through the sale. But I told him I'd stand behind the horse. He bought the horse through the sale, x-rayed him, and found a sesamoid problem. He'd given $350,000, and he didn't want to take the chance. I took the horse back. And I needed the money, but you have to live with yourself. Before all this money came into fashion, we didn't have any more problems than we do now. You were protected by a handshake instead of an X-ray.

LS: *At age ninety-two, what is it that keeps you going?*
SW: I go to the deliveries. Got my arm broken last year foaling one. I just love seeing new life. You always want to know what it's going to look like when it comes from your mating. I'm going to take you out to this field and show you this gray filly we have, to show you why I love this business. When I took over this farm, it was an agricultural operation. Every post, every plank that's on this farm—and a lot of the buildings—we did it ourselves with farm labor. We called ourselves the Messy Construction Company, of which I am the president. It's been a lot of fun.

31

John T. L. Jones Jr.

KNOWN TO HIS BEST friends as "Alphabet" because of the various letters comprising his name, **John T. L. Jones Jr.** made hefty impressions in both the Thoroughbred and quarter horse worlds. He was equally at home on the dusty Texas plains collecting belt buckles for his champion quarter horses as he was making trips to Europe to import Thoroughbred blood (Alleged and Nureyev) that impacted the breed. Jones helmed Walmac Farm for decades and was a principal in the Four Star Sales company. His collection of Western art and artifacts filled his office, and Jones always carried the aura of a larger-than-life figure wherever he went.

2004

Interviewed at Walmac, Lexington

Lenny Shulman: *You started with quarter horses.*
John Jones: My father was in the insurance business but he had quarter horses, and I was riding them at five or six years old in Quanah, Texas. He showed horses as a hobby. After he died, I spent a couple of years doing his insurance business but have been with horses ever since. I built a training center and stallion operation in Quanah where we broke horses, then I moved to New Mexico to train. I worked for Walter Merrick, a legend in the quarter horse business.

Then I met Marvin Warner, who was looking for a manager, so I moved to Cincinnati and worked with him in quarter horses for a decade. I started this place [Walmac] in 1977. I had it in my mind to move to Thoroughbreds, and I switched Marvin over to them. I was fortunate in that I had started going to Europe in 1973.

LS: *You are most associated with the European stock you brought back here.*
JJ: I got acquainted with Robert Sangster and Alec Head before it got crazy with importing horses from Europe. I got to be a very good friend of Robert's, and he had controlling interest in Alleged and put the deal together. I was just leasing Walmac at the time. Will Farish was involved with me in it before he started his operation [Lane's End] in 1984. Sangster and Farish were great partners.

John T. L. Jones Jr. (Keeneland Library *Thoroughbred Times* Collection)

Everyone was running after Alleged, and Robert stayed with me until I could get the deal done. He was a horse who had won the Arc, and it was just a matter of price, and Farish backed me putting up the money, and we had him syndicated quick.

The Nureyev syndication—I thought the horse would work here so I went to Europe and did a deal to bring him here not knowing he wasn't a particularly fertile horse. We bred him around the clock, and Dr. J. D. Howard did a great job with him. Then he broke his leg, and we missed part of 1987 and 1988, but we were back breeding the first of April 1988. We built him his own barn out there. I've been pretty lucky to be at the right place at the right time.

LS: *How tough is the stallion game?*
JJ: I've had failures with stallions, but not an enormous amount. Probably got a leg up on most places as far as having luck with them. A lot of it is instinct and listening to other professionals' opinions. But in all honesty, you never know. Gotta be luck involved. There are so many factors it would take days to decipher it all.

But when push comes to shove, nobody knows what's in the genetic bank. You can have some indicators, but it boils down to you can't say anything is an absolute, because the stallions who have been top stallions sometimes didn't have a lot of pedigree. But if you want to increase your odds, you'd want to go with pedigree. It's all an odds game, a matter of being right more times than you're wrong. But I don't know that anyone has a secret formula.

LS: *How else can you increase your odds?*
JJ: Most successful stallions in my lifetime have had a freakish ability. Not that there aren't good horses who could win races and make a lot of money. Raise a Native didn't start many times; Nureyev didn't start many times; Danzig didn't start many times; Red Ransom didn't start many times. But they all showed uncanny ability. I don't think there's many horses who make stallions that get good at age four and grind out some handicaps. To me, they don't do as well as studs. I'm not saying some of them haven't, but in general.

LS: *Were you surprised that Alleged and Nureyev turned out to be so good?*
JJ: Northern Dancer was a sire of sires, and those were marquee horses at the time. The best breeders in the country were involved. Now, Nureyev never got the best mares because everybody knew he wasn't that fertile. They sent nice mares, good mares—don't misunderstand me. The Niarchos family always bred good mares to him, but overall, he didn't get the elite. The feeling was, "We'll take a shot on Nureyev." Alleged was a different kind of horse; obvious.

Miswaki was a horse I just saw in the paddock at Saratoga and was so good-looking I felt I needed to get him. I thought he could sire some speed and also had a lot of stamina in his pedigree. And it happened like that (*snaps his fingers*). He was by Mr. Prospector and out of a great family. A little instinct on that one.

LS: *Any notable disappointments?*
JJ: I thought Risen Star came along at the wrong time in the industry, around 1988. He was a big horse, and we stood him for too much money. Had we not done that, I think he would have had a better opportunity to make it as a stallion. For a horse that won the Preakness and Belmont Stakes, we didn't get a lot of people jumping on his bandwagon. The economy was lousy, and at seventy-five thousand dollars he was overpriced. People took a shot the first year, then backed off. He was also a stayer, and the whole game was switching toward more speed.

LS: *What has changed the most in your time?*
JJ: When I came here you could drive up and down this road [Paris Pike], and all the farms bred to race. Dixiana, Greentree, Whitney, Elmendorf. Now it's totally flipped, and everybody's breeding to sell.

Back then, your better trainers would have thirty or forty horses. Now they have two hundred. I'm not being negative. There were a lot of people in the game back then that it was their lifestyle and their hobby and the way they wanted to spend the money they earned. Not wanting to be foolish with it, but they enjoyed the lifestyle. I'm sure there are people like that today, but it's gotten to where it's all business. When I came up you didn't have the government to worry about, having to show a profit two out of seven years for tax reasons. That's where it changed. I don't know if it's for the good or bad or whatever, but I think it was a more genteel sport twenty-five years ago than it is today.

While the accent has always been on speed, it's different today. I think I stood Shecky Greene for $2,500. A champion sprinter was still a sprinter—a poor man's horse. Today, they have a great deal more respect for them. The sporting people used to breed to win the Gold Cup or the Derby. Today, there aren't many bred to run a mile and a quarter or a mile and a half. Obviously, if there's ten drunks in a race, a drunk's gonna win the race.

Also, when I came here, you went to the sale and sold your horse, and it was sold. Now you got the veterinarians and all, and it's taken a lot of fun out of the game. You bought a horse, and you depended on the integrity of the people sell-ing it. Usually, they made it right if you had trouble. And if they didn't, they would lose out on business. It's taken some fun out of the breeding game to never know what you've got till you x-ray them. A lot of sale horses are overdone, and some people bring them up there way underdone. With the emphasis on selling, a lot of these yearlings are hot-housed and don't get enough free movement. They're protected from growing up to be a horse because of the money involved.

When the Nuckols brothers or Claiborne raised a horse, you knew they weren't pampered. Today, with millions of dollars at stake, the tendency is to put them away in a smaller paddock so they don't get their hock kicked. That's just human nature.

LS: *Who are some of your best clients and also great characters through the years?*
JJ: Sangster was a true sportsman, the epitome of high society. John Magnier has been a close friend of mine the whole way through. I have a lot of friends and not too many enemies. I've done a lot of business with Dee Hubbard through the years. I raise a lot of quarter horses with Hubbard and Toby Keith, and we've been on a good roll with that.

The two most colorful people I've met are Jim Scully, who bought Wajima; and Billy McDonald, who was a Texas Ranger and who I don't even know how to describe other than a real character. Scully was a biochemist who liked horses, had a gravel voice, worked for the *Bloodhorse*. Billy drank way too much, but everything was fun. He ran with the wealth of the world on a shoestring.

There are characters in the horse world. Some are guys who never got out from under a shedrow, and some are guys who come to Keeneland with billions of dollars. It's not boring. There's winners and losers, good years and bad years, good luck and bad luck. Anything you do with any animal, you've got to expect some bad news, and you have to be somewhat of an optimist and overlook that. It can be a little outside the plan from what most people think. From a breeding standpoint, there's not instant gratification. It's a long, drawn-out affair.

Bill Young [Overbrook Farm] was an amazing guy. His demeanor; he had a long-term plan, and that's why he was successful. He told me it took him ten years to develop any business he'd ever gotten into. So he wasn't looking to win the Derby in one year. He set up a program and did it right. Most people who have patience will come up with a good horse, but they can't tell you whether it will be in the second year or the eighth year. It's not an exact science.

John Gaines is a character, very opinionated but smart. His ideas have always been in fast-forward, and he's always been a good person for the horse business. Leslie Combs was a real character. He enjoyed bringing people into the game and spent an enormous amount of time entertaining. You don't see that anymore.

A lot of good people, and a lot of outlaws. As far as people being dishonest or unethical, Wall Street makes us look like a bunch of Sunday School teachers. This is a small business, and most of those guys get herded out. They may last a while, but they don't last indefinitely.

LS: *What does the future hold for you?*
JJ: I go out to Texas and Oklahoma once a month for a week or so. I like to hunt and golf. I've got a ranch, and range cattle back in Oklahoma. I collect Western art. I'm no connoisseur, I just buy what I like. I can't afford any Remingtons, but I have a decent collection. I have saddles, one that was made more than one hundred years ago.

I'm going to turn seventy this year, and I'm selling this place to my son. I can't sit around here and hang on forever, and I don't want to. If I'm lucky enough to live a few years and help out and have some influence on good stallions, fine. But I can't hang on till the last breath.

Part V

Veterinarians

THE ROLE OF VETERINARIANS IN THE THOROUGHBRED WORLD IS EVER-CHANGING AND INCREASINGLY CONTRO- VERSIAL. WHILE VETERINARY PRACTICE WAS RELATIVELY primitive a century ago, vets' rise to prominence has coincided with medical advances but also as medication use has become ubiquitous at all points in a horse's life and race career. Many grouse that veterinari- ans do more training on racehorses than the actual trainers do. And others, who seek to sell horses at sales, complain that vets have taken over that process as well and are paid to find fault in every horse, mak- ing it significantly tougher to move trade along.

Since the middle of the twentieth century, however, it is easy to appreciate the great contributions doctors have made to the sport of horse racing. For nearly every prominent racing star one can name, there is a story of how that horse's career was saved through medical care. Where breeding was once done by trial and error, today reproduc- tive specialists can tell exactly when a mare is ovulating and the opti- mum time to get them covered. Surgery specialists apply the latest knowledge, equipment, and procedures in helping the horse in every phase of its life. Foot specialists today save what would have previously been dead-end cases of laminitis.

There is no doubt, however, that racetrack remedies have often skirted, if not made a shambles of, rules and regulations and best prac- tices. Particular vets using homemade elixirs and operating in gray areas were said to have played an enormous role, for instance, on who would ultimately win races such as the Kentucky Derby. Recently, illegal drug use and rogue vets have tarnished the reputation of horse racing at a time when it can ill afford the black eye of scandal. Lack of federal guidelines has led to a patchwork of state-by-state regulations that have proven ineffective. Today, with animal welfare on the ascendency, veterinary medicine is under scrutiny as the industry moves, slowly, toward universal rules.

The reputations of the vets profiled below, however, were—and are—never in question. They each represent a dedicated breed of doctor striving to do what is best for the equine athlete. Not surprisingly, they are also engaging and gregarious by nature, and each can be proud of the contributions he has made to horses, the breed, and the sport in general.

32

Dr. Robert Copelan

IT WOULD BE IMPOSSIBLE to overestimate the effect that **Dr. Robert Copelan** has had on the Thoroughbred. Small enough to have galloped and exercised race-horses early in life, Copelan used his horsemanship skills to great effect, first as a racetrack vet and then as a trailblazing surgeon who pioneered techniques that have aided horses for the past half century. He has influenced all who have fol-lowed him. A dynamic man into his nineties who can still recite poetry by the stanza and recall significant dates from decades past down to the day of the week, Copelan's intellectual curiosity has never wavered. He often served horses on the racetracks of Florida and Illinois in the morning before flying home and per-forming surgeries at his clinic in Kentucky in the afternoon. He saved the racing careers of dozens of prominent runners and was the driving force behind the American Association of Racetrack Practitioners (AARP), today the most influ-ential organization of its kind.

2018

Interviewed at Chester Park Farm, Paris, Kentucky

Lenny Shulman: *Was it always your goal to become a veterinarian?*
Robert Copelan: No. I wanted to emulate my father, who was managing editor of the *Cincinnati Times-Star*. He cautioned me not to go into journalism, but when I got out of the Army in 1949, I went into journalism at Ohio State University. It was the first day, and I arrived for class early and was looking out the window. Right across the road they were unloading a racehorse at the College of Veteri-nary Medicine. His name was Talked About, and he was a Calumet castoff. I got up from my chair, went down the stairs, crossed the street, and never came back.

All the people there were men about my age, so nobody said, "What are you doing here?" And I watched them block that horse's leg and fire that horse, and he had no reaction to the 1,100-degree heat they were putting into his ankles. I was mesmerized. I had to know more about how all that worked and how you did that.

LS: *You could have become a jockey.*

RC: When I was a kid, I got ruled off at Coney Island because I took a stick on the pony ride. My grandfather told me I was going to be a rider. He told me I could sue the City of Cincinnati because they built the sidewalk too close to my ass. During college, I would exercise ride at Beulah Park. I got a job breaking yearlings at Darby Dan's farm near Columbus. Olin Gentry was there at the time and sent me down to Calumet in Kentucky.

That summer I got assigned to belly [lie on a horse to get it used to bearing weight] on a Bull Lea colt named Hill Gail, out of Jane Gail. Hill Gail had a big laceration on his shoulder, and I assisted Dr. Art Davidson sewing it up. I got to break him and drive him on lines, and all of that. He was quite a handful. In 1952, my father got me a press pass for the Kentucky Derby, and I was on the roof with the cameraman. Of all the things that have happened to me in my life, nothing topped that feeling when Hill Gail won the Kentucky Derby.

LS: *How did your vet career get started?*

RC: My first job was a six-week stint at Belmont Park with Dr. Manny Gilman, who taught me so much in the paddock every afternoon. He would ask me, "What about that horse? What about that conformation? What do you think of his hocks?" I'd say, "They look OK." And he'd say, "No, the angle of those hocks, is that satisfactory?" And he wanted an answer right away. I liked his way of going.

He saw I had a hole in my pants, and gave me one hundred dollars to go into New York City and get some clothes. I went to Brooks Brothers and bought a suit, a shirt, and an extra pair of pants. He said I could have gotten a lot more if I had gone to Richmond Brothers. He was good to me and taught me so much.

I got twenty-five dollars a day and that was like finding money. I got to meet all the great trainers—Max Hirsch, Mr. Fitz ["Sunny" Jim Fitzsimmons]. One day at Hialeah Mr. Fitz was leading a horse down to put him on the train—he was bent way over and couldn't see—and I said, "Hello, Mr. Fitz." And he said, "Hello, doctor." Boy, what that meant to me, that he knew my voice. He was such a lovely man. And Hirsch Jacobs. You'd say good morning to him and his response was, "It's no use."

LS: *What was the state of surgery then?*

RC: There was only one guy operating on horses: Bill Reed, who had a place across the street from Belmont and another at Hialeah.

LS: *What happened after those first six weeks in New York?*

RC: I went back to Ohio and worked at Randall Park and Thistledown, which were right across the street from one another. My job was to watch the horses come to the gate and make sure they weren't lame. Early on, I called the stewards and told them to take a horse out of the race. They said, "Let's get one thing straight here: You're going to *suggest* to us to take the horse out." I had a lot to learn.

I met Dr. [Gary] Lavin there. We'd spend the time waiting for the horses to come to the gate by trying to knock a can off a fence with clods of dirt. I developed quite a nice practice there. But I was still learning. The Ohio Derby that year was won by Traffic Judge, and I'm talking to the starter about how impressive he was, and he says, "What happened to that horse who broke down at the three-eighths pole?" And I sprinted to my car and drove like mad to get back onto the track, and the horse's front leg was broken off, hanging by a piece of skin. I pulled out some strychnine, which is what we used back then, gave it to him, and threw the syringe in the trunk. I look up, and here's the horse running toward the grandstand with his leg flapping. Buddy Cunningham, the assistant starter, ran him down, and I gave him some more strychnine and put him down. I've never been fired in my life, but I came close on that one. I learned a lesson to pay attention instead of hanging out and socializing.

LS: *How did the surgery practice begin?*
RC: I did my first surgery while standing on a hind leg. It was for a broken splint bone on the lateral side. I hadn't remembered from my anatomy class that the great metatarsal artery lies under that splint bone. I cut down on it, and nobody else had taken to doing that, but something in me said that this is the way I was going to make a reputation. So I cut down and removed the fractured splint bone with the great metatarsal artery right there. After I sewed it up and it worked out fine, I realized the Good Lord was watching over me that day that I didn't bust that artery.

LS: *What was a case that stands out for you?*
RC: I operated on Susan's Girl here for a broken sesamoid. She'd already won two championships [champion three-year-old filly of 1972 and champion older mare of 1973]. On the third postoperative day, she still hadn't eaten or taken a drink of water, and she was running a high fever. She demanded a lot of attention. I was giving her water through a stomach tube every six hours around the clock. I had worn out my assistant, and he didn't show up for the midnight procedure, and I was by myself, and there was no way I could put a twitch on and use a stomach tube and pump at the same time. And there were no cell phones back then.

So I said to her, "Well, old girl, we're up to our ass in mud here. So I'm gonna stick this tube in there and I need you to stand still. Just hold right there." And she never moved a muscle. I pumped the water into her, but she still wasn't eating or drinking on her own. So the next day I took a blood sample to the lab. My wife, Pat, was with me. I said to her, "I'm going to lose that filly, sure as hell. I've done everything, and I don't know what else to do." Pat said I ought to ask God for help. I was an agnostic. But I thought about what she said. So in a quiet moment, I said, "I know I've been a badass. I'm not asking for me, but it would be a shame to lose that filly. That's all I have to say."

When I got back, I went to the barn to look at her. The bucket of water was half gone; the feed was gone from the tub. And she recovered, and I've never since been denied anything that mattered that I've asked for.

Later that year she won a stake in Louisville, and the next year [1975] she was named champion older mare again, and she became the greatest money-winning female of all time [more than $1.2 million]. Mr. [Fred] Hooper owned her, and he didn't have much humor about him, but years later Susan's Girl had a foal and he called me up, trying to be funny. "I've got this little colt down here, a little runt, and he reminds me of you, and I'm going to name him Copelan," he says. I asked him who the sire was, and it was Tri Jet, on whom I'd also operated, and who set a track record at Saratoga that stood for a long time.

Copelan won a bunch of races [he was a three-time grade 1 winner of nearly six hundred thousand dollars] and looked like a contender for the Derby. But in the Blue Grass Stakes, Marfa, a horse I had treated earlier in the day with Lasix, comes over on Desert Wine, and Copelan got smacked into and bowed. And he was out for several months.

LS: *Any others?*

RC: Calumet had a two-year-old named Her Bull down at Hialeah in January 1972. He was making a noise, and I looked and found he was paralyzed on the left side of his throat. So I passed a tube down his trachea, and before you operate, you pump it up like a balloon at the far end to block it off. So we throw his head down—we're on beach sand outside the barn—anesthetize him, hog-tie him, and put him on his back. We stretch his neck and head, and I make the incision on the bottom of his throat and do the procedure. As we're getting done, he comes out of the anesthesia and jumps, and throws a bunch of that white sand into the incision. And I looked at the other doctor and said, "We killed this @#$%& horse."

But we still had the tube in there, so I pulled it up and instead of letting the air out of it, I pulled it up inflated and pulled all the blood and sand up with it to the incision site, and we poured water in there and cleaned it up best we could with gauze sponges. I thought about him all that night. Next day, he's perfectly OK. On July 4, 1972, Her Bull made his first start, at Belmont Park. Beat another first-time starter that day named Secretariat. That was one of the ones you look back on.

LS: *You became the go-to man for joint problems.*
RC: Any kind of orthopedic problem. I built my own surgery center here at the farm in 1966, and at the time that was probably one of the earliest facilities specifically for orthopedic surgery for horses in the country. I borrowed $100,000 to build it, and I had a lot of friends who sent horses that I operated on and that had good recoveries. I did one surgery per day.

I would do my racetrack work and then come here and start operating at four o'clock. If I was out of town in Miami or Chicago, I would fly back every Friday morning, and do surgery that afternoon. I don't know how I did it. I just did. If I thought about it . . . I just had to do it, and that's all there is to it. Yeah, I was tired. But I'd been given an opportunity, and gosh, nobody had that kind of a thing going. I had it, and I did the best with it that I could.

LS: *Were you conscious of being a mentor?*
RC: I was. It was important at the time, and I thought if anyone made the effort to come ask me to help them, there was no way I could turn them down. And it remains that way to this day. Of course, everybody knows everything now. What I knew then, maybe I was a little ahead.

LS: *Dr. [Larry] Bramlage said the most important thing he learned from you was ethics, and to speak up when a trainer tried to force a vet into doing something that wasn't the right thing.*
RC: Yeah, there was so much of that crap going on. There was a guy who graduated from Ohio State who said he was really going to make some money now treating these horses with all kinds of stuff. And I said, "Don't tell me that. You won't last doing that." And he didn't. You never treat horses illegally. If the rule is this way, you have to adhere to it. If you don't like it, raise some kind of hell about the rule. But don't let anybody say you ever did anything wrong. My dad always said that to me: "Keep your nose clean."

LS: *Did the Ruffian case change the way equine medicine evolved?*
RC: I was thankful I wasn't in on that. That was a thing where public opinion forced Bill Reed to make the decision to operate on a horse that had just come off the racetrack with all the anesthesia they had to give her right after an athletic

185

performance. They should have waited three days. Certainly, until the next day. Everybody had a bad taste about it. Among ourselves we talked about what could have been done. I think the possibility existed that maybe they could have put a cast on there.

LS: *You were instrumental in the success of Overbrook Farm.*
RC: A guy named W. T. Young called me one day. Didn't know him. Asked me to come over and look at an Alleged filly he had just bought on the advice of Joe Taylor and John Gaines, who were standing right there during my evaluation. So he was really putting me on the spot. They said they wanted to race her, and I said, "She might be a broodmare prospect, but you won't keep her racing sound because she's so badly calf-kneed." She was likely to fracture carpal bones if she raced. And they blanched.

I figured I'd never see Mr. Young again, but he calls me that night and says he wants to hire me. I did bloodstock work for him, which I'd never done previously. Looked at yearlings. Also got him Wayne Lukas as a trainer.

Larry [Bramlage] and I together operated on both Storm Cat and Grindstone. Storm Cat had a knee fracture, and he had it when he ran second to Tasso in the Breeders' Cup Juvenile. Mr. Young wanted us to correct that, and it was the early days of endoscopic surgery, which Larry was doing at Ohio State, so we took Storm Cat up there. And he came back and ran some.

LS: *And then turns into one of the great sires. Do you take pride in that?*
RC: You take pride only in retrospect. You're supposed to do what you do. You can't say, "Look what I did." After years go by, you think of some of these things and think that maybe your life wasn't all wasted.

LS: *And Grindstone?*
RC: We operated on both knees and both front ankles with the scope, under the same anesthesia. He had another fracture on a hind ankle, but we didn't operate on that because it would heal with the time necessary for what we did up front. That was August 18 of his two-year-old year. I didn't even know the horse's name at the time. In November, Lukas came in for the sale and asked me when that horse was coming back to him, because he was going to figure big in the Triple Crown. And I told him he was smoking that stuff again and people would catch him.

And sure enough, he wins the Arkansas Derby but then lost his next race, and I thought, "Triple Crown my ass." I was quick to condemn. Then he comes back and wins the Kentucky Derby. I go over to the barn afterward, and I'm standing at the sawhorse outside, and Marcelino, his groom, is walking

Grindstone and sees me standing there and brings the horse over. The horse put his head right in my chest. That was a tough deal, trying to keep my composure.

LS: *Talk about founding the American Association of Equine Practitioners (AAEP).*
RC: It was the year after I graduated, and a vet named Joe Solomon asked me what I thought about forming an organization of racetrack vets because there were guys out in California we never met, and it cost an arm and a leg to call them on the phone. I thought it sounded like a great idea. So three of us got together, wrote down the names of every vet we knew, and sent invitations to meet at the Brown Hotel in Louisville in December 1954. Eleven of us showed up on the third floor in the Louis XVI Room. We hammered out a constitution. We shared scientific information. Now we have ten thousand members in fifty countries. Of all the things I've been associated with, gosh, it's a big thing.

I graduated from OSU June 12, 1953, and I quit practicing June 12, 2018. Sixty-five years, and I said, "That's it for me. I'm never going to pick up another instrument." And the next day somebody called, and I was right back in it. But just vaccinating and doing a little bit of practice.

The horses have been a good life for me. I can't imagine what life would have been like without horses. They were my heroes. There were things they did when I knew that every breath they took was scorching down into their lungs, but they kept on, and that was the difference.

33

Dr. Gary Lavin

DR. GARY LAVIN IS as good a storyteller as he was a racetrack veterinarian. The grandson of a doctor and son of a racetrack executive, Lavin grew up on the track and left it only to establish his Longfield Farm outside Louisville. His family is racing through and through, with wife, Betsy, having served on the Kentucky Racing Commission, and their son Allan involved in bloodstock and son Kevin in equine insurance. Lavin, besides his doctoring duties, used his knowledge to establish a successful boarding and breeding business as well, partnering with the likes of his neighbor, the legendary breeder Warner Jones Jr. Majestic Prince, Pine Bluff, and Winning Colors are just a few of the headliners with whom Lavin was associated.

2009

Interviewed at Longfield Farm, Goshen, Kentucky

Lenny Shulman: *When did your family get involved with horses?*
Gary Lavin: There wasn't a horse person in the family when they came to Lexington from Ireland in the 1850s. My father went to training the West Coast string for Greentree, and then World War II broke out, and he put us on a train for El Paso while he got on a train with the Barnum & Bailey Circus. He came back from the war and worked on the gate crew at Oaklawn, Fair Grounds, Keeneland, and Churchill. He ended up being the racing secretary at Delaware, Oaklawn, Keeneland, Churchill, and Ellis Park.

I was around the racetrack my whole childhood. I was too young to get a license for the backside, so I worked in grandstand maintenance, straightening up the benches. I hung out in my father's office for scratch time, then went to work straightening benches and sweeping the roof and raising the flag at noon. On days when they had steeplechasing, there was a law you needed a stretcher and two bearers. So I had the high responsibility at Delaware of being one of the guys who had the stretcher at the water jump. And sure enough a horse fell. The jock didn't get hurt, but we made him lay down on the stretcher anyway and carried him off.

LS: *How did the doctoring begin?*
GL: Every kid on the backside wanted to be a veterinarian because the veterinarians were independent and they drove big cars and most of them were fairly clean and respectable. And they could talk fairly well. But it was the independence more than anything that was attractive. We didn't realize, in fact, that they worked for everybody. Plus, my grandfather was a doctor.

Until I graduated medical school at Penn, I spent part of every summer at Delaware, then we'd go wherever there was an opening. The best place was Randall Park, which was the best racing Ohio ever saw and ever will see. It so happened that the racetrack vet there at the time was Bob Copelan, before he got important and went to Arlington.

Dr. Jack Robbins would come out to Delaware whenever a California horse shipped in, and he would spend afternoons in my father's office talking horses. Johnny Longden would come in to ride them on that deep Delaware surface, and he had a pom-pom on his hat, and I used to kid Robbins that by the time they got to the quarter pole you could see that little pom-pom going to the back of the field. He'd laugh and pull out another cigarette.

LS: *You settled outside Louisville at some point?*
GL: Betsy and I got married in 1960. When I got out of school, I didn't want to move around, and my father's farm was right up the road here. Joe O'Farrell, who my father knew, told me one very important thing: If you're going to be in one place all the time, you better know something about broodmares. Which I knew nothing about. I got to ride with Dr. William McGee for a winter in Lexington, and the following spring I came here to work for Warner Jones at Hermitage. Years later we became great friends, but I couldn't work for him.

He decided at some point that palpating mares messed up their cycle and wasn't good for them, so he decided not to palpate mares anymore, which took most of my work away. I decided to go find something else to do, but we did buy a piece of land on the back corner of his farm, and we learned more from him . . .

A couple years later, I bought a Court Martial mare, and Warner calls and asks what I'm planning to do with her. I had claimed her for $6,500, which was a lot of money for me, and I told him I'd like to breed her to Bold Hour, but I don't have a season to him. He said he'd get one, and I hemmed and hawed, and he said, "You'll make more money owning half of that mare with me than you will owning it all by yourself." Well, he was right. He could be truthful once in a while. We bred her to Bold Hour and took the filly up there as a yearling and got thirty thousand dollars for her. The next year we took a Crimson Satan up there on a ten-thousand-dollar stud fee and got sixty thousand dollars. She became the granddam of Rodrigo de Triano, who won the Guineas, and that's one of our main claims to fame.

Betsy and I had four mares and started up the farm, and we began having success selling yearlings. We didn't own any more mares with Warner Jones, but we syndicated a number of horses together and did very well with that, except I sold my share in Raja Baba too soon, but everyone makes those kinds of mistakes.

We've sold yearlings for $250,000, $500,000. You might say, "So what" anymore, but we were paying ten thousand dollars for the mare and selling them off a ten-thousand-dollar stud fee.

LS: *And you were working at the track at the same time?*
GL: At that time, it was the glory days for horse racing. We didn't have things like Lasix and flexible endoscopes, the ruination of any normal lifestyle. I was the track vet at Miles Park for a couple of years—you can do anything when you're twenty-eight—and the farm was a sideline. I never would take jobs where my father worked because I never wanted someone to think he was doing me a favor. But I took one at Miles Park. I had to be there early in the morning, and I could do all my work by lunchtime, come back to the farm, and be back for night racing. Made for long days—maybe that's why we only had two children (*laughs*).

There was plenty of farmwork at the time. Warner had four or five stallions; farms in Bowling Green and Indiana I did work for. We've always been lucky enough to have one core patron that allowed us to go on. When Dan Lassiter left to build his operation in Ocala, he left his Kentucky mares with us. In 1989 we bought the Hermitage annex, and ten years later we bought another farm, so we have seven hundred acres all together.

LS: *How did your vet work change through the years?*
GL: It was much simpler years ago. Seems like everything we did cost six dollars. That was a shot of antibiotics; floating teeth. There was a scope, but it was a straight rod. The racetrack has changed so much from what it was early on. I think Sunday racing is one of the worst things to have happened for the people and the infrastructure of horse racing. It took the culture and turned it upside down. Every Sunday in the summers my father would pack up the car and we'd go to Washington, DC, Gettysburg, Valley Forge, Philadelphia, New York City. Racetrack families don't do that today. When we had our own family, I could do

my job at the racetrack in Kentucky and get back in time to drive to Cincinnati and we'd watch the Bengals play.

LS: *You had a pretty good stretch working on Kentucky Derby winners.*
GL: My favorite story is Majestic Prince in 1969. A week before the Derby, my father carded a three-horse race for Majestic Prince, Fast Hilarious, who was a really fast horse from Chicago; and a gray horse from Texas whose name I don't remember. They were going seven furlongs, and at the half-mile pole Majestic Prince takes off after Fast Hilarious, and he's ten lengths in front before they got to the three-eighths. The Derby comes up, and Majestic Prince just does beat Arts and Letters [by a neck].

The Derby winner would be the last stop I'd make on my rounds before I called it quits. So by the time I get there, it's dark. All the lights are off in the barn except one—I could go right to that stall today—Barn 39, the second stall. The one light that's on is in that stall. Majestic Prince's groom, a pencil-thin Hungarian named Valentino Szot, is sitting there rubbing on the horse's legs, saying, "The Kentucky Derby. The Kentucky Derby." He was absolutely overcome. Damn near brings tears to my eyes.

Dust Commander the next year was fun because his trainer, Don Combs, is a good friend and was a client at the time. Canonero in 1971 was a story. They made one attempt to fly him here, and they had to turn the plane around and go back to Miami. They wouldn't put him on another plane. He got to Churchill after a van ride and looked absolutely awful. And nobody could speak English. Joe Rodriguez, who was in the paddock for years hanging saddle numbers, would come over every day, find out what had to be done, and then we'd give the horse fluids. He was obviously a good horse down in Florida but had to overcome that plane ride to win the Derby.

LS: *That's three in a row for you.*
GL: Copelan and I used to keep track of who treated more Derby winners. The year [trainer Johnny] Campo came in with Pleasant Colony [1981] the vet who came in with him didn't have a Kentucky license, so I wrote out the health certificate. And when he won, I claimed to Copelan that counted in my column. He went crazy.

I could have had another one in 1982. Hostage was going to win the Derby by as far as you could throw a rock. He beat El Baba in the Arkansas Derby from here to the church. The trainer, Mike Freeman, wanted to work him the Saturday or Sunday before the race, but his rider, Don MacBeth, had big mounts out of town both days, and he comes in Monday to work Hostage. Hostage breaks a sesamoid during the work, and that was the end of his career. Mrs. Hexter, who bred and owned him, came by wanting to see the X-rays. She's quite proper, and I show her the ankle fracture, and she says, "Gentlemen, I thank you for taking such good care of my horse." And she reaches inside her Burberry raincoat, pulls out a pint, unscrews it, and says, "Would you like a sip?" And she takes a big slug.

We raised [Preakness winner] Pine Bluff for Loblolly Stable. We sold his sister Angel Fever. We went out to Stone Farm to see her yearling by Mr. Prospector. Arthur [Hancock] leads out this horse, and he absolutely stops you. He was ready to go in the ring right then and there. But his momma was nutty as a fruitcake, and I didn't know if he'd like the sales experience. Pine Bluff could lead the Mardi Gras parade and never turn a hair, but Angel Fever, you never knew what she was going to do. But that was Fusaichi Pegasus [2000 Kentucky Derby winner]. He had presence, and that makes a big difference. He was a sale topper who won the Derby, and I said at the time he was the best-looking yearling I'd seen since Royal Academy.

Devil's Bag won the Derby Trial in 1984 and was going to be the next Secretariat. Champion two-year-old and multiple grade 1 winner. So he wins the Trial, but not like you thought he would. [Trainer] Woody [Stephens] is sick, and he's not coming around, and Claiborne, which is handling his syndication, sends word to go over the horse and see if I can find anything. I'm not going to tell you everything we found, but it was enough. I called Seth [Hancock] and told him the horse's career was over, and he asks if I'll call the owner to talk about it.

Well, I'm not good at that. But I called Mr. [James] Mills and told him what was wrong in one leg, and he said, "Isn't that too bad?" And then I told him what was wrong somewhere else, and we went through that three different times, because there were three things there that would have put an end to any horse. He couldn't have been more gracious and was so concerned for the horse. Those are the kind of people who make this business worthwhile.

34

Dr. Larry Bramlage

WHEN ANYTHING GOES WRONG with a prominent horse anywhere in the United States today, you can bet your bottom dollar on trainers and owners saying the following: "We're sending him/her to Dr. Bramlage for evaluation." And if the horse isn't sent to **Dr. Larry Bramlage,** its X-rays are. Like Dr. Copelan before him, Bramlage is a product of the Ohio State University Veterinary College. He eventually made his way to Lexington to serve in the capital of the Thoroughbred world at Rood & Riddle Equine Hospital. Bramlage was establishing himself as the practice of arthroscopy was in its infancy and became its most prominent practitioner. Bramlage will always be known as the doctor who saved Personal Ensign and enabled one of the most storied runners in history to thrive, but in truth his clientele is a who's who of Thoroughbred history books. His published papers have pushed the industry forward, and his energy in aiding horses seems indefatigable.

2014

Interviewed at Rood & Riddle Equine Hospital, Lexington

Lenny Shulman: *How did you get involved in horses?*
Larry Bramlage: Not by design at all. My grandfather had a pensioned Thoroughbred, and when we were kids, we'd ride him on the weekends when we visited. My dad worked for a cattle company, and we always had quarter horses that we moved the cattle with. I was a junior in college when I first went to Fonner Park [in Nebraska] to watch horses train. I thought the training of Thoroughbreds was the most amazing thing I ever saw, so I kept going back. If you had to draw a horse, to me the Thoroughbred is what a horse should look like.

Eventually I started going to the races at AkSarBen in Omaha. I thought I might want to go to the racetrack and practice. When I was close to graduating Kansas State, the head of the equine section said I should consider doing surgery. So I interned at Colorado State with Dr. O. R. Adams, who wrote the original lameness book, and I ended up doing a residency at Ohio State. And I got interested in bones around the time Dr. Bruce Hohn, an orthopedic surgeon, began bringing screws and plates in from Switzerland. The first courses for bone plating were held at the veterinary school. Originally, it was all done on cadaver limbs; today it's done on plastic limbs.

LS: *You became known for your arthroscopic work.*
LB: As luck would have it, the arthroscope came along just as I got interested in orthopedics. A sequence of fortuitous events. I also went to the first human arthroscopy course in Ohio. At that point, they only used the arthroscope for human knees and horse stifles. I started coming to Kentucky and doing some arthroscopic surgeries with Dr. Copelan on a regular basis. Nelson Bunker Hunt's Bluegrass Farm had 180 mares before he tried to buy all the silver in the world, and I'd come down every week and operate at the surgical facility they had there. Mr. Hunt would come into the recovery stall with us and talk horses.

Three years later, when I was the head of equine medicine and surgery at Ohio State, I realized I didn't have the patience to be an administrator, so I took a position at Rood & Riddle.

LS: *How did that grow into what it has become, where everybody everywhere confers with you?*
LB: It's important to specialize. There's no substitute for experience in an area. I've been asked if I'm tired of doing arthroscopy and taking out ankle chips. It's still very interesting to me because the pathology of the disease is not simply taking a stone out of your shoe. It's not just the piece in the joint. That piece sheds debris in the inside of the joint that disrupts the normal lubrication mechanism, and that interests me. So having a specialty is key.

Secondly, we've done a pretty good job of using our experience as the laboratory for the veterinary profession to determine what the prognosis for a problem is. We've done thirty or forty papers on the follow-up results of treatment of condylar fractures, stress fractures, sesamoid fractures, OCDs. We keep looking at problems and whether or not you treat them with surgery, and write papers. That experience adds up and is a big plus. You don't know the percentages unless you take those horses and go back and look at an injury and see how many of them raced and how well they raced. We've published quite a few papers that way. And we've perfected surgical techniques along the way.

I was lucky enough to develop the surgical procedure for fusion in the fetlock joint, where there wasn't any solution for that back in Ruffian's day. I was interested in biomechanics and in bone plating, and I spent a lot of time in the post-mortem room, and we finally came up with a surgical technique that worked. A horse in New York named Noble Dancer got the same ruptured suspensory apparatus as Ruffian, and they called. We did the surgery and it worked, and he became a stallion. Then we did Saratoga Six, and then a lot of [prospective] stallions and broodmares. So that surgical procedure established the credentials.

LS: *You are famously associated with the great and undefeated Personal Ensign.*
LB: That was a milestone as well. She split that pastern, and when [trainer] Shug [McGaughey] called, he said they just wanted to save her as a broodmare. We did the surgery, and she came together so well I told him I thought she had a chance to race again. He didn't believe me. But she kept getting better and better and was ready to train. She went back and trained well and went on to do what she did. That procedure took the injuries you put together with screws and gave them the kind of credibility that not only were they possible, but they were practical. Now we don't think too much about it when a horse with a condylar fracture comes back. Little Mike won the 2012 Breeders' Cup Turf and the Arlington Million. Condylar fractures are not big stories anymore.

But the first horse that really proved you could do that was Personal Ensign. She fractured her pastern after her second race and comes back and wins eleven more in a row. That's still amazing. I don't think I appreciated how hard it is for a horse to be right—like her and Cigar, who won sixteen in a row—every time you lead them over there. It's a special horse that can do that every time, who doesn't say, "I'm not running today."

LS: *Is the number of consultations you're asked to do overwhelming?*
LB: It's difficult sometimes. Digital X-rays are a plus and a minus. It used to be you at least had the time it took for a client to FedEx the X-rays. Nowadays they say, "I just sent you a set of X-rays. Have you looked at them yet?" Sometimes I want to say, "Yes, I was just sitting here hoping you'd send me something." I get about twenty-five to thirty sets a day, plus the stuff we do here. Sometimes I get a backlog. We try to do them for our clients, and certainly for all the people in this practice. Over time, the doctors here learn what my opinion is, and they gain more experience themselves. The farms, when they're surveying their yearlings and if the right yearling has a problem—if he was supposed to be the mail carrier this year—that's an emergency for them.

LS: *How do you let down after doing surgeries all day?*
LB: We have a small place up near Georgetown where we raise cattle. That's therapeutic for me. When I've had a busy day in surgery like today, where we operated from 7:30 a.m. to 5:00 p.m., it's a change to go feed the cattle, and it recharges me.

If I just went home and had nothing going on, I'd crash in a chair and go to sleep. Your adrenaline has been up all day long. We have twenty-four cows, and they're calving right now, so that gives me something else to do.

LS: *Are there common injuries by age, from babies through broodmares and stallions?*
LB: Absolutely, even within each season of a racehorse's career. We see the OCDs in the yearlings, which are accidents of bone formation that happen for different reasons, but especially when they're growing fast. A horse reaches maturity in two years, and they also grow to five times the size of a normal person, so that's a factor of twenty in horses compared to humans. If bone formation gets disturbed by an accident or a bruise, it might end up with a fragment.

When horses get to training, we see an epidemic of stress fractures in shins—the advance form of bucked shins—which always start around November of their two-year-old year and run through the following March. Horses aren't born with racehorse skeletons; they literally mold them into what they need to do in response to exercise. In their first three or four starts, there are a lot of knee chips because that's when the horse's lungs, heart, and muscles have matured enough so they're peaking, but the skeleton is slower to come along.

With older horses, ankle chips are an occupational hazard. The fetlock goes in full extension and they hit in front. If you take a horse from a solid track to a deep track, that can happen. With racehorses, most injuries are products of stress fractures or multiple loads. No one load is heavy enough to break a bone, but if you do that same load over and over, it accumulates damage. Some horses will break down no matter how you train them, and some are so tough that they can take whatever you throw at them. Serena's Song raced thirty-four times in three years, and retired clean-legged, and then she became a good producer. She's an example of a horse that can take anything.

LS: *Is there an optimal time to start a racing career?*
LB: It's a mistake to try and do that by the calendar. Remember in fifth grade when some guys were already shaving? Some horses mature early and may be good two-year-olds, but the ones that develop at three and four will be way better and pass them by. Each horse develops at its own rate, and training each horse according to its progress is far better than training to the calendar.

But it is important that all horses train as two-year-olds. I don't know how that wives' tale that we train them before they mature still hangs on. Every scientific study shows that horses that start training at two do better. And it makes sense. When they reach maturity at two, if you don't give the cells and that blood supply a reason to hang out, they atrophy away. If you wait until three, you have to re-create that support system. It doesn't mean you have to race at two, but you need to train at two.

LS: *Has the breed changed in a significant way?*
LB: The commercial market has had an effect. Go back to the 1950s, when the Vanderbilts, Phippses, and Galbreaths were selecting the stallions. They selected the horses that were good to them over a long period of time, selecting for durability through three or four or more years of racing. Today we select for brilliance as a two-year-old, for speed. And the two-year-old who shows speed and precociousness is doing that on genetic ability, and will breed truer than a horse who got good because he was trained into being good. So we're selecting more for brilliance and less for longevity.

I think we have changed the breed. If I remember correctly, just looking at height, the Thoroughbred is a hand taller today than he was in 1900. So we've obviously changed their height. And I think we've also changed the look of the Thoroughbred from the time I first saw them at Fonner Park. I went to the first Gold Cup in Singapore, and they were tall, angular horses that stood knock-kneed. Here, our Thoroughbreds are broader-chested and have the tendency to be offset in the knees, and have more speed. We don't reward the long career. Kitten's Joy might be a big surprise that way.

LS: *What are the biggest factors that lead to injury?*
LB: The easiest thing to pinpoint is year-round racing. It used to be there was an enforced one- or two-month break, and that was important because that's the time needed for a horse to recover from being track-sour. The horse that's overtrained loses form, with pain mostly coming from the bottom of the cannon bones.

LS: *What about medication?*
LB: I think we're better now in managing horses than we were ten or fifteen years ago. We've moved to short-acting steroids where you get the job done and the steroid goes away and you get the chance to read the horse again. If you used just long-acting steroids, that can lead to a horse getting injured. If you inject him too often you have some residual steroid from the last injection, and you lose track of where the horse is. He can't show you his problem.

Thresholds for uniform medication recommendations are based upon the idea that the medications we use aren't bad; it's how we use them that can be bad. Drugs that last the longest are more apt to hurt horses. You can't have more than one nonsteroidal aboard at the same time. It's not appropriate now to have medication in a horse that renders you unable to know where that horse is.

LS: *Which are the horses that stand out to you for having come back from adversity?*
LB: I have two favorite horses. Personal Ensign, because she was kind of a landmark. And Rachel Alexandra, because she was owned, originally, by Dolphus Morrison and Michael Lauffer, who were not big-time horse people. They thought she had some talent, and then she gets this big chunk in her ankle in November as a two-year-old. [Trainer] Hal Wiggins was about to go to Oaklawn for the winter, and we take it out and she does really well and comes back and does what she did. That Kentucky Oaks she ran—the best race I ever saw was Personal Ensign winning the Breeders' Cup Distaff—I was yelling for her. But Rachel's Oaks was on a par with maybe Secretariat's Belmont in the way she just ran off and left everybody. And she did it for those people for whom she was their first big horse. So she's a favorite of mine because of the connections and what she did for them.

Part *VI*

Kentucky Derby–Winning Owners

THE MOST DIFFICULT INTERVIEWS I'VE HAD TO DO THROUGH THE YEARS HAVE BEEN THOSE IMMEDIATELY FOLLOWING THE KENTUCKY DERBY. FOR TWENTY YEARS, MY ASSIGNMENT was writing a story on the winning owner, which, on the surface, seems like it should be fairly easy. However, in the minutes and even hours after someone accomplishes a lifelong dream, they rarely are sufficiently composed to transfer their feelings and emotions into words. Yes, they are ecstatic; they just can't communicate very well until gaining a measure of perspective.

And make no mistake: Winning the Kentucky Derby is the foremost dream of nearly every owner who gets into the game of Thoroughbred horse racing, at least those in the United States. The Derby winner's circle at Churchill Downs—which is used only once per year—represents the most valuable piece of real estate in the sport. Some spend a fortune trying to get there; others run lucky and hoist the Derby trophy after more modest outlays. It is winning the World Series and the Super Bowl and the lottery all wrapped into one.

"It's hard to put into words." "I can't express how I feel." "It's unbelievable." "It hasn't sunk in yet." These are the answers that come in the immediacy of a Derby victory and in the postrace press conference. The toasts haven't yet been offered, and the alcohol, which tends to loosen the thoughts and the vocal cords, has yet to be consumed. Dozens of viewings of the race replay will come when the winning owners return to their homes. And dozens of subsequent meetings with business associates and perfect strangers who, when they discover a person owns horses, ask if they've ever made it to the Kentucky Derby, and then, if they've ever won it.

Those who can answer "Yes" make up a most elite club.

Occasionally, I had the benefit of interviewing Derby winners far removed from the magical day(s) in which they carried the roses and spoils of their triumph at Churchill Downs. Those conversations are presented herein. I was also fortunate enough to write up, at one time or another, nearly every person who has won multiple Kentucky Derbys since Calumet Farm's domination of the race in the mid-twentieth century. Interviews with a couple of these multiple winners appeared in previous chapters—Penny Chenery and her Meadow Stable are included in the "Legends of the Industry" section, and Arthur Hancock III and his Stone Farm appeared in the "Kentucky Hardboots" section.

35

Bob and Beverly Lewis

BOB AND BEVERLY LEWIS burst on the racing scene in the 1990s from their Southern California base and became the faces of Thoroughbred racing in the United States. Unfailingly upbeat, Bob Lewis seemed to see the world through rose-colored glasses, and for good reason. Nearly everything he touched turned to racing and breeding gold. He and Beverly raced top colts and fillies, made stallions, and sold successfully at sales. The former beer distributor and philanthropist found good even in the most dire circumstances. Needing a Heimlich maneuver one evening to avoid choking, Lewis later said the problem was caused by a "delightful piece of chicken." The Lewises' horses were truly delightful—they raced not only Derby and Preakness winners Silver Charm (1997) and Charismatic (1999) but also the Hall of Fame race mare Serena's Song, who became an illustrious broodmare for them.

2004

Interviewed in Newport Beach, California

Lenny Shulman: *What was it about racing that first attracted you?*
Bob Lewis: I hate to admit it, but I went to the races when Santa Anita opened in 1934 and when Del Mar opened in 1937. It was a family ritual to go to the races on Saturdays. What impressed me is it seemed to attract a meaningful group of people—the men in handsome, double-breasted suits and felt hats, and the women in their lovely styles. It seemed like an uplifting place to go. My parents were enthusiastic about horse racing even though we were in the midst of the Depression.

I can't truthfully say the horses grabbed me right away. But then I had the opportunity to see Seabiscuit and the other great horses of that era, and they left a lasting impression. The first year Beverly and I were married we went to the Santa Anita Handicap, and Vulcan's Forge won and paid forty-five dollars, and we had a couple of dollars on him and thought it was all the money in the world.

LS: *Mrs. Lewis, did you know you were in trouble when you spent your honeymoon at the racetrack?*

(*Left to right*) Robert Lewis, Beverly Lewis, and Bob Baffert (Keeneland Association by Bill Straus)

Beverly Lewis: When we began dating at the University of Oregon we'd go on dates to the racetrack in Portland, Portland Meadows. And he was so lucky.

BL: I always say that's why she married me. I couldn't get her to say "yes" until I showed her my winning ways at the racetrack. And it was absolutely dumb luck. We'd go on Friday nights and have a delightful time. I got Beverly back to her sorority house after-hours and snuck her through the side door.

LS: *Did you decide at a young age you wanted to get involved in horses?*

BL: The first ten years of our marriage, we starved. I worked for breweries in Northern California and sold to the racetracks up there. Later, I actually delivered the beer to Santa Anita, which was one of my largest-volume customers. I would take the beer there and eventually would go out in a supervisory capacity and hang out at Clocker's Corner during racing season once or twice a week. One day my sales manager ran into a friend whose son had just begun training, and we had reached a position where we could justify investing in Thoroughbreds. That was 1990.

LS: *I read where you said racing represented a new dimension in your lives.*

BevL: It's taken over.

LS: *In a way you probably couldn't have foreseen in 1990.*
BL: Oh, good God, no. You couldn't expect it. The first two horses we bought were at the inaugural Barrett's sale. One was a filly named Destiny's Devine who we realized after six weeks was a wobbler and had to be put down. The second one was a colt named Deduction who finally won in his eleventh start, up at Pleasanton. For some unknown reason—why we didn't pull the plug on it at that time I don't know—we had gotten just hooked enough. I don't know why, because we certainly hadn't had any great experience of winning anything.

We have a daughter who at the time was a sorority sister at the University of Arizona with a young lady named Melissa Baffert, who was a cousin to Bob. So we would talk at Clocker's Corner, and one day I ducked my head in his barn and said, "Bob, if you're looking for a client for a horse, call me and maybe we can make some music together." He bought us a horse named Ebonair, who won the California Cup Juvenile in 1991. That's the first time we'd been to a winner's circle.

LS: *Were there tough lessons to be learned at the beginning?*
BL: No, I didn't know any better from that standpoint. As a practice businesswise, if I employed a manager or executive in a position of responsibility, I always felt it was in our collective best interests to let them run with it. I employed them, I gave them the opportunity to excel, and most of the time it worked. When it didn't, we would stop and make a change. And I believe that with horse trainers. I don't select these horses. The trainers do. My philosophy is if they're only interested in getting their day money and filling a stall, I'm not interested in them.

On the other hand, if they're aggressive in their approach—when I went with Bob Baffert he was a struggling young trainer who hadn't won the Breeders' Cup with Thirty Slews yet. Or if they have a meaningful record—about that same time I joined with Wayne Lukas, who was far and away the leading standard for trainers in the industry. Wayne and Bob have become great friends of ours, and we enjoy their company and the association.

LS: *Did you have a business plan starting out? Was it possible to run your horse operation as you would your other businesses?*
BL: (*laughing*). There wasn't anything particularly unique at the beginning. After the first ones didn't work out, we went on and bought a few more, kind of got into it with both feet, and somewhere along the line our level of enthusiasm was heightened, and we got into it pretty good.

Along with the brewing business and Anheuser-Busch distributorships, I owned a number of automobile dealerships. And that taught me about keeping your hands in a multiplicity of areas. A car dealership has new car sales, which they don't make any money on; used car sales, where maybe you can generate a profit; and parts and maintenance, which governs. If you're pulling your weight in your maintenance department, it's covering your overhead, and you can make a profit.

Beverly and I had the experience of having a filly such as Serena's Song. She won $3.3 million on the racetrack, and now she has foaled seven foals for us, and as a result there has been a multiplicity of highly respected offspring which have brought in a whole bunch of money. We're also fortunate enough to be standing three stallions right now, and have had the good fortune to have covered a lot of our expenses in the horse business through them. We have broodmares that are exceedingly well-bred.

Silver Charm is now the top second-year stallion in the country. So it's important to have multiple areas of income that can offset expenses.

LS: *Among stallions, breeding and selling, racing, or pinhooking, what is the area of greatest profit?*
BL: Well, we learned quickly we shouldn't be in the pinhooking business. We tried that, and it didn't work out. We've been fortunate with the stallions, and they've complemented the bottom line. Exploit brought a lot of money. Charismatic was sold to Japan. We sold Composure and Orientate for good sums.

LS: *How much of your success is luck, and how much is having the right people?*
BL: That's very easy. In my opinion, 60 percent is the horse, 20 percent might be the right trainer, and 20 percent the jockey. Every horse has only so many races in him, and Wayne and Bob have been so successful in bringing the horse, their training skills, and the jockey skills together on the first Saturday in May, and that's what it's all about.

LS: *Talk about the Kentucky Derby.*
BL: It's the biggest thrill we've had.
BevL: Especially the first one. Then the second one came along, and it was just as exciting.
BL: When you're standing out there, you're like, "This just can't be." You're pinching yourself trying to determine if it's for real. Beverly's knees were quivering. There are other great events in racing leading up to the Derby and magnificent races after, but nothing equals the Derby. You're standing out there in the face of 140,000 other people, and they're screaming their heads off for your horse after

you've won. And there are the other thrills like the walkover from the backside to the saddling area, and all the people along the way. It's awe-inspiring.

LS: *Everyone knows about Silver Charm, but can you talk about Charismatic, who actually ran in a claiming race?*
BL: He was the combination of hope, disappointment, and courage. I refer to him as our six-week horse. He first showed his ability with a second in the Bay Meadows Derby, then was fourth in the Santa Anita Derby. Wayne called and said, "Bob, I think I've found the key to this animal." And I said, "Who are you talking about?" He said, "Charismatic. I'm finding the more I work this horse, the happier he becomes. When I put the coal to him, he's responding and getting better." He asked if I'd agree to run him in the Lexington Stakes, and sure enough he won it. Two weeks later he won the Derby. Two weeks later he won the Preakness. I believe the reason we didn't win the Belmont is because it was a three-week span. He laid off too long (*laughs*). It all happened in six or seven weeks.

Of course, we didn't know until the day after the Belmont the horse had an opportunity to be saved from his broken leg. Charismatic seemed to sense everyone attending him were working in his behalf, and he was a marvelous patient.

LS: *You used Chris Antley, who was down-and-out with substance abuse problems, to ride Charismatic. You've been outspoken in your support of Pat Valenzuela, who has had similar issues. Are you attracted to underdogs?*
BL: Having been in the alcohol industry all my life and having dealt with recovery facilities, it is my opinion that we do people with those illnesses a grave injustice if we give up on them. I think it's our moral responsibility to stay after it and realize you don't recover from alcohol or drug usage overnight. You may have to go back on numerous occasions and go through it again. I've had many employees go through rehabilitation who have come back and done a really marvelous job, and their whole lives are opened up again for them.

When you see a young man like Pat Valenzuela with the talent he possesses— and it's true of Chris as well—there is something about that man that can communicate with a horse. During his last break from racing he was in my employ—he would go to retail outlets and the people just loved him. That positive spirit and personality he possesses was as evident there as it has been in the Thoroughbred industry, and I want him to have every opportunity.

I believe there are certain people who have an innate ability to communicate with the horse. That may sound crazy, but somehow that animal senses the positiveness of that person who is riding or training him.

LS: *I spoke with Bob Baffert the other day, and he said the thing about you is you can come out to the races for a twenty-thousand-dollar claimer and have as much fun as you do for a stakes race.*

BL: That's true.

BevL: It's exciting no matter what.

BL: To hit that winner's circle is always good. If you're an owner and winning 20 percent of the time, you are really doing well. You also are losing 80 percent of the time and getting really calloused. If I've learned anything over the last fourteen years, it's that it does take an investment, and you have to have a multitude of horses. Right now, Beverly and I have twenty-seven two-year-olds, and foolishly or otherwise, I'm going back to Kentucky and maybe buying more.

If you get one out of that group who does really well . . . if you get one out of every ten horses, you'd be in clover. Because that one can pay for the other nine. Or it can happen that he pays for the whole twenty-seven. We were too new and naïve at the beginning to truly recognize what we had. Serena's Song won, what was it, eleven grade 1 races? There we were, a couple of California dummies who didn't know much.

LS: *When people see you on TV, their impression of you is you're one of the happiest men on earth. How close is that to the truth?*

BL: I have the blessing of looking at everything in a very positive way. I enjoy being optimistic and being enthused about doing things. I'm a product of the Depression era, and that has had some bearing on my outlook. I saw my father suffer significant business losses, and I recognize what that did to him. But he accomplished a great deal and was the legislative representative for the brewing industry in Sacramento.

In the late forties and early fifties we used to entertain distributors, and they'd be talking about going to great nightspots and traveling to Europe and Hawaii, and Beverly and I couldn't afford to get out of San Mateo. By 1956 I started in business with Anheuser-Busch. I drove a truck, and Beverly kept the books. We had one employee. When we sold the business recently, we had 250 employees. We've been fortunate to have growth everywhere we turned.

LS: *You've been an active member on many boards in horse racing. Why is that important to you?*

BL: This industry has been so good to Beverly and me, it seems only right and fair to give back. I think you have a responsibility to get involved. One of this industry's biggest failings is the trainers have run the show, and the owners succumb to their wishes. If you're going to be critical or offer any kind of analysis of the industry, you'd better get in and express your feelings and put yourself in a position where you can have some influence.

LS: *Talk about your involvement with philanthropy and various causes.*
BL: We created the Bob and Beverly Lewis Family Cancer Care Center about ten years ago in Pomona. It's a free-standing facility with two linear accelerators; sophisticated equipment. We have the blessing of people coming to us and saying, "You made the concluding period of life for my [relative] much more pleasant." Or, "I'm a survivor of cancer and appreciate that very much."

At our alma mater, the University of Oregon, we have the Robert and Beverly Lewis Neuro-Imaging Center doing brain research. I've served on various hospital boards and support all kinds of equine activities like Grayson Jockey Club.

LS: *Do you get recognized when you're out at the grocery?*
BevL: It happens much more often to Bob, not as much to me.
BL: What do you mean, not as much? You're the beauty of the group.

LS: *So it's been a good idea, getting involved with horses?*
BL: We've had absolutely the most phenomenal and exciting career. We've had such good fortune, certainly more than we deserve. If you put us on a comparative basis with others in racing, there are many who through generations of families have invested huge amounts of money and never won the Kentucky Derby. And they've had magnificent horses. And here we are, a couple of dumb yokels, who have won it twice.

36

Paul Reddam

AS A FORMER UNIVERSITY logistics instructor, **Paul Reddam** would have realized the odds against winning the Kentucky Derby once, let alone twice. But that didn't stop the Canadian-born Reddam from switching to Thoroughbreds after an initial dive into the harness racing world. After settling in California and developing and then selling a popular mortgage company, Reddam stepped up his involvement in horses, yet has managed to do more with less. Playing in the middle of the market, and in concert with trainer Doug O'Neill and his brother, bloodstock agent Dennis O'Neill, Reddam has reached the mountaintop twice, when I'll Have Another won the 2012 Derby and Preakness, and Nyquist turned the Derby trick in 2016. Our first interview came nearly a decade *before* his first Derby victory. His story was updated, of course, after his success in Louisville.

2003

Interviewed at Santa Anita Park, California

Lenny Shulman: *It's well known you're a fan of hockey and the Detroit Red Wings, but how did you become a fan of horse racing?*
Paul Reddam: Traditionally, Canadians have always been involved in harness racing. Where I'm from—in Ontario—there's a track every fifty miles. So I grew up on the harness races. In high school, my best friend was a groom at Windsor Raceway, our home track just across the border from Detroit. He used to bug me to go out, and I finally did and caught the fever.

The first time I was even at a Thoroughbred race was after I moved out to California in 1979. Out of curiosity I went to Santa Anita at the time when Spectacular Bid was a four-year-old and dominating the big races. I still have a vivid memory of the Big 'Cap—there were only four horses—Bid, Flying Paster, Relaunch, and a horse I don't remember. I bet every dime I had on a Bid-Flying Paster exacta, and down the backside Relaunch was way out in front, and I said, "Oh, shit, I'm going to be broke." But sure enough at the wire it was the Bid by five

208

or six and then Paster by ten. I wasn't used to the way Thoroughbred races went. But that was a powerful experience.

LS: *How did you get into ownership?*
PR: I had gotten a scholarship from the Canadian government to work on my PhD at USC, and I was teaching logic there. USC waived my tuition, so I had extra money and bought a Standardbred with my old high school friend. He raced back in Canada. Eventually I talked my friend into moving here. I had a student whose husband was a doctor, and I convinced him and some of his doctor pals to cough up some money, and we bought a few Standardbreds who raced at Hollywood Park.

LS: *And the move to Thoroughbreds?*
PR: I had a few claimers in the nineties, and then decided to get back into it around 2000. I asked my attorney to interview some trainers, and he came back and said Wally Dollase's son Craig seemed enthusiastic. He had won the Breeders' Cup Sprint in 1998 with Reraise, so he seemed like a good choice. He earned my trust by going to a sale in Ocala with my OK to buy some horses, and he didn't buy anything. And I thought, "How unusual is this?" I still hadn't met him, and normally if you told somebody you'd never met to go buy a horse or two, they'd come back with three or four.

He bought one horse at the Keeneland sale that year—Zillah the Hun, who ended up winning a graded stakes. I thought that was pretty good on Craig's part. Then he bought Swept Overboard out of the 505 dispersal, and that turned out well.

LS: *Did you have a business plan for the Thoroughbreds?*
PR: The answer there would be "No." There's no grand plan. You hear of the 80/20 rule in business, that 80 percent of the production is done by 20 percent of the people? In Thoroughbreds, it's the 95/5 rule. Ninety-five percent of the people will lose, and 5 percent will get all the money. I think that we've been very lucky. My goal was really to have a good time and not blow too much money. When we sold Swept Overboard to Japan, that pretty much paid for a lot of purchases.

It's pretty clear to me that you have to make your money through the residual interest in the horse. Meaning that the real money isn't purse money, it's in the breeding side or sale of breeding stock. In buying horses now, I ask what the potential is for the horse. And that doesn't mean buying every Storm Cat at the sale. It's more like, "If this athlete pans out, is there an upside here?"

With fillies, you need to decide whether you want to get into the breeding end. We have Elloluv now, a graded stakes winner, and we haven't decided yet, but the temptation would be to sell her. I'm going to get heat for that from my wife.

LS: *How do you reconcile your background in academic philosophy with being in the horse business?*
PR: That's easy. Logic is about possibility. When you buy a racehorse, you're always dreaming about the possibilities. That goes for everyone in this game. Not what is, but what could be. Everybody who buys a horse has a dream about the Kentucky Derby or winning something big. The philosopher closest to the racing game would be the British empiricist David Hume, who wrote a lot about causality. You assume a lot of things in life; we go through presuppositions about everything, but it doesn't need to be that way—things can turn out in all different ways. Turn back the clock to when you were a kid—would you think you'd be writing an article for the *Bloodhorse* on Santa Anita Derby day? You just don't know.

LS: *You are aggressive in placing your horses.*
PR: Yes, I do get involved in twisting Craig's arm to put a horse in a stakes race that he doesn't want to. Swept Overboard in the Met Mile, Elloluv in the Hollywood Starlet, and Logician in the San Felipe were all examples that worked out well. He's in a difficult spot because he doesn't want to tick off a major owner, but at the same time he wants to win races. And usually, when an owner gets too involved, it's a bad thing for the management of the stable. But my thought is, "What's the downside to running in a stakes race?" You miss an allowance race where you'd be odds-on and win thirty thousand dollars in purse money. You can always come back and run in that allowance race if it doesn't pan out, so if that's where you fit, you'll get there eventually.

LS: *You're a risk-taker.*
PR: The point is, if you think the horse is good enough and you're on a certain path, there could be lots of reasons that he throws a clunker. If I'm confident in something and it didn't turn out, I make the play again. Back in the eighties I had a bookie. I bet my horse heavily at a harness track and was convinced he couldn't lose. He went off as the chalk and finished fifth. I owed the guy six thousand dollars and didn't have the money to pay him. I told him I'd meet him at the track Saturday night to pay him, and also told him the horse was back in, and I wanted to bet a thousand across on him. He goes off at 10–1 and wins. I meet the guy and say, "Well, I guess I don't need to pay you now since you owe me."

LS: *You took a risk with cheesy commercials—I remember you being on TV—for your mortgage business.*
PR: Like a lot of things, a lot of it was luck. Often, the best ideas are really simple. I'd been in the mortgage business for a number of years, and it had been boom-and-bust. I didn't understand why somebody didn't go on television and give out the rates like a weather report: "Today's rate is this. If you want it, call us up." I bounced it off some guys from GE Capital. and they looked at me like I was nuts.

Call me stupid, call me naïve, but I think people want to get the straight stuff blared right at them. I gathered up what little money I had, started DiTech, and did a radio spot with today's rate. The first day there were six calls, and I figured I was in trouble. Then the next day the phone rang more, and soon it blasted off like a rocket. Then I'm driving down the freeway and see a billboard from a radio station saying, "This is the song and artist we're playing right now." And I thought, "Why can't you do that for interest rates? Today's rate is such and such." So I bought a couple of billboards, and it exploded.

Then we ran TV spots during the O.J. trial on a local channel. The air time wasn't that expensive, and everyone was glued to that thing in the summer of '95.

As far as rating my performance, Steven Spielberg hasn't called with any offers.

LS: *You've bought two-year-olds, runners from Europe, horses out of dispersals . . .*
PR: The one place we haven't bought is the most common place—yearling sales. I believe they're the riskiest sales, other than buying weanlings, I guess. When you look at the prices at yearling sales—which are all over the map—and you consider, "What are the odds this horse is going to make it to the races?" It's pretty low. If you buy at a two-year-old in-training sale, you're still paying up, but at least you've seen him move under tack. Obviously, you're taking a huge risk there, too, but we've been fairly lucky at that so far. Elloluv is paying for everybody else.

You have a hope and a plan for every one you buy, but sometimes they don't come anywhere near that. We bought a horse after he won two legs of the Triple Crown in Argentina, and he got beat twenty-eight lengths in the UAE Derby last week. So now, we don't know what we bought. We paid a lot of money for Castle Gandolfo, thinking if he wins a graded stakes, he's stallion material—he's by Gone West and his dam is a half sister to El Gran Senor. But so far, he's been a dud. You don't know. You have a secret hope that things are going to turn out well. It's a game of high highs and low lows, and more low lows than high highs.

LS: *Later today you have Elloluv running in the Santa Anita Oaks and Logician in the Santa Anita Derby.*

PR: She's done enough already to go to the Kentucky Oaks [Elloluv would finish fourth in the Kentucky Oaks], so we're going to go to Louisville anyway, and we'd like to take Logician to the Derby. But if he doesn't go forward today, we'll say we tried, and so it goes.

Almost everyone who gets interviewed says the only way they'd go to the Kentucky Derby is if they think their horse has a legitimate shot, and I think half those people are lying. If the horse gets in, they're going. My honest answer is if he qualifies, we're going with him. Everything changes quickly, and you just don't know. If he races badly today, you don't want to go on and make a fool of yourself. [Logician did not race in the Kentucky Derby.]

If someone tells you the Kentucky Derby doesn't mean that much to them, they're all liars. I was thinking that if we ever got in the Derby and won, that would be the time to get out of the game. You see people who win it and then spend millions and millions trying to repeat the experience. And it's not going to happen. You hit the top and that's it.

2012

Immediately after winning the Kentucky Derby with I'll Have Another, Churchill Downs, Louisville

Lenny Shulman: *Were you confident heading into the race?*

Paul Reddam: Well, with Ten Most Wanted [who finished ninth in 2003] I was highly confident, but I've learned to be less confident just on the probability aspect that there's a 95 percent chance you'll lose. To me, this horse is the real deal, and I thought he was going to run the race of his life. The question was, "Is he good enough?" To win the race, you've got to have the right, lucky trip. We were in the exact position we talked about wanting to be in. I looked at the tote board and the half went in :45 and change and he was sitting off it, and I thought, "Man, did I dream this or what?"

And then, truthfully, I lost sight of him. I heard the call that Bodemeister was in the clear. But I know the way our kid [Mario Gutierrez] rides—just when it looks like he's waiting too long, he goes. So when I saw someone coming, I said, "Is that him?" And it was, and then I saw we were going to win, and then I don't know what happened.

It all went according to plan, and how often does that happen? Like, almost never. I might be dreaming. Who knows? I'm just so excited for the whole team. I don't know that anything could be bigger than winning the Kentucky Derby.

LS: *Is this a bigger thrill than drinking from the Stanley Cup when the Red Wings won it in 2002?*
PR: Yes, this is above drinking from the Cup, are you kidding me?

2016

Immediately after winning the Kentucky Derby
with Nyquist, Churchill Downs, Louisville

Lenny Shulman: *How can you explain winning two Kentucky Derbys?*
Paul Reddam: Well, one of your colleagues [Steve Haskin] told me years ago I was the luckiest guy in racing. I think that's how I'd explain it. I'm just very lucky to be with these guys [trainer Doug O'Neill and bloodstock agent Dennis O'Neill]. It's as simple as that, really.

37

Jerry and Ann Moss
and Mike Pegram

SPECIFICALLY TO GET THEIR perspectives on having won the Kentucky
Derby, I interviewed **Mike Pegram** and **Jerry and Ann Moss** together eight years
after Pegram's Real Quiet won the race and one year after the Mosses took it with
Giacomo, a 50–1 longshot. Both Pegram and Jerry Moss are significant players in
the Thoroughbred world for a number of reasons. Pegram, who started out giving
a couple of quarter horses to a young kid named Bob Baffert to train in Arizona,
is responsible for having started the Hall of Fame trainer on his journey to great-
ness. Pegram has owned numerous champions, including Silverbulletday, Midnight Lute, and Preakness winner Lookin at Lucky.

Moss, a member of the Rock & Roll Hall of Fame for the success of his A&M
Records, which he founded with trumpeter Herb Alpert, has long been involved
with racing Thoroughbreds. In 1993, his Sardula won the Kentucky Oaks [the
distaff version of the Derby], and he also campaigned Zenyatta, one of the greatest racehorses of all time. She won her first nineteen starts and remains the only
female to have won the Breeders' Cup Classic. Moss named Giacomo after what
one of his label's stars—The Police's Sting—named one of his sons.

2006

Interviewed at Santa Anita Park, California

Lenny Shulman: *So when you meet people who find out you own horses, do they
invariably ask if you've won the Kentucky Derby?*
Mike Pegram: That's exactly the way it happens. People ask what you do, you tell
them you're in the horse business, they ask if you've ever had one in the Derby,
and then they look at you and ask, "You haven't won it, have you?"

Before I won it, I'd always tell them it was a one-in-a-million shot. You
tell them there's forty thousand foals each year and you don't have a chance.
You got a better chance hitting Powerball. Since I won it, I try to downplay it.

I'm ancient history now. I say, "You can't remember my horse. It was a long time ago."

Jerry Moss: We're the freshest face now, having won it last year. But if we don't win it again somehow this year, we'll be like Mike. We'll be "last year's people," and things will slow down. It's been an amazing roller-coaster. The year after you win it is absolutely incredible. People still look at you and shake their heads.

MP: My most treasured book is the one with all the Derby photos that Churchill Downs put together. You open that thing and relive it. I'm getting goosebumps now thinking about it. Even though it gets a little more distant, it stays with you. The neatest thing about the Derby is you're so happy for the people who win it after you because you know the feeling they're experiencing when that horse hits the wire. It is a once-in-a-lifetime experience. You never feel like that again.

Ann Moss: It's a complete thrill. We have friends in the entertainment business who called us and said, "This is like winning an Oscar, an Emmy, a Grammy, a Tony, all in one shot." They were really impressed, and they're used to winning great awards. We still tear up every time we watch it.

JM: We watch the tape once a week to pump ourselves up. And if somebody comes to the house, we're like, "Oh, you haven't seen the race? Let us show it to you." Same ending. Fantastic. It was incredible. He was a come-from-behind horse. We lost track of him. He showed up and won the race. Just amazing. It was a beautiful day.

MP: I still pop the tape of Real Quiet in every time I lose a ten-thousand-dollar claimer, just to remind myself why I'm in this business (*laughs*). Then, when I get real high on my success, I throw in the Belmont Stakes tape [in which Real Quiet loses his chance at the Triple Crown by a nose] and get back to real life (*laughs*).

LS: *Mike, you got into horses through your father. Jerry, you got into them through a partner and a friend. When does the Kentucky Derby become a goal? Is it in your mind from the very beginning?*

MP: I never dreamed of winning the Kentucky Derby. Even in the week leading up to it, I would never allow myself to think about it. I got there and figured I'd use up my thirty thousand dollars' [the entry fee] worth of fun by Thursday. The morning of the race, I thought, "Wouldn't it be great if I was just in the hunt turning for home? Just give me something to root for." But winning is just too much to dream; too much to ask. I grew up ninety miles down the road from Churchill Downs, but it's just too big to think about.

LS: Your trainer [Bob Baffert] told me just today that you guys knew you were going to win it.

MP: When are you going to quit believing him? In fact, we have a horse in the fourth race today I named Forgivable Bob. I did have a unique situation in that Derby because Indian Charlie was the favorite, and I owned half of his sire, In Excess, and a win would have really put the stallion on the map. Also, the man who introduced me to Bob was Hal Earnhardt, who owned Indian Charlie. We started in the quarter horse business with Bob, so there were a lot of emotions there.

JM: We were completely under the radar. We were 50–1 and nobody was paying any attention to us. So we were just having a good time. Nobody was interviewing us. The last morning, the guy from *Sports Illustrated* came around and said, "I've interviewed everybody else; I may as well talk to you just in case."

From where I came from to get to where I'm at, I've always dreamed big. We've won the Santa Anita Handicap and the Met Mile and the Kentucky Oaks, but we'd never had any Triple Crown experience. And I'll tell you, it's totally different from anything else. We've always tried hard to get into it because I've always wanted to be a part of that sort of action.

To walk out at the Kentucky Derby in front of 160,000 people, my God, that's Woodstock. A Day on the Green in San Francisco. The most amazing festivals of our time. And everybody is there to have a great time, and you can feel that energy. It's overwhelming.

AM: This business is a game of hope. It's all built on hope. You hope you get a baby. You hope it grows up. You hope it wants to win. You hope it gets good luck. You hope nothing goes wrong. It's all about hope. So it was very exciting and part of the magic around Giacomo. We were happy to be part of the twenty entrants.

LS: Mike, you run a string of McDonalds. Jerry, you're in the music business. What are the parallels in the success of your horses to the success of your other businesses?

MP: You surround yourself with good people and try to be as honest and have as much integrity as you possibly can, and you hope that old saying that good things happen to good people comes true. It's the old racetrack saying: "Keep yourself in the best company and your horse in the worst company and you're going to make a lot of money."

JM: I agree with Mike. You try to have the greatest people around you, and you're all sharing the same dream or vision, and if you have the integrity and try hard and do the right thing, good things happen to you. They just do.

LS: *What does racing give you that your other business doesn't?*

MP: It makes me pray every time they hit the quarter pole. It's like going fishing. You never know what you're gonna get. It keeps you humble. When you start getting cocky in this business, you're going to get buried. If you start thinking about making your reservations for Louisville, that's the kiss of death. You can't really plan. You can lay it out, but the Racing Gods are in charge of this thing. It's all so fragile, you learn to enjoy the good times.

JM: The entertainment field is an emotional business. We've developed ties with people we like and respect, and then see the acclaim they get and how they handle it and how they reach people and the good they do and the joy they create. Building a company that has earned respect throughout the world, that was pretty good. I started coming to the racetrack because it was a good diversion. I love sports, and the thing about this sport is, it's over in a minute and a half, and you're either on top of the world, or it's, "Oh jeez."

But that level of excitement, I just love everything about it. And that's why I've stayed with it all these thirty-five years. I got out of it for a few years but got back into it because I missed that charge. And I kept dreaming that someday, somehow, it will happen, and all of a sudden up pops Giacomo, who does everything right, and here we are.

LS: *Real Quiet was two-for-twelve going into the Derby and had lost twice in New Mexico. Giacomo had lost six in a row after breaking his maiden. What is the dialogue like between you and your trainer?*

JM: All [trainer] John [Shirreffs] kept saying was, "This horse hasn't done anything wrong. He's done everything we've asked him to do." There were excuses in every race. John concentrated on keeping the horse progressing and feeling good. After the Santa Anita Derby he had two incredible works and was doing well, and we felt if he gets lucky, he's going to win.

I've been with lots of trainers, and I've believed every one of them. These guys work so hard, and they're putting in gargantuan hours every day, and I have the highest respect for them, especially John. I put my trust and belief in people, and I expect them to tell me the truth. Charlie Whittingham used to say that there's nothing more dangerous than an owner with a condition book. And it's absolutely true. Thank God we've been with him, and Bobby Frankel, Ron McAnally, Brian Mayberry. All these guys are just incredible.

MP: Let me tell you about New Mexico. Bob and I were flying with my grandson, Gator, and we're over New Mexico and Bob punches him and says, "See that track down there? Real Quiet got beat there." And Gator said, "No way. He wouldn't have run at a track that doesn't have a turf course." You're right, we got beat twice in New Mexico, but we had also run at Churchill the November before the Derby, and Real Quiet finished third there after a horrific trip. So we knew he liked Churchill; we knew he could handle adversity; and we knew he could travel.

What Jerry said is true: You have to have total trust in the people who are handling those horses. Everybody has an opinion, but there's one guy who's back there working with the horse every day: the trainer. And you have to listen and believe him.

The losses? We were just going for the price, man.

LS: *What was the vibe like when you got to Kentucky?*
MP: That whole city lives for that one week. It's being at the barn on the backside in the mornings. That's what makes the Derby, going back there and seeing 2,500 people there. The clockers' stand is full. The buzz is all around—"Here comes so-and-so." You see all the media—those free doughnuts bring you guys out. That's what makes it so special—everything leading up to it.
AM: Just sitting there and staring at your horse is fun. The whole community is horses. Everyone is living and breathing horses. It's a wonderful life, a good feeling.
JM: The time goes. There are farms to visit, places to go, people to see. We're not big social people, but we get around.
MP: They had to put up with us from Monday on. The recycle man liked us, I'll tell you that. We recycled a lot of cans.

LS: *Now it's Derby Day . . .*
MP: It's so big, and you're enjoying yourself, but you can't get caught up in what it would be like to win. I've seen some stall-walking owners, and I don't want to be like that. I don't have to ride the horse.

LS: *You hear athletes in the playoffs say, "It's just another game." But the Derby is not just another race.*
MP: No, it's not. I'll go back to when we got beat in the Belmont, and people asked me, "How can you still be happy?" Well, I've just had the best five weeks of my life. I've been walking on air. Moonwalking. And now I'm going to be sad because I got nipped on the wire? Nah. Now, if that had happened in the Derby, I would have been totally deflated. But I could say, "I still won the Derby. And the Preakness." So how can you be mad after that happens?

LS: *Looking back, were there any omens that the Gods might have been smiling down on you?*
JM: The way everybody was downrating us, that kind of encouraged me. Again, I can quote Charlie. When I'd get nervous before a race and ask Charlie if we had a chance, he'd say, "If you're in the race, you've got a chance." Plus, the day after the Derby was my seventieth birthday.
MP: I had a perfect week. Everything fell into place. I woke up Derby morning and a friend had left one rose outside my door with a note that said it was my job to bring home the rest of them. That's something you never forget.
AM: Close friends of ours got married that day, and after the race we flew back to California and went right to their house and brought them the roses. They put their wedding outfits back on and we drank Champagne and watched the race.

LS: *In the moments after you win the Derby, are you conscious of what's going on?*
MP: You're talking about an eerie feeling. My grandson and I watched the race from the rail. When that horse hit the wire, I looked over and my brother was standing next to me. We had no idea we were next to each other until that moment. One hundred and sixty thousand people, and we end up in the same place. The emotion from that point on . . . that's impossible to describe. You just did the impossible. And that's the reason I believe in Racing Gods.
AM: I remember every moment of it. Time went really slow. I remember everyone's faces.
JM: We did the press conference, spent some time with the horse, and had an escort out of town.
MP: The night before I had fifty people with me and we were at a little pizza joint, and when the owner found out I had a horse, he said if we win, we had to come back. I said, "If we win that thing, we'll be right back in here tomorrow night." And that's what we did. But after that, I wouldn't go to bed until I saw the newspapers. I still couldn't believe it. I waited for the Sunday paper in the hotel parking lot.

LS: *When the Derby winner continues to race, how special is that to watch?*
MP: Those horses have their own personality, and he was the king of the barn. Then he got to his stud career, and when people start knocking him, it's like they're knocking your kid. I'm pretty easygoing around the racetrack; everyone has their opinion, and that's what it's all about, but when they start knocking your horse, man, that's tough. It really is.

JM: I just want him to be fine and have a good time. He's done for us everything you could ask a horse to do. If he's lucky enough to win a couple more grade 1 races for us, that would be amazing.

LS: *You're in a small fraternity of Derby winners. Did you hear from others after you won it?*
AM: We had a nice moment with Beverly Lewis on Derby Day and gave her a rose and told her it was nice to be part of her club. Debbie Oxley [Monarchos] sent us a nice note. I get music CDs from Arthur Hancock. It's a great club, and we're so proud to be part of it.
MP: I had dinner with Mack Miller [trainer of Sea Hero] soon after the Derby; we did a thing on the Derby at the Smithsonian. Probably the most memorable dinner I've had in my life. Mack knew more about my horse than I did. What a great human being he is.

LS: *Do you think about the immortality of it?*
JM: Very much. We're in the history books. It really strikes home when we remember we lost Sardula the year after she won the Kentucky Oaks. Her mortality lasted four years, and it was so horrible to lose her.
AM: To have your name attached to the biggest race in the oldest sport in America is pretty good.
MP: First thing I did after they remodeled Churchill Downs was to go back and find Real Quiet's sign [the names of all Derby winners are displayed on plaques around the grandstand] and find out where they put it. You can't take that away from me. It was perfect. They put it right under the beer stand.

Acknowledgments

THANK YOU TO ALL the interviewees who have trusted me with their stories over the past twenty-plus years; thank you to Evan Hammonds, who made my two decades at the *Bloodhorse* as much about fun as it was about work; and thank you to Roda Ferraro for her gracious help and kindness.